VOICES
FROM THE
CHICAGO GRAVE

THEY'RE CALLING.
WILL YOU ANSWER?

VOICES
FROM THE
CHICAGO GRAVE

THEY'RE CALLING.
WILL YOU ANSWER?

BY SCOTT MARKUS

WITH FOREWORD BY BILL MOLLER

Holt, Michigan 48842

Voices from the Chicago Grave
by Scott Markus

Published by
Thunder Bay Press
Holt, Michigan 48842

First Printing, August 2008

15   14   13   12   11   10   09   08   8   7   6   5   4   3   2   1

ISBN: 978-1-933272-19-1

This is a work of fiction.

Illustrations by Mary Gutfleisch
All photos by Scott Markus and Mary Gutfleisch
Front cover image by Shelley Anderson
Book and cover design by Julie Taylor

Printed in the United States of America
by McNaughton & Gunn, Inc.

CONTENTS

Chapter 1

Chapter 2

Chapter 3

Chapter 4

Chapter 5

Chapter 6

Chapter 7

Chapter 8

Chapter 9

Chapter 10

Chapter 11

Chapter 12

Chapter 13

Chapter 14

FOREWORD

I don't believe in ghosts… or, perhaps I should say, I don't think I do. Heck, I've seen a lot of things in my twenty-seven years in the news business, the violence of man and nature, but never something that could not be explained. Like most adults, I dismiss the possibility of hauntings, spirits, and the paranormal as just so much bump-in-the-night fear and fantasies of children. If it cannot be measured or detected by the conventional sciences or fit into a nice, tidy classification, only a fool would believe in such hokum. Right? That's the convenient rationale of adults who would harrumph at anything for which there isn't a ready explanation. And yet, who hasn't been in a room where something felt not quite right or heard or seen something that could not be explained… an eerie light or a shuddering cold. There are perfectly rational people who are convinced they confronted a figure or apparition beckoning them in a dream… or were they awake?

Whether or not you believe, you have to accept the fact that there are many strange and unexplained things in the world.

Skepticism is good. To blindly accept without questioning can leave one vulnerable to being deluded by lies. Yet, when someone refuses to allow that there are still unexplained "things," then they limit themselves to the possibilities of experience. Don't wait for science to reassure you. Science, you see, cannot account for all the forces at work in the universe.

It is natural when we encounter something that appears out of the ordinary to try to find a normal and rational explanation for it. When all reasonable analysis fails, then the experience must be placed under the heading of the unexplained or paranormal.

Call them ghosts, call them energy abnormalities, or merely call them uncategorized phenomena… it really doesn't matter. The point is, strange things happen! And they're happening all the time. Consider the sheer volume of ghost stories... not the Halloween goblin variety told around summer campfires but the detailed serious accounts as chronicled in countless books and Web sites.

The tales and pictures that follow are fascinating and bizarre. They are as varied as the definitions of what a ghost is. The spirit of a dead person unable to leave this world... a manifestation of psychic energy from a violent act. Some think of them as tall tales sprung from unknown sources or calculated mischief.

What follows is not just a journey into the strange and unexplained but a passageway to the shadowy back streets and neighborhoods of Chicago where many of the city's hidden treasures are tucked away. You'll visit the scenes of the city's violent past where the spirits of the *Eastland* Disaster, the Iroquois Theatre fire, and infamous gangland murders may still walk among us. You will see Chicago as a city rich in characters and commoners. You will read, hear and see things that have been thoroughly researched but for which forensic analysis has no answers. You will learn, you will wonder, and you may be left questioning and feeling a little uncomfortable. It's best not to think about it too much; what is not of this world cannot be interpreted by the science of this world. I seem to now be talking like someone who does believe in ghosts. Believe... perhaps. Understand... not in the least.

BILL MOLLER

ACKNOWLEDGEMENTS

Without a supportive environment, there is no way creativity can bloom. Therefore, the bulk of my praise for assistance in this book is to my very patient parents, Larry and Dianne Markus.

Every project is a team effort. This particular project started in 1999 with the filming of our documentary *Voices from the Grave*. My partners on that were Jeff Lord and Jason Jacobs. In 2000, my partner in crime in exploring haunted Chicago was Mary Czerwinski. She was a dream to work with, pulling triple duty as photographer, navigator, and expert.

In addition to her masterful illustration of this book, Mary Gutfleisch has been one of the most inspiring and encouraging people I've ever met, working on projects with me from Chicago to Hawaii with stops in between.

Since the book was first self-published in 2003, countless readers e-mailed the Web site, slimpictures.com, with their personal accounts, tips on new stories to cover, and historical information. Their contributions greatly enhanced this book, as they have helped to improve every chapter. Indeed, the people of Chicago in general are largely to thank. Restaurant owners, the residents of Archer Avenue, and Dan Melone and Buzz Spreeman's Robinson Woods contributions were the definite highlights. These neighbors from the suburbs to the Loop, businesspeople and farmers, Sox fans and Cubs fans are all linked by this great "city on the make."

Countless others, though unaware of it, were major driving forces. JP Maurer of People Technology has been a great friend and an immeasurable help for most of the projects I've worked on, ranging from Web sites to video projects. Teachers like Pat Gonder, Teresa Aguinaldo, Carole Johnson, and Jim Jackson, though I have voiced my appreciation, will never fully know how much their work has impacted my life.

I need to thank Dr. James Dorsey for setting an example by the way he lived his life, bringing a sense of community to everything he approached and continuing to push local history to the forefront. He and his countless efforts will be missed by many.

I would be remiss to overlook the great mentors and colleagues who've shaped my professional life, particularly Liz Long, Wainani Tomich, DJ MacHale, Bernie Axelrod, Tony Farmer, Ursula Bielski, Ed Shanahan, Mikey Eberle, and my co-host on *The Mothership Connection*, Dobie Maxwell.

Bill Moller has set the standard of ethics and professionalism that discriminating Chicago viewers expect out of their news anchors. I thank him for bringing the same level of talent, attitude, and style to writing the foreword of this book.

Pat DiPrima helped me take the next step n the world of the paranormal. She exposed me to new theories, ideas, and stories, and she unselfishly helped me book speech after speech.

Perhaps most importantly, I survive by the amazing group of friends that surround me with their support and positivity. Where would I be without Heather & Eric Butner, Travis Cameron's clan, Melissa Carlson, Nora Graham, Ammi & Akia Lane, Rachel Lipanovich, Kathlyn & Jeff McLane, Rob Otterson, Chris Pry, Scott Ray, Lara Shaffer, Sara & Giddeon Silence, and Mike Winget? I don't know, and I don't want to know.

This book is dedicated to them and my entire family.

INTRODUCTION

On a summer night in 1999, some friends and I were bored. We started telling stories, and it wasn't long before the conversation turned to ghost stories. The night was full of goose bumps as there appeared to be a never-ending supply. Our storytelling session started at 9:00PM, and by the time we came up for air it was four in the morning. Those seven hours disappeared in a flash.

Impressed by the enthusiasm from the night before, I started my quest to learn about local ghost lore. Realistically, I didn't think I'd find much, but I was greatly mistaken.

Simply learning the tales was not enough. I applied my background in television and created a feature-length documentary. We were able to explore some of the more famous stories, such as Resurrection Mary and Bachelor's Grove, as well as uncovering the "Sunnybrook Asylum," the scariest location I've ever covered. I quickly found, however, that there was too much content and not enough time to do everything I wanted in a single documentary.

After the documentary, I teamed up with Mary Czerwinski to explore and report on nearly ninety Chicagoland locations in the first edition of this book, which was published in 2003.

I thought my involvement with supernatural Chicago was done. Again, I was greatly mistaken.

Thanks to my Web site, slimpictures.com, dozens of people submitted their own stories and shared the independent research they've done to help make the book an evolving process.

The decision to write a revised edition was an easy one. In addition to incorporating the new research, firsthand accounts, and locations, there were simply too many updates to the existing locations. For example, some no longer exist. The Red Lion Pub, Sunnybrook Asylum, and the House of Crosses are lost to the wrecking ball.

As always, the book will be a continuing work. Readers can visit the site (specific addresses will be posted throughout the book) to find additional information, message boards, and literally thousands of additional pictures.

CHAPTER 1

THE LORE AND URBAN LEGENDS OF NORTHERN ILLINOIS

"The Gate"

SLIMPICTURES.COM/CHAPTER1.HTM

On December 3, 1818, Illinois became part of the United States of America when it was admitted to the Union. The land where Chicago is now was considered by England to be a part of Virginia. The French, however, who were the first to discover the Great Lakes, set up posts throughout the Midwest, including Illinois, as early as the mid 1500s. Further back, a number of tribes, together called the Iliniwek, called this land home. As we'll see in the following pages, to know local ghost lore is to know local history, as some of the ghostly tales date back to Native Americans and Chicago's first European settlers.

However, most of Illinois' past is unwritten. This is both unfortunate and thrilling in that it often takes a lot of hard work to uncover the hidden and nearly forgotten truths. Many events from the past are simply passed on verbally from one generation to the next. Due to this, much of Chicago's past exists as a "talk story." Our history is part true, while errors and embellishment, intentional or not, are used to tie up the loose ends. The human-nature-fueled interest towards stories of the macabre leads to their repetition at a higher frequency. Therefore, these stories mature and morph more quickly and drastically between generations than more tame fare. At the same time, these stories become so well known that, for the residents neighboring the locations where these events took place, the stories don't even need to be told. They are simply part of that community's collective unconscious. The "collective unconscious," first noted by Swedish psychologist Carl Jung, usually refers to archetypes but can easily cross over into other situations where a group of people share a knowing that doesn't necessarily have to be stated in order to be understood. When the collective unconscious is based on a talk story that is more embellishment than truth and if the topic is of a darker nature, then an urban legend is born.

Urban legends in Northern Illinois are plentiful and immensely entertaining. In recent years the story of "Bloody Mary" (mentioned in this chapter) was even used as the basis for *Candyman*, a horror movie shot in the Cabrini Green housing project in Chicago's near West Side.

An interesting aspect of urban legends is that they are based on some evidence of truth. As the people are being drawn into these stories, most of what is heard is taken in with a cautious ear. Knowing that truths can often be few and far between, the listener is often confronted with a dismaying decision to make: How much of this is real?

"The Bloody Hook," one of the more popular and easy to dismiss urban legends in America, is actually based on a lot more truth than one might expect. In it, a couple at a lover's lane make a reluctant exit from their romantic evening after hearing a radio report about an escaped killer on the loose who has a hook for a hand. They arrive at home to find the hook hanging on their car door, ripped from the killer's arm — a sign they pulled away moments before they would have met their demise.

The tale comes from a real-life lover's lane killer that preyed on couples in Texarkana just after the second World War. The fact that the media nicknamed this elusive menace the "Phantom Killer" only added to the mystique.

There is a comforting feeling knowing that the horrific story being told is padded with fiction, but the fact that it is based on an undisclosed amount of fact leaves an unsettling feeling that breathes life into the urban legend for yet another round.

The tales contained in this chapter are not all urban legends. Some are merely unique stories that seem so "out there" that they could easily be dismissed as the campfire banter of grade school children. The only problem with easy dismissal is that those tend to be the true stories. Other stories in this chapter are urban legends unique to Northern Illinois. With mentions of a slave catcher, a family massacre, and an escaped criminally insane convict who stumbled across a sleep-away camp, it will be your task to decipher how much of this actually happened.

"The Gate"

To follow in the footsteps of countless Lake County high school students whose rite of passage involves a trip to the gate, you will enter the north suburban town of Libertyville. Traveling down the four-lane highway of Route 137, you exit onto the desolate River Road. River Road can often be an experience of its own, especially at night. The road is long and narrow. The left side is bordered by the Independence Grove Forest Preserve while the right side is dotted with houses. The car's headlights provide the only illumination as there are no streetlights along this thoroughfare. Often, the experience is even more heightened as the ponds to the left of the street mix with summer air to form massive banks of fog that drift over the many low points of this hilly street.

After a journey of about two miles down this road, it makes an abrupt ninety-degree right turn. Directly ahead sits a horse ranch; to the left of that, set back farther from the road, sits a menacing vision. This is what local residents commonly refer to as "The Gate."

According to the widely-known legend, the gate marked the entrance to an all-girls' school in the 1950s. All was well in the area until the fateful day when the principal snapped and killed four of his students. As the legend goes, it was at this very gate, on the posts, that the heads of the young students were placed after they were removed from their bodies.

The stories, namely who the killer is and what the location beyond the gate's walls were, vary depending on where the story is being told. According to some, instead of being a school, it was a sleep-away camp, an orphanage, or even an asylum. Some versions of the story assert that it was a madman, escaped from an institution, not a principal, who stumbled across this location and went to work. Others talk of an escaped convict who caused the mayhem, and those who believe the location was an asylum state that it was a counselor who, after spending year after year in the company of mentally unstable persons, ended up joining their ranks and lost his sanity as well. As would be expected from a sensationalized story, the final death toll often gets inflated well past four.

The sheer predictability of the tale is the first clue that this is an urban legend. More than one location covered in this guide of haunted Chicagoland also share this or a strikingly similar story.

The type of residue left behind also differs depending on the story. Libertyville and Vernon Hills high school students often talk of people visiting the gate at night only to find blood from the decades-old slaying still running down the gate's wrought iron bars. Other versions state that on Halloween and the anniversary of the slaying, at the bewitching hour of midnight, the phantom heads of the fallen girls reappear on the posts. The legend about the fence, when told by a Wauconda resident, claims that a small boy has been seen on numerous occasions walking or staring out from behind the entrance.

Sorting out the truth from the speculation is a difficult challenge when forced to rely on eyewitness accounts rather than printed documents. Most towns across the country have their fair share of skeletons in their respective closets. It is customary for a verbal history of a neighborhood to get edited by their residents in order to preserve a peaceful illusion of reality.

Libertyville is already the home of the "Murder Mansion." Straight out of the pages of the Amityville Horror, in 1980, Bruce and Darlene Rouse were brutally murdered by their son. Understandably, the resale value of the house couldn't get low enough to entice a typical buyer. The stage was set for the Chicago Mafia, who wasn't put off by the violent past of the home, to take over residency. Specifically, it was the Ferriola street crew that owned the home in the mid-1980s and operated a casino in the same house for the Chicago Mafia. Modern era gangsters like Salvatore DeLaurentis, Rocco Infelise, BJ Jahoda, and Harry Ferriola brought in a reported $800,000 every month just from gambling at this location. In September of 1984, the Murder Mansion was also the location of another slaying when independent bookmaker Bobby Plummer was killed on the second floor. The house gained a small and mostly rumor-based haunted reputation, though the most recent owners have publicly made statements to the contrary. The house itself met its fate in a mysterious fire that left it a darkened shell of a building in 2002.

This being said, in recent years Libertyville has shown its resiliency in being able to bounce back from negative press. Though a number of very famous murders have happened, catching wind of it is often a difficult task. Usually, the only time these events are mentioned anymore is in the press on TruTV or on an MSNBC look back in time but hardly ever in a local newspaper.

Libertyville has been mostly successful in hiding unnatural deaths from just twenty years ago. If alleged events happened in 1950, then there's more than half a century for people to forget.

It is possible that a horrific or tragic event did, in fact, happen at "The Gate," but over the years the legend grew to the absurd state it is today due to overactive imaginations. If this were the case, then there could very well be a legitimate haunting at this location that is based on a real-life event in history. What can be said for sure, however, is that a trip to "The Gate" can be quite the harrowing experience. On humid summer nights, a fog forms in the distant fields, rolls in, and hovers just beyond the entrance. The mere presence of the structure leaves some to keep the door of possibility open. Obviously, there is some reason for such a massive structure to stand.

What can be said of the legend that is true is that at one point in time the land behind the gate, originally known as the Dodridge Farm, served as nearly all of the incarnations reported in the various urban legends. It started as the Kathrine Dodridge Kreigh Budd Memorial Home for Children. The orphanage was home for one hundred children at a time and opened in 1926 (construction began the year before). The two hundred acres were then sold off to the Chicago Archdiocese in 1940. It served as the Catholic Youth Organization Camp for Boys. According to Jim MacAyeal, who is researching the Dodridge Farm, during this incarnation it also took in, "... orphans from the war in Europe. More buildings, more paths, and roads were built. Five hundred were now able to stay at the camp." Next, it served as the St. Francis Boys Camp in 1955. In 1974, the name changed to Camp St. Francis and was an all-girls camp. The Archdiocese sold the land to the Lake County Forest Preserve in the 1980s.

Outside of that, the only certainty is that it will continue to lure curiosity-seekers and lovers of the paranormal for years to come, much to the chagrin of the residents of the neighborhood.

One of the most chilling firsthand paranormal encounters ever relayed to me came from Sean Ellis Dotson and centers on "The Gate." After midnight on Easter 2003, he and a friend named Justin found their way to the gate for their first visit. After getting over their initial intimidation, the trip felt like a disappointment. After all, there was no blood, phantom children, or disembodied heads.

They walked through the gate, down the Des Plaines River Trail, and into the darkness. Upon coming to a T-intersection, they were able to faintly make out another option. This is a mostly hidden and completely off-limits trail called the Upper Loop Path that leads to the ruins of the orphanage and camp buildings, which were demolished in 1979. They didn't make it that far.

> "I knew I had heard something strange because both Justin and I stopped breathing. In that brief, rare moment I was able to stretch my hearing to absolute clarity, and what I heard frightened me in a way I had never before experienced.
>
> ...Voices, was the thought which first crossed my mind. Very faint, very distant, yet most

assuredly voices. Not just any voices either...
but the voices of children. I realized they were
the voices of children.

...Oddly enough, I did not make the connection
between the voices of children, which I was
rapidly becoming more and more convinced
I was hearing, and the urban legend which
motivated us to visit in the first place. My
first thought, which I held onto for as long as
I possibly could, was that there were indeed
children on the trail. Not the restless ghosts
of children, but real kids, probably out doing
the same thing we were—looking for ghosts,
never mind that it's 2:00 A.M. Easter morning.
It was the way the sound reached us which
caused me to doubt myself, which frightened
me so thoroughly and gave me chills—it was
so ambiguous, so ethereal. Was it one voice or
a dozen? Girls or boys? A mile down the trail
or around the next bend?

...What snapped us out of that weird, almost
hypnotic, state and slammed us back into reality
was something that frightened me so badly I
cannot remember what it was. I remember
the voices, which had been fading in and out
the entire time we were listening, faded down,
down, and were gone. I tried to get my ears to
follow them, straining, stretching my hearing
as far as it would go. Imagine listening as hard
as you can in near perfect silence, listening
that closely, that quietly, that carefully... that is
when the screaming started.

...I remember thinking very calmly, very
rationally. What could make that noise? A

person? No. Surely not. Certainly not. I felt sure no human being could emit the horrible cry that pierced my ears. A deer? Rabbit? Some animal? If it was, it sounded like no other animal I've ever heard, at least none indigenous to this area. It sounded... wrong. That's the best way I can describe it. It rose up from somewhere deep within the woods, twisting and winding higher and higher, reaching its zenith, sustaining, and dying off as quickly as it came."

After Sean and his friend made the decision to run back to the car, their story was far from over.

"As we ran down the gravel path towards the gate and, just beyond, to freedom, it became terribly apparent that the sound was following us. At first quiet, then growing... We ran, and we heard that terrible cry get closer and closer, and we kept our eyes on the road in front of us, paved and sane and safe. Safety, a hundred yards away... ninety... eighty... and still the howl behind us grew closer and louder.

When we were no more than fifty yards away, I suddenly became terribly, deathly certain that soon we would hear another sound right in front of us, the sound of cold, ancient steel dragging across gravel. Then we would see the giant wrought iron bars of the gate itself begin to shut—slowly, of course, to mock us. We would run faster, harder than we ever have, ever could, but it would be too late. We would reach the gate and its mouth would be shut, its big metal teeth clenched, smiling its boneyard smile."

Thankfully for Sean, Justin, and their hearts, which, by this time, were on the brink of failing, the gate remained open and they returned safely to their car. In the safety of their escape vessel, they could still faintly hear the screaming. The sound chased them from the Upper Loop Path but did not continue past the gate itself.

It would be easy to dismiss a single report of a haunting; however, shortly after the posting, a response was offered by someone else who encountered the same event at a different time, in a different part of the property.

One day, while researching the Dodridge Farm, MacAyeal located three additional building foundations and a swimming pool.

"If you are truly brave," writes MacAyeal, "beyond the swimming pool through the woods southwest is the well and water tower base. I ask anyone who claims to have psychic abilities to be able to even approach it. It is here that I have concluded that a terrible thing happened. It is also where I too heard screams. The screams sounded unreal, like bizarre dogs fighting or something. And yes, those screams follow you."

MacAyeal wrote in a later post that he is not a believer in ghosts even though he cannot explain his encounter. "I can tell you now that I do not believe in hauntings. The concept of spirits stuck on Earth for whatever reason just doesn't jive with my way of thinking. I work as a volunteer in my parish and consider myself a pretty good Catholic. But there is something. I cannot tell you what it is."

The stories don't end there either. There are additional stories regarding the houses that stand across the street from this north-side landmark. An easily dismissible but strangely well-known fallacy is that the neighborhood is full of devil worshipers. However wild and random these claims are, a number of reputable stories have been told about the area. Several people have made the statement that they are sharing their homes with past residents who move about in shadowy forms.

After giving a speech at Libertyville's Cook Memorial Library on Milwaukee Avenue, not far from the gate and just down the street from St. Sava's Monastery (covered in a later chapter) I was approached by a woman from the audience.

Her question was, "I just moved to Libertyville, and I want to know why my house is haunted. I live across the street from the gate."

She went on to talk about seeing shadowy forms in her basement—a room her dogs refuse to enter.

In my speech, I talked about the gate, which, until now, had only been a landmark to the woman. It must have been quite the experience for this new owner of a haunted house, on a fact-finding mission, to run into a paranormal researcher talking at length about what was just beyond her front door.

In addition to the nearby homes, Ursula Bielski reports in *More Chicago Haunts* that hunters in the area have come across nearby farms only to see long deceased gangsters in 1930s-era clothing. In recent years, the number of Mafioso in Lake County has decreased. Of course, this is only counting Mafioso in the county with a pulse.

On a final important note, I will reiterate that many of the foundations can only be found off the trail, which is not permitted. It is also quite frequent that people visiting after sunset get arrested for trespassing. Lastly, the road outside of

the gate is a no parking zone. To visit the gate, use the main entrance to the Independence Grove Forest Preserve during daylight hours and walk or ride a bike down on the trail.

The House of Crosses

Some of the best stories we hear have never been reported. This also represents some of the more exciting moments for us. Locals can be our most valuable resource. These are people who grew up in one part of the city and know more about it than any historian. Often, it is these people who know the true diamonds in the rough, the great stories that are too bizarre to print. While conducting a search of the Red Lion Pub, one of these stories presented itself to us.

An area man when asked, "Do you know of any haunted places in the area?" was more than happy to tell us about "The House of Crosses."

The story he relayed was almost too far-fetched to be real. In the process of writing this book, however, we've learned to give anything a chance.

"There's this house not too far from here," the man started, "where a guy for no apparent reason killed his wife and his kids—the whole family—and then went out to his car parked in front and killed himself."

Sounding rather typical of a generic urban legend at first, this is where the story started to become unique.

"So, all of the neighbors were obviously sad, and they decided to remember the family by placing little crosses on the door and in front of the walkway. It was like, no matter how hard they tried, the neighborhood just couldn't forget so they kept putting up more crosses. If you go there now, you'll know which house it is right away. There's gotta be a couple thousand crosses on the house."

Taking in to account the predictability of a family massacre and adding in the fact that this story was being told to us while at a haunted bar, skepticism was still running high.

The house on Chestnut Street, demolished in 2007, was located in a predominately Hispanic neighborhood and seems no different than any other residential part of Chicago. The Loop and major highways are near, so the sound of the city loudly breathing is constant. Children play on the streets and sidewalks as would be expected, but it is the unexpected that causes travelers to slow down after taking a moment to catch their breath. Among the rows of two-story row houses stands an ominous house that probably bears more crosses than can be found in all of Vatican City.

If the story was true or not, reason would dictate there had to be a story behind this house. The resident of the house across the street simply stated, "She's very religious," as the obvious answer to this puzzling question.

After first being reported in this book, the house gained notoriety and became an attraction in the *Weird Illinois* bus tour.

The display lent itself easily to rumor. Several of the crosses were placed on parts of the house that didn't face a street or couldn't be seen at all unless a real effort was made. One of the more peculiar shields contained a sword broken in two pieces. A symbol of strength broken usually symbolizes a life cut short. Often these symbols of strength are pillars, trees, or even elephant tusks. A sword would easily fit in to that group.

The front door of the house was on the second floor, so access to the house could only be gained by climbing a staircase from the ground. However, boards containing even more crosses seemed to bar the entrance.

Walking down the side alley, I noticed a mess of cluttered crosses continuing around the side and even the back of the house, totally out of the line of sight of any observers. Another structure sat farther back on the property and followed suit completely: covered on all sides from ground to roof with crosses and looking completely vacant.

"I stood at the front gate and just knew that something wasn't right there," said our friend from the Red Lion Pub. His sentiment echoed loudly during our trip there. The more we saw and asked about, with neighbors who didn't seem to have many answers, the more our list of questions and speculation increased.

Our theory sounded just as outlandish as any Hollywood horror movie. "Perhaps the elderly woman moved into the house and quickly realized that she wasn't alone," we thought. "She then went on an ongoing rampage to post crosses in order to protect herself and cleanse the house of the evil spirit of a mass murderer." When it came down to it, a sight this strange simply needed a story to explain it, so the urban legend was created.

Shortly before the house was razed, the mystery of the house was finally cracked by *Weird Illinois*. Owner Mitch Szewczyk began decorating the house with crosses in 1979. At this point, the house already had one hundred years of history. Was he ridding the house of evil forces? In one sense, the answer is yes.

The first cross was placed when Szewczyk was dealing with gangs and crime in the area in hopes that the sight of a cross on the home would deter criminals. It seemed to work, so he continued.

In time, it morphed from a crime deterrent to a shrine to honor multiple influences on Szewczyk's life, from movie stars, to fictional characters and saints. He constructed a shrine on the house to Pope John Paul II that was actually visited by the Pope during his 1979 visit to Chicago.

Szewczyk died in the mid-1990s, and family members continued to live in the house until they sold the weakening structure in 2007.

In the end, there are no ghosts or horror stories associated with the house. However, this lost landmark served as a perfect example of the lifespan of an urban legend, which, in this case, needed almost no facts at all to start and evolve.

Heroic Elephants Remembered

In a devastating event that could easily be placed in the chapter about Chicago's most deadly and devastating disasters, some unlikely heroes were made.

At four o'clock in the morning on the day of July 21, 1918, the train for the Hagenbeck-Wallace Circus entered Hammond, Indiana. The train never made it to its destination, and eighty-six people, including the president of the Showman's League of America, never made it to another show again.

While the circus train stopped to repair an overheated wheel-bearing box, an empty troop train manned by Alonzo Sargent, who had a history of falling asleep on the job, crashed into the stopped circus train, destroying the last three of the twenty-six train cars and initiating a devastating fire.

The victims who weren't killed on impact died a horrible, fiery death. Several people were trapped in the wreckage, so the cars containing elephants were unloaded to enlist their brutish strength in moving heavy timbers and other flaming debris.

Unfortunately, in the process of saving lives, several elephants ended up losing their own. The Showmen's League of America has a section of Woodlawn Cemetery, more than a football field long and fifty feet deep, in Forest Park reserved for their members. All but thirty of the eighty-six who died in the train wreck are buried here.

Due to the informality of the profession, even those who could be identified still went nameless. Examples include gravestones bearing the names "Baldy" and "Four-Horse Driver." However, the vast majority of the victims went unidentified due to the severity of the fire. Most of the graves of those who died in the train wreck are only identified with a sterile, lonely phrase such as, "Unknown Male, No. 30."

Elephants who died in the fire are also placed in this section of the cemetery. Rather than marked graves, five statues of elephants with their trunks symbolically bowed and their tusks cut represent them.

Since the erection of the elephant statues, the faint sounds of elephants roaring has been noticed on an almost daily basis. These phantom sounds serve as a constant reminder of the lives lost and the heroism exhibited by the Hagenbeck-Wallace Circus elephants.

One problem though: this haunting isn't true.

The train wreck, the events around it, and the mass burial at Woodlawn Cemetery are factual. However, mention of elephants being buried here is purely fictional. Not only were the elephants not used to save lives, but there weren't animals of any kind on this train. The Hagenback-Wallace Circus utilized three trains total, and the animals were on a completely separate train, so there couldn't have been any elephants present. Certainly, there are no elephants buried at Woodlawn Cemetery.

The five elephant statues were used because they are so symbolically associated with the circus. In fact, the elephants appear in silhouette on most of the gravestones as well.

However, animal sounds were, in fact, heard at the site. As far-fetched as it may seem, were these sounds manifestations of a memory of one of the individuals buried there? The answer, in retrospect, was remarkably simple: "no." Under the right conditions, during the slow traffic hours when it was most quiet and when the wind was blowing in the exactly correct direction, the sounds of wild animals are carried by the wind from the nearby Brookfield Zoo.

The phrase "out of sight, out of mind" provided the difficulty in locating the source of the sounds, which led to the overly elaborate and incredible story.

The Curse of Cap Streeter

Chicago has changed a lot since 1886. It's different not only in the size of buildings and the fact that cars replaced horses but also in its geographic borders. In the Wisconsonian Period of the Ice Age when the Great Lakes were formed by massive glaciers, the edge of the lake extended much farther into downtown Chicago than it does today.

In the mid-1880s, a sandbar began to form about four hundred feet off the coast of the northern part of the Loop. In 1886, a wily captain named Cap Streeter accidentally landed his boat, *The Reutan*, on this sandbar and decided that it was as good a place as any to set up residence with his wife.

Streeter's nickname of "Cap" came to be not because he was a boat captain but because he was a captain for the Union during the Civil War. Before becoming the most famous "squatter" in Chicago history, Cap worked countless jobs including stints as a steamboat operator on the Mississippi River and even as a circus performer.

Over the next several decades, Streeter allowed developers to dump building scraps on his sandbar. In the end, this tactic filled in the land between his boat and shore, creating 186 acres of new land. Streeterville was born. Cap's claim was that the Illinois border was defined by the former coast, so the new land was not technically part of Illinois and was therefore a new territory. He named this territory the District of Lake Michigan. This real estate debate between Cap Streeter, City Hall, and The Title & Trust Company lasted nearly fifty years when the claim to the land was finally dismissed.

The wealthier landowners in the area were initially content to let Cap stay, for the moment, because they saw the opportunity. Potter Palmer, in particular, looked to take advantage of the new land, overseeing the development of the Gold Coast north of Streeterville after the first road was laid in Streeterville. This road, Lake Shore Drive, connected downtown to the North Side.

Cap was bankrupted by his first wife in their divorce settlement. To survive, he ended up selling or giving away plots of his land to lawyers in exchange for their services. Attempts to evict Cap from the property in question was difficult as disputes were often tied up in court, while Cap frequently defended his property with a shotgun. This came to an end when Cap allegedly killed a trespasser. There is speculation that Cap was framed in order to get rid of a nuisance.

In 1921, Cap was laid to rest in Graceland Cemetery at age eighty-four. As the story goes, Cap, never wanting to give up the battle for his land, cursed the land, still called Streeterville to this day, before his death.

The most notable structure in Streeterville is the Hancock Tower which at the time of its completion in 1969 was the largest building in the world. Standing in with one hundred floors, the Hancock Tower delivers some of the best views from some of the most expensive residential suites in the city.

Believe it or not, the land where the Hancock Tower stands has even more of a shady past. Anton LeVay was born on that very spot. LeVay went on to form the Church of Satan.

Strange events have been the rule more so than the exception when it comes to the Hancock Tower. A bizarre march of spiders, sounding like something out of the Old Testament, occurs twice each year. Hundreds of spiders gather and march up one side of the massive building, cross at the top of it, and then march down the other side.

Deaths and suicides with peculiar circumstances also occur at the site. The most famous is the death of Lorraine Kowalski on August 12, 1971. Though the double-paned glass of the high-rise windows were capable of withstanding 280 pounds of pressure per square foot, this 130 pound woman somehow went through it. Her clothes were left in a pile within the apartment as her boyfriend was in the bathroom and out of sight when the apparent tremendous suicide happened.

A famous but far less strange death occurred on December 18, 1997, when former *Saturday Night Live* and emerging comedy star Chris Farley died from a drug overdose.

Frequently, the February 1, 1988, death of Heather O'Rourke is linked to the Streeterville curse. Heather will forever be known by horror film enthusiasts as the little girl in the *Poltergeist* films. Scenes of the third *Poltergeist* film took place at the Hancock Tower and at the nearby Streeterville site Water Tower Place. Heather died of medical complications due to intestinal stenosis. Mistakenly, she is often rumored to have actually died in Streeterville, which is not the case. Also, if O'Rouke's death is associated with a curse, Streeter is in competition with the famed *Poltergeist* curse, which has followed production, crew, and cast through three films.

The most recent freak incident happened on March 9, 2002. It involved three deaths and eight injuries when scaffolding fell over forty stories to the sidewalk and street below during a windy weekend day.

Whether or not the curse of Streeterville is a true story or purely a number of strange coincidences, it is an interesting part of Chicago's history that allows one unique individual, Cap Streeter, to have eternal fame. At the very least, the marching of the spiders is a difficult event to overlook.

Do You Believe in Mary Worth?

Perhaps the best known urban legend outside of the Lover's Lane bloody hook killer is the belief that stating the name Bloody Mary a specific number of times into a bathroom mirror in a darkened room can summon a woman named Mary Worth from beyond the grave.

Most children practicing this ritual at sleepover parties don't think to question this routine, but it seems to be based in as many cities as there are people who have heard the story of "Bloody Mary." Chicago is no different.

In one of the most northern towns of Illinois, Wadsworth, another narrow, hilly, and poorly lit street, very similar to the one that "The Gate" sits on, holds St. Patrick's Cemetery. This is allegedly where the infamous Mary Worth is buried.

As the story goes, during the time of the Civil War, Mary Worth owned a farm complete with house, field, and barn. It is in the barn where Worth gained her notoriety, for it is at this location that she captured runaway slaves.

Lake County is dotted with Underground Railroad stations, even before the Civil War. Waukegan had a church and house that served as stops on the Underground Railroad. The Bonner farm is another site, and Reverend Dodge in Antioch even led a congregation where a prerequisite to join the church was support of the Abolitionist movement.

Residents secretly trafficked runaway slaves through Lake County into ships docked in Lake Forest harbors on Lake Michigan. This was common and occasionally openly practiced. From there, the ships would go to Washington Island off the peninsula of Door County, Wisconsin, before completing the journey to Canada. Not all of the slaves made this difficult journey.

Perhaps the smuggling of runaway slaves was practiced a little too openly. Mary Worth took it upon herself to capture as many runaway slaves as she could. She also took it upon herself to dole out the punishment.

Worth reportedly was a witch, and it was her macabre hobbies that earned her the name Bloody Mary. The manner in which she dealt with the slaves she caught was cruel and ruthless, especially when taking into account all that the slaves had gone through and how close they were to freedom by the time they were caught.

Her much more liberal neighbors eventually found out about Worth's satanic practices and decided to take a page out of the Puritans' book during the famed Salem Witch hunts of the 1600s. Worth was given a punishment appropriate for a witch: burning at the stake. The practice of execution by burning at the stake was far from common in the Midwest (especially in the more modern 1800s), but apparently a desperate situation necessitated a break from the norm.

After the burning, one story relates that Worth's remains

were interred down the same street that her house was on, Dilly Road, at St. Patrick's Cemetery. It is here that the repetitious beckoning of Mary Worth's name started. It is believed that those who are brave enough can walk up to Mary Worth's grave and boldly declare, "I Believe in Mary Worth," and walk away to tell the story. Those who are fearful and not sure of themselves will have quite a different story to tell. Those who state their claim with insincerity are punished violently with a scratch across the face so deep that blood is drawn.

There are many who are suspicious that a Catholic cemetery would ever allow the interment of a known witch. Those who don't believe Worth was placed at St. Patrick's Cemetery point to the former Worth residence as the more likely burial site.

Later, the barn was destroyed, but another farmhouse was soon built on the same location. Apparently, this same location where the gruesome tortures purportedly took place witnessed another death when a later tenant killed herself there.

In Ursula Bielski's thorough book, *Chicago Haunts,* she relays a story told to her by Larry Rawn. This story states that after the suicide, the former Worth property was purchased by another family with the intent to live on and farm the land.

While clearing his field in preparation for his crops, the man of the house came across a square stone. Not thinking anything of it, the man removed the stone from the field and brought it back to his house. Almost immediately, odd things started happening at his property. These events ranged from objects moving from shelves only to break on the floor to the woman of the house repeatedly and inexplicably being locked in the barn.

It was at this moment that the man knew it was not just any rock that he removed from his field. Rather, it was a gravestone. Furthermore, it was believed to be Mary Worth's gravestone.

Attempts were made to restore the stone to its original location, but after the soil had been plowed, this was impossible. By 1986, the house no longer existed due to an alleged arsonous fire.

By the mid 1980s, Lake County was at the beginning of a massive population boom, and formerly unused farmland became highly sought-after real estate. The Worth property was no different—on the surface. The first three contractors to purchase the Worth land all went bankrupt before earth could be broken. The fourth contractor was able to build a number of houses on the land, but, reportedly, the house built nearest to the barn where Worth used to torture slaves has burned twice as of 1998. Any burnings since then have not been recorded.

While this is quite a compelling story, it is merely one of the hundreds that claim to be the basis of the legend of Mary Worth. It may be true that there was a slave catcher and killer who was severely persecuted by the townspeople who found out her secrets. It may also be true that the land where the evil deeds were done may still bear a psychic residue, but there is no guarantee that this is *the* Mary Worth.

On a factual basis, a look at the listings for those buried at St. Patrick's Cemetery in Wadsworth reveals that there is no Mary Worth interred there. Also, the first woman to earn the nickname "Bloody Mary" was Mary I of England whose five-year reign, starting in 1553, included executing nearly three hundred Protestants that refused Catholicism.

There is also the claim that Mary Queen of Scots, who served as queen from 1542 to 1547, earned the moniker Bloody Mary after killing her husband.

The most urban legend part of the story—stating "Bloody Mary" in the mirror or at the gravesite—has several versions. Instead of scratching the caller across the face, Bloody Mary is also said to merely present herself in the mirror on top of the caller's image. Rather than repeating the name or "I believe in Mary Worth," alternate statements include "Bloody Mary, I have your baby," and "Bloody Mary, I dropped your baby."

Though some queens have found their share of celebrity in being nicknamed Bloody Mary, most American folklorists believe that the urban legend of Bloody Mary has American, not European, roots.

The possible names aren't even always Bloody Mary or Mary Worth. The list also contains the names Black Agnes, Agnes, Bloody Bones, Hell Mary, Mary Whales, Mary Johnson, Mary Lou, Mary Jane, and even other common names like Sally and Kathy.

Sometimes the story even detours from the story of a slave catcher. Occasionally, Bloody Mary is the victim of a disfiguring automobile accident or a sympathetic mother who tragically lost her baby (e.g., "Bloody Mary, I dropped your baby").

The true origins of the story of Bloody Mary may never be known since there are so many theories and claims to the story from credible sources. One thing that can be said: Wadsworth has an intriguing past that is still being felt today by residents of Dilly Road and visitors of St. Patrick's Cemetery, which has been the target of vandals and cult worship for many years now.

The Devil's Stomping Grounds

The most amazing paranormal experience imaginable would be an actual encounter with the devil. An intimate encounter with the Evil One witnessed by a crowd would make for an even more unforgettable tale.

The random question, "Have you ever danced with the devil in the pale moonlight," sounds like nothing more than a pretty sentence from Tim Burton's 1989 film *Batman*, but according to Chicago lore, there is one woman who can answer the question with a definitive, "Yes."

The scene was Chicago's Bridgeport area in a dance hall during the early days of the First World War. Attempts to escape the horrors of war often included evening entertainment at a dance hall, safe from government newsreels. It was at just such a dance hall, the Kaiser Dance Hall on Archer Avenue near Loomis Street, where a young woman was taken by the hand by a dashingly handsome gentleman.

The two were enjoying a delightful, light-hearted evening of dancing, laughing, and music when something near the ground caught the woman's eye. A scream filled the room and the musicians stopped playing. A group of people, thinking the woman was in trouble, rushed towards her. The man she was dancing with began to run away, and the mob gave chase.

Cornering the man against a third-story window, they were horrified and surprised to see the man jump through the window, seemingly to certain death. Walking to the window, the crowd was even more amazed to see that not only was the man still living, but he was actually running from the building.

After asking the woman why she screamed, she exclaimed that she looked down only to see cloven hooves emerging from the gentleman's pant legs. Later observation revealed two hoof prints sunken into the concrete below the window. (A popular tradition in lore is that when the devil takes human form, the only parts of his body that do not transform are his feet.)

The legend of the devil in Bridgeport is a unique one, but not for the obvious reason. Rather, it is unique because the story takes place in Chicago and not in Europe or Latin America where it is more common.

There was even a version of it floating around Danzing, Germany, as early as 1875, as it related to a ballroom called The Vineyard. Generally, the stories have a religious motif. Usually, the woman is partaking in this inappropriate activity—dancing—during the religious time of lent. Other times the girl is not obeying the fifth commandment, by not honoring her mother's wishes. Often, it is a combination of the two.

Variations of the story include the man running into a bathroom and disappearing rather than jumping from the window. After disappearing from the bathroom, the only thing that remained was the malodorous stench of sulfur. Other times, the man does jump from the window, but his hoof marks are burned into the dance floor rather than the pavement below. Another tale tells of a man jumping from the window with the girl. By the time the onlookers reach the window, the man has vanished, but the lifeless body of the woman is on the sidewalk.

The versions of this story coming from Latin America often have Satan and the girl dancing in the middle of the room where the orchestra notes the odd legs and feet on the man. The orchestra quickly changes tune to a religious hymn. The couple dance faster and faster until the dramatic exit is made in a large puff of sulfur-smelling smoke. Often the woman is abducted by the devil himself. Also, rather than cloven hooves, the tall, dark, and handsome man ends up having chicken legs and claws.

Most researchers of lore and urban legends claim the story came from Latin America and has spread to few other countries. They also tend to claim that as far as North America is concerned, it has only reached the Southwest. The fact that the legend is also active in Chicago and has been for around ninety years is still quite an enigma to most historians and researchers.

The Warrior at Lake Shore Drive

Every square inch of land in America can be linked back to Native Americans. The massive totem pole overlooking Lake Shore Drive and facing Addison Street looking directly at Wrigley Field is a constant reminder of this.

The founder of Kraft Incorporated, James L. Kraft, purchased it in 1926 from Vancouver, British Columbia. Kraft, whose name is still upon Kraft Cheese products, was an experienced collector of art.

Three years after the acquisition, the totem pole was placed on Chicago Park District land between Lake Michigan and Lake Shore Drive and dedicated to the schoolchildren of Chicago. The problem is that it faces inland and not Lake Michigan. It is traditional for the totem pole to always face water. Many believe this is where the problems began.

First of all, there is the almost constant thread that occurs at haunted areas, that of orbs and mist appearing on photographs but not seen by the human eye. On photographs and their negatives, this appears as a definite area of fog. The ectoplasm isn't always circular, but the edges do tend to be well defined.

The orbs are easily discounted as the location is near the lake and a busy highway. Water and dust particles appear in still images as orbs. It's my practice that orb pictures are ignored unless there extenuating factors, such as a simultaneous cold spot or a spike on an electromagnetic field (EMF) reader to substantiate it.

The more curious unexplainable occurrence is that photographs taken at different times, when compared, show that the totem pole has changed. The story the totem pole tells is that of a great warrior hunting down a whale. The warrior is half way down the whale's back with one arm extended and the other holding a spear. The whale's head is nearest the ground while a mighty bird is perched on its tail at the top of the totem pole.

From photograph to photograph, the warrior can be seen with his arms in different positions and even with his entire body turned to a different side of the pole. Though the position of the photographer and the time of day could create minor optical illusions that could be the reason for these changes, most of the differences are far more extreme than that.

The original pole developed a scar in the form of a massive, unsightly crack running through the wooden structure. This was most likely a result of being in Chicago 365 days a year from 1929 to 1985 withstanding wind chills of -93°F to heat indices up to 119 °F and not due to any paranormal activity.

The 1970s marked an interesting time in the history of the totem pole. First, stories of the moving warrior graced the printed pages in two of Chicago's most respected publications, the *Chicago Tribune* and the *Chicago Sun-Times*. Soon after, it twice became the victim of vandals. The first simply threw red paint on its base, but the second was an arson conducted by Richard Skyhorse in protest of the looting at Washington's Bureau of Indian Affairs.

Then Chicago Mayor Harold Washington gave the nearly two-hundred-year-old totem pole back to British Columbia in 1985, partly due to the weathering it had suffered over the course of fifty-six Chicago winters but possibly also to deter curiosity seekers in search of the paranormal.

Kraft, Inc., hired a Native American artist to replicate the

totem pole. In 1986, it was placed in the exact same spot as the previous pole and, again, with its back to the water. Almost immediately, the pole took on the same characteristics of the previous Native American artifact, right down to the crack in the exact same spot that runs from tail to head of the whale.

The totem pole sustained heavy vandalism shortly after being erected for the second time. One vandal actually broke and stole the arms off the warrior; later, it was even shot several times.

To this day, the Kraft Totem Pole stands where Addison meets Lake Shore Drive and faces the home of the Chicago Cubs, and it continues creating mysterious visions in person and on film. Some even blame it for the exceptionally long World Series drought the Cubs endured.

Hungry Fences

To say the least, Chicago is a unique city. Whether it's cow statues marching down State Street or randomly placed couches scattered along Michigan Avenue, there is always something to catch the eye of a local driver. A more inconspicuous item to catch a driver's eye is metal, vertical slat fencing, typical along a number of city cemeteries.

Bohemian National Cemetery has stood on the North Side since 1877. On the West Side stands Mount Olivet Cemetery, which has been around since 1885, while Holy Sepulchre Cemetery dates back to 1919. Suddenly, for some unexplainable reason, a common thread linked all three of these locations. The fences that defined the borders of these cemeteries and protected the monuments inside from uninvited, after-hour guests for many decades developed an appetite.

The rash of odd automobile accidents into cemetery fences was first noted at Mount Olivet Cemetery in the late 1970s. Regardless of time of day, from the late 1970s throughout the 1980s, it was routine to see about one car per week crashed into the cemetery fence along 111th Street in front of the cemetery. Reportedly, there were nearly nine times as many accidents at this location than there were at the fence of Mount Greenwood Cemetery located immediately across the street. Not long after the first reports of these random accidents at Mount Olivet Cemetery, Holy Sepulchre Cemetery and Bohemian National Cemetery reported similar events.

All that the hapless drivers could recall was that they were driving down the road and the next thing they knew their car was at rest against the bronze cemetery fence.

As these events continued, an investigation ensued. The result of the investigation concluded that each driver had suffered an epileptic-like seizure caused by rapid flashing off the cemetery gate bars from the car headlights. In the instances where the bars of the gates could not be the culprit, the blame was placed on reflections from shiny headstones nearest to the roadside. For crashes that happened during the daylight hours, the reflection from the sun was to blame.

The conclusion was very plausible, but many questions were still left unanswered. To start, hundreds of cemeteries in the state have the very same style fence, so why were these other cemeteries not affected? Since these cemeteries have been around for almost as long as automobiles have, then why isn't there a consistent record of this type of accident happening? Also, if this incident was so easily occurring, it would obviously happen all over the country—even all over the world. So, why is this localized to being a Chicago phenomena? The reasoning behind these "hungry fence" accidents may not be related to any paranormal activity, but the explanation given so far seems insufficient.

To counter the problem, Mount Olivet Cemetery removed large portions of their vertical slat fence and replaced it with a less decorative green cyclone fence. The accidents drastically decreased. A similar story holds true for Holy Sepulchre Cemetery, which replaced all of their fencing along 111th Street.

Bohemian National Cemetery on Pulaski Road has the same fence, and the accidents are continuing. This anecdotal evidence does seem to link the accidents to the metal slat fencing, but there are still gaps in reasoning that need to be filled.

As recently as the 1990s, a fourth Chicago cemetery has added its name to the list of locations with a hungry fence. The much-famed and historic Rosehill Cemetery has been the site of numerous car accidents as recent as the printing of this publication. The border of Rosehill Cemetery along Western Avenue is completely straight, but driving alongside of it in the daytime is morbidly comical due to the many visible scars on the fence from the numerous accidents. Severely damaged sections have been replaced and are easily identified by the different shades of green. The section's more recent accidents are covered by massive sheets of plywood while the newest scars haven't been addressed at all as the bars are bent drastically or even broken.

In addition to the road being straight, it is also well lit, and normally, there's even a row of parked cars in addition to the sidewalk, providing a buffer zone between the road and the fence. Driving past the fence in day or night does not produce a flashing effect because the fence is covered with a dull green matte color. Also, beyond this fence is nothing but trees, so no reflections are coming from tombstones. This section of the cemetery isn't yet being used for interment. No reasons or guesses for the accidents at this location have been ventured.

CHAPTER 2

FINE FOOD AND SPIRITS

"Ole St. Andrew's Inn"

SLIMPICTURES.COM/CHAPTER2

As Michael Jordan is associated with Chicago, so should be fine dining. There may be more restaurants than haunted locations in the city, which is saying a lot. This being said, it is natural for the two to overlap.

With Chicago being one of the main stops for settlers moving west from New York as they moved across the country, a number of cultures have left their mark on Chicago's food business throughout the years.

From "hole-in-the-wall" Thai places throughout the South Side, to the much more commercial "eatertainment" industry on Ohio Street in the Loop, to the many frat-boy-infested pubs around Wrigleyville, options for the hungry are numerous.

The spirits active at these Chicago eateries range from employees still on the job to regulars who considered the site a home away from home to a fiery-tempered bar owner who makes for a very interesting ghost, light on humor and heavy on activity.

Ghosts sitting in with the band, ghosts helping out during peak hours or playing tricks on customers, and even one spirit who made the journey from England to Chicago are all available to meet here in the Windy City.

Cheap Labor

Thanks to the transcontinental railroad in 1869, the East Coast now had a link to the West Coast. The mechanical feat was possible thanks to the Chinese, who made up eighty percent of the workers. At the completion of the railroad, most of these Chinese workers were living in the California region; however, it was made clear they were not wanted.

There were many riots against the Chinese throughout San Francisco and Los Angeles. Another major blow was a law that was passed in 1863 that forbade a Chinese person to testify against a white man. This led to a rash of race-inspired violence that today would be classified as hate crimes.

It is interesting to note that the railroad was finished in

1869, and the first wave of Chinese moving to Illinois happened in 1870. The first Chinese settlers in Illinois established themselves in Morgan County in Southern Illinois. The first Chinese person to settle in Chicago is believed to be a man named T. C. Moy, who, in 1878, wrote to his friends and family on the West Coast that Chicagoans were much more friendly than Californians.

By 1900, Chicago boasted around six hundred Chinese-owned businesses. The first Chicago-Chinese community was established in 1905 near the intersection of Clark and Van Buren Street. However, when news of the hostile treatment towards Chinese on the West Coast reached China, China began boycotting American trade. To counter this, landlords drastically raised rent in the Chinese neighborhood. A majority of residents were forced to move south to an area that was an Italian and Croatian community at Cermak and Wentworth.

This area quickly became Chicago's new Chinatown. Unfortunately, preexisting city plans and international events made life very difficult for the residents of the new Chinatown.

First, the 1933 World's Fair in Chicago brought about the extension of Cermak Road through the community. Roughly half the residential portion of the area was demolished. Then, in 1949, China was taken over by the Communist Party, and, as a direct result of this, Chicago saw its largest increase of Chinese immigrants. Unfortunately, at the same time Chinese immigration to Chicago was peaking, even more housing areas were being demolished to accommodate the new Dan Ryan and Stevenson Expressways.

Ethnic neighborhoods still exist today and serve a functional purpose in the city. They ease the immigrants' transition from one culture to another before they move off to another Chicago neighborhood or suburb. Their absence is quickly filled with a new immigrant.

Today, the first Chinatown still exists but is referred to as Small Saigon, since most residents are now from Southeast Asia and Vietnam. South Chinatown is still fighting the same problems that it has been facing for more than half a century. New land for housing is being bought in the Bridgeport area as the constant southward development continues. Serious efforts are being made to reduce crime and to diversify their economy. Right now, the vast majority of businesses in Chinatown are restaurants who are forced to lower their prices to compete against each other.

Within seconds of exiting the expressway, people quickly forget that they are in Chicago, Illinois, or even America for that matter.

Driving down the streets on a sunny summer weekday afternoon, the Catholic schools in the area release their students who are almost exclusively of Asian descent. Asian Chicago police officers patrol the many crosswalks the school children use to go back to their homes. It is this environment that acts as a living museum for Americans to view a modified, but local, foreign culture.

Triple Crown Seafood is one of the many authentic Asian eateries in the area. It is in this building that a former occupant never officially "punched out." In actuality, the spirit that still inhabits the Triple Crown Seafood Restaurant died in the building long before it was a restaurant, but it seems that the spirit has been able to adjust to the changes.

Two-eleven West 22nd Place was first an apartment building. Eventually, On Leong Businessmen's Association bought a large number of buildings in the area to create South Chinatown. Over time, this apartment building was converted to its current state, the Triple Crown Seafood Restaurant, but not before one occupant of the apartment hanged himself in the area that is currently the bathroom.

The psychic problems with the building may not have started with the hanging but rather with the land the building is on; it was reportedly an Indian burial ground. Building on an Indian burial ground has seemed like little more than a horror movie plot point ever since *Poltergeist;* however, it is a sad reality that has been repeated countless times across the country.

It is not uncommon for very old burial grounds to be disturbed, as we'll see again in Lemont's St. James of the Sag Cemetery. It is almost commonplace for construction workers building subway tunnels in New York to stumble across mass burial grounds for slaves that date back to the American Revolution.

While the majority of ghost stories talk of spirits going about their own business, unaware of the physical world around them, this spirit seems quite aware of the current state of the building. As workers of the restaurant approach the sink to wash the pile of dirty dishes that routinely grows on busy nights, they find the work already finished. Reportedly, the dishes weren't washed by another coworker but rather by something else.

Patrons of the restaurant have also claimed to see a shadowy figure milling about in the area of the restrooms. Similar stories have been told relating to a number of private homes in the area. According to local lore, a number of past residents have hanged themselves to death in homes along 22nd Place. There is the possibility that one true story is being recycled and accidentally linked with several other locations incorrectly. However, the fact that the land was formerly a burial ground is good cause for the area to be haunted regardless of whether or not a suicide was committed on the grounds. Perhaps additional occurrences will reveal more clues to the origin of the haunting.

A Mischievous Ghost Remains

The energy around restaurants is usually light and positive since most dining experiences are a pleasure. Friends and family spending time together or people celebrating a promotion, birthday, or a wedding can leave the residue of positive energy in the environment. It seems most eateries and bars in Chicago have their own group of regulars who attend the establishment on a nightly basis because they care so much for it. Perhaps some deceased regulars may return in search of more good times with friends. Many believe that adding alcohol to the situation at the time of death only complicates matters for the recently deceased during one's transition to the other side. One can only imagine that this transition is a major one that can be confusing for anyone and much more confusing for someone who is intoxicated.

Although not for certain, this could be the case involving the Country House Restaurant in Du Page County. It appears that in 1958 a woman named Sharon was very distraught when she was exiting the establishment at 241 West 55th Street. She requested to leave her child with the workers at the restaurant for a short time, but her request went unfulfilled. Seemingly distraught, the woman left the area with her child.

Within a few minutes, the woman was dead. Her car came to rest after crashing directly into a utility pole. Fortunately, her child was unharmed.

Some claim the woman left angrily after an argument with one of the bartenders. Easy guesswork speculates the woman may have been confronting the father of the infant child.

Apparently, witnesses to the car accident, which happened less than a mile from the restaurant, claim that the accident was no accident at all but rather a successful suicide.

By 1975, the Country House Restaurant opened under the management of David and Patrick Regnery. It wasn't long before odd sounds put the new owners on their toes. Though initially dismissed as common creaks of an older structure, the owners soon couldn't ignore the sounds anymore.

A friend of the owners, after entering the building, made a joke implying that rather than a restaurant Patrick and David were running a brothel. The reason for the comment came after the friend saw a pretty young blonde woman beckoning for him to come in from a second story window. Upon checking the upstairs, no one was found.

This woman was first seen from the second story window facing the parking lot, but she has also been seen standing at windows facing 55th Street. It was at this point that the Regenery boys had to face the fact that their business was haunted. It was when psychics were invited to evaluate the situation that the link to the woman's apparent 1958 suicide came about. A phone call to the previous owner confirmed the story of the woman's death.

Getting Fresh

It may be alcohol that helped fuel Sharon's haunting at the Country House Restaurant. However, it's well documented that Frank Giff was under the influence when he passed at Ole St. Andrew's Inn at 5938 North Broadway.

This bar has gone through many incarnations through the years. It held the names The Castle Pub, Pancho's Place, and Frank Giff's Bar. It was under the direction of bar owner Frank Giff that the location came to be known as The Edinburgh Castle Pub.

Giff's ownership of a bar was like a sad case of a kid in a candy store. After closing nightly, Giff would sample from the bar's vodka collection to the point of passing out. The employee opening the bar the next morning would invariably find Giff sitting on a barstool, passed out on the bar.

One morning, the discovery of Giff was not a pleasant one; he was dead. How Frank actually died isn't clear-cut. Some believe Giff simply drank himself to death while others believe Giff died of head trauma after passing out and falling off his stool backwards, hitting his head on the floor behind him. The one aspect of his death that is pretty much beyond dispute is that Giff was drunk when he died in his bar.

Giff's wife Edna continued the business a short while before selling it to Jane McDougal in the early 1960s. Under McDougal's control, the Edinburgh Castle Pub became a Scottish bar called the Ole St. Andrew's Inn. As can be the case, a dormant spirit is awakened or simply springs to action after the location has undergone change. This can be in the form of additional construction to the place, destruction (in rare cases), but most commonly after the place has undergone a remodeling.

After the Ole St. Andrew's Inn was remodeled, it quickly became evident that former owner Frank Giff was still present and not too fond of the changes. After all, the actions of the spirit were easily compared to that of an unruly drunk.

There was a rack that hung over the cash register where glasses were suspended. Glasses suddenly appeared to propel themselves from the rack to the floor. To prevent this, bartenders went so far as to actually tape the glasses to the rack when they weren't in use. Oddly enough, the glasses continued to smash themselves on the ground. Giff appeared to be stubborn.

The glasses were not alone in being the victim of Giff's protests. Glass ashtrays also flung themselves from the bar to the floor below, shattering on impact. Most remarkable was the case involving a metal lion statue, which was used to add to the Scottish décor. Giff saw otherwise. One morning the lion was found with its legs and tongue mangled and bent completely out of shape.

Giff's nightly binge sessions also continue. It seems that up to a quarter of a bottle of vodka, Giff's drink of choice, vanishes overnight.

Giff died while sitting at the bar, but the bar was shortened in order to make room for additional seating at tables. Initially, booths lined the walls, but right after Thanksgiving of 2000, the booths were removed and replaced with tables. Upon entering the establishment, if one were to take the first table along the far wall, they would be sitting at the precise location where Frank Giff perished.

Frequently, patrons who sit at this exact location experience the most phenomena. Cold spots or drafts brushing along the legs of patrons are common despite the fact that the nearby bar should redirect drafts coming from the front door. Women tend to get the most attention from Giff. On several occasions women have been grasped on the shoulder or on the knee by a cold, clammy unseen hand. Apparently, this only happens to redheads and blondes. It is interesting to note that Giff's tastes haven't seemed to change at all. His wife was a strawberry blonde.

Boasting free jukebox plays on Wednesday, the cozy bar is still very much in business and open to talk of the paranormal. There is a framed newspaper article about the bar's ghost behind the bar.

Margaret Dillard, a veteran bartender at the pub, can attest that there is truth in the stories although it is rare for things to happen to her. When we spoke to her in 2001, she had been working at the pub for over thirty-five years but only had three or four encounters with Giff's rowdy ghost. Apparently, the addition of Margaret, a no-nonsense redhead, to the staff was a change that Giff welcomed.

On the Edge

Like the Ole St. Andrew's Inn, Tito on the Edge has been around for a while, mostly in other incarnations. The difference is that the Ole St. Andrew's Inn has a long history of being a bar, whereas Tito on the Edge had been quite a different type of business. Originally, this was Coletta's Funeral Parlor. That business, started in 1908, has since moved down south.

The very clever name comes from the fact that the bar is located on the edge of two of Chicago's cultural enclaves: Chinese and Italian.

"Back a long time ago, the city was broken down into sections. Around here were Chinese, Irish, Black, Italian, and Croatian. So, every two or three blocks there was another funeral home. If someone died they'd be laid out at their nationality's place," stated part-owner of the bar, Bob Tito, "and if two Italians died on the same day, one would be waked out and the other would have to be held over until the following day."

Bob Tito, who grew up in the area, purchased the building with his brother Russ in 1992, despite the fact that they had visited the location in the past to pay respect to their own deceased family and friends.

Though they have owned it for about a decade, the Tito brothers still, "have friends who won't come in here because of their memories. They get as far as the doorway but just can't do it," said Bob.

The then and now of the building is morbidly humorous. Where the casket was placed on display is now where the bands perform. In that same area there is a recessed opening in the wall where a cross was hung. Now, a disco ball is suspended in front of it. Where mourners sat to listen to the service is now the dance floor. It also holds a number of large tables for dining. Those in the mood for something to eat might be disheartened with the knowledge that the kitchen was formerly the embalming room.

Tito is quick to point out that the freezer in the basement never held bodies; however, the room behind it was the holding area. This room stands out visually because red-fire bricks were used to construct the wall so it would stay cool and dry for obvious reasons.

A funeral parlor is a highly unlikely place to be haunted. Many haunted locations tend to be places that were significant to the individual, like a house or a place with fond memories. Cemeteries are also somewhat rarely haunted. Theories for hauntings at cemeteries are varied but mostly revolve around the connection between spirit or energy and the physical body.

Tito on the Edge seems to be the exception.

Evidence of hauntings started quickly after the building was transformed. Staff members, rather than customers of the bar, experience most of the happenings.

Television sets change for no reason, and the ceiling drips water though there are no problems with the plumbing in the upstairs apartments. The most dramatic experiences include mists and an actual apparition of a man wearing a black trench coat near where the bar is now. The apparitions have been seen appearing at the bar and moving to where the caskets were displayed before they vanish.

"I've never seen it, but a lot of the bartenders have," stated Bob. "They claim they see what's like a wave of energy floating near the archway." The archway frames where the caskets were displayed.

Though superbly transformed into a locally popular bar, the layout of the building was obviously not created for a bar. Upon entering the structure, one must walk through a small greeting room. It doesn't take much effort to imagine a guest book near the doorway and a line of mourners standing behind it. Due to the necessity to have a large amount of space for funeral seating, there now seems to be a lot of wasted space in the main room for a bar.

Bob and Russ Tito have created a warm environment for those who wish to patronize the location after browsing through Chinatown. The fact that the place is haunted and was a funeral parlor is no secret, as bartenders, patrons, and the owners alike enjoy telling the history of the building to anyone interested in listening.

Just as the bar has a difficult time doing business to those who have personal ties to the funeral parlor, the Titos have a difficult time renting out the six apartments over the bar, mostly due to superstition.

"The Chinese are very superstitious people," warned Bob. This explains why, though on the border of Chinatown, there are few, if any, Chinese sitting at the bar on any given night.

The cause for the haunting is up to debate. Many believe it is psychic residue of a half a century of people being mourned at the site, but there's possibly something more to it than that. Like the story of Frank Giff, a former owner or employee of the funeral parlor might still be residing at the location. While this person obviously helped hundreds of Chicagoans cope with their losses, perhaps this man is having difficulty dealing with his own death.

There is also the possibility of psychic manifestations still filling the building, or at least the main room, with a sorrow-filled energy. Considering Bob Tito has operated this bar for nearly a decade and yet some of his close friends still refuse to enter the building because of their associated memories, it shows the depth of feeling these people hold for the building. Since 1908, a great many people have entered that building and endured much sorrow and sadness in the same place people are currently drinking away their worries.

Could this energy, comprised of the sadness of thousands of people, be coming together to manifest itself? In this undefined world of the paranormal, the only thing that's a certainty is that everything is a possibility. For the time-being at least, only the man in the long black coat will know for sure.

A Transcontinental Ghost

Enter yet another North Side bar with great character. Time will tell if the next version of this bar, which is planned to open on the same location after the original is renovated, will have the haunted reputation of its predecessor.

The original Red Lion Pub closed late in 2007. The building was gutted completely with plans to reopen in fall of 2008 after slowly deteriorating over the previous 120 years.

If you had the fortune to visit the Red Lion prior to 2007, you would have found a telephone booth that looked to have been directly imported from jolly old England. Farther from the door were rows of booths for dining. Then, out of the left side of your peripheral vision, a white flash would catch your attention. One of the bus boys has thrown a towel from a doorway in an attempt to startle yet another wide-eyed ghost hunter.

These owners and staff embraced and celebrated the bar's haunted reputation, as opposed to the countless others who tried to conceal it.

The stairway to the second story was near the front door. Halfway up the staircase was an eye-catching stained glass window. The second story held a smaller version of the bar from the first floor and another large dining area. This was considered to be one of the most haunted places in Chicago and by far the most haunted restaurant in northeastern Illinois.

When observing a haunted location, it is always important to look into the history of the building and sometimes even the land it is built on. Though the Red Lion had been operating since the mid 1980s, the building itself was constructed in

1882. Throughout time it was a grocery store, a country and western bar called Dirty Dan's, and even an illegal gambling parlor in the 1940s. An interesting fact is that it is situated across the street and about a hundred yards away from the Biograph Theater where the infamous gangster, John Dillinger, was shot. The pub is also within walking distance from the site where Chicago's most notorious Mafia act took place: the St. Valentine's Day Massacre.

The second story of the building was almost always used as apartments. This is where one of the ghosts linked with the site originates. A young, mentally-handicapped girl named Sharon lived in this apartment and died after a long illness. This contradicts several other readings by psychics who identified Sharon as a flapper during Chicago's roaring twenties who was either killed or committed suicide. Her two elderly parents also lived and died in the apartment.

In addition to being responsible for a pungent smell of lavender filling the upstairs, Sharon is often the one who is blamed for the happenings in the second story women's bathroom. Perhaps the most famous story pertaining to the bathroom happened one evening when a Chicago police officer was spending his time off duty in the bar. Suddenly, the peacefulness of the atmosphere was broken by a horrific scream of terror that emanated from the women's bathroom. The police officer, with gun drawn, quickly approached the door and shouted to whoever was inside. There was no answer. The man tried to open the door, but it was locked from the inside. Fearing that a woman was being attacked, he kicked the door down to find the room absolutely vacant. There are no windows through which someone could have escaped or from which an outside sound could have come.

In addition, on more than one occasion women have found themselves trapped in the bathroom for a chaotic fifteen minutes at a time. Somehow, the door seems locked despite the fact that the door locks only from the inside. Then, for whatever unknown reason, the door is free and opens easily.

The next ghost that has been identified in the pub is linked to the stained glass window on the landing of the staircase to the second story. When John Cordwell purchased the bar with his son Colin in 1984, he decided to commemorate his father with it. Below the stained glass window is a plaque dedication to his father who is buried in England in an unmarked grave. There is no headstone on his actual grave because he was uncomfortable with the idea of having weight placed upon him.

Soon after the window and plaque were added, those using the stairs would often feel a presence, be tapped on the shoulder, or even suffer dizzy spells. In addition, at the very top of the staircase where the second-story door is, cold spots are frequently felt.

"A huge cold breeze just came out," explained my partner Mary Czerwinski during our first visit as she opened the door to the second floor. This was in the middle of a warm summer afternoon. The second floor bar was not in use, so there was no air conditioning on at the time.

Just past the second floor door, a presence was felt on the first stool of the bar. This has been reported by many people, particularly members of Twilight Tales, a group of horror and mystery writers who held their meetings at the Red Lion Pub and will continue to do so when the bar is reopened.

If this actually is John Cordwell's father, it means that in his afterlife he traveled all the way across "The Pond" to America to be close to his son and at the one place where his name stands in memoriam. This does seem fitting since John's father made a promise that he would try to make contact again after death.

The hauntings did not begin with the Cordwell's ownership of the property. Dan Danforth, who owned Dirty Dan's, had his own experiences in the second story during renovations. After working for a while, he would take a break only to return to find his work destroyed and his tools scattered around the room. The destruction of his construction efforts went as far as nails actually being pulled up from the wood.

Believe it or not, in this small Chicago building, these two spirits are not alone. A number of other spirits have actually materialized in different locations throughout the bar. The rest of the "cast" include a man who walks up the stairs and through the downstairs bar, a blonde Russian-looking male, a bearded man donning a black hat, and even a man in cowboy attire. These spirits occupy the second story bar, commonly calling out the names of other people at the bar and even throwing things around on occasion.

Some of the happenings on the second floor can only be witnessed from the first floor. Frequently, the sounds of heavy footsteps are heard walking across the floor on the second story. Other times it sounds like a destructive customer is throwing things. While people on the first floor are hearing this, people on the second floor are completely unaware of it. Most of the time there are no people at all on the second story when these sounds are heard.

Luckily for ghost hunters, there is even a best time to hear these sounds. They appear to be the most common between 3:00 and 5:30 P.M. According to some, Sunday is the most popular day for such an occurrence

Despite the fact that on slow days the deceased outnumber the living in the quaint English pub, a relaxed and comforting atmosphere is experienced by nearly all who frequent it. The owners, bartenders, and regulars are open to conversation on the unseen guests of the bar, and it's not uncommon to find a recorded presentation of the History Channel's Haunted History airing on the television behind the bar.

Monday nights are especially popular at the pub, as the second story is the site of readings from members of Twilight Tales. Many of their works are compiled into books that are for sale through their Web site (www.twilighttales.com). One of their works is *Tales from the Red Lion* and is a collection of many of the real stories associated with the pub.

A Sad End to a Lot of Pain

It takes a certain type of character to run a bar, especially in a big city. Dealing with the area regulars, roughnecks, and wayward tourists can be a handful to deal with in addition to the grind of attempting to keep a business above water in this highly competitive market. A bar cannot successfully exist without a unique atmosphere to set itself apart from the rest. Wally Bochenek's cachet for his bar, the Parakeet Lounge, consisted of actual parakeets flying throughout the bar.

Like the Red Lion Pub, the Parakeet Lounge (now The Bucktown Pub) was a common Mafia hangout. Those wise to the inner workings of the city know that Mafia families have run the day-to-day operations of the city about as much as the politicians, and there are the cases where the two overlapped. During the prohibition era, the bar continued to sell and distribute alcohol. Once prohibition ended in 1933, the establishment became a legal bar and has been one ever since.

Ultimately, the pressures of running a bar and his own personal pressures came to a head for Wally. The largest factor was Wally's long and futile battle with cancer. A man who controlled his bar with a strict and knowing force lost control of his own life thanks to the powerful sickness. Wally took control of his life again with one final and decisive action. On August 11, 1987, Wally pulled the trigger of a gun he was holding to his head. Wally was rushed to the Illinois Masonic Hospital, but to no avail. Wally's life had come to a tragic end in the apartment above the bar, which he shared with his wife Anna.

Anna continued to live in the second story apartment and sleep in the same room where her husband shot himself for several more years. The bar was closed, never to reopen as the Parakeet Lounge. In 1991 Mike Johnson purchased the property and opened the Bucktown Pub with Krystyne Palmer.

Under the new management, the parakeets were replaced with an impressive, comprehensive, and, if anything, cluttered collage of pop culture icons.

It would appear as though the changes to the bar weren't accepted by all of the former regulars of the Parakeet Lounge. The one who was the most unhappy with the changes was Wally himself. Phenomena generally categorized as poltergeist activity, primarily movement of objects, quickly became commonplace. Bottles would be rearranged, and napkin and coaster placements would also be altered.

It wasn't long before these things were linked to Wally.

While the bar was flourishing as a new Bucktown hot spot on the first floor, Wally's widow, Anna, continued to live in the second story apartment where Wally had retired after work and eventually retired permanently.

"Could you imagine living in that place?" asked manager Krystyne Palmer rhetorically. "I think she talked to him," she continued. Apparently, Anna would go on about conversations that she had had with her departed husband.

Without the struggles of running a business and beyond the pain of cancer, Wally was still able to keep up to date with his wife and the goings on in the bar below.

Anna has since passed away from natural causes. "I think she's up there [in the apartment], too, now," mused Krystyne. "It's just my feeling, my intuition."

"She never used to leave," remembered a former bartender named Jimmy.

Krystyne agreed, "Yeah, we used to say to her, 'Come on, let's go out and do something,' but she'd just say, 'No, Wally wouldn't like that.'"

A former bartender named Holly found her way to Wally's bad side.

"She was walking around back here [behind the bar] hitting stuff, throwing things around, and just abusing the place," explained Krystyne. Wally was happy to tame her by dropping a plaster Rolling Rock statuette from a high shelf directly behind her as she passed it, breaking it in the process. She did not challenge Wally again. The broken Rolling Rock statuette still sits upon the shelf overlooking the bar as a reminder that Wally is doing the same thing.

A regular named Bill loudly disputed Wally's supernatural existence; that is, until one day when he was proven wrong. After again calling the thought of Wally's ghost a joke, a shelf along the bottom of the bar broke, dropping a number of bottles a few inches to the floor. "Then every bottle rolled a different direction," said Krystyne. "He didn't talk about Wally at all after that."

Krystyne became a believer even before she owned the bar. When she first made her bid to purchase the bar, someone else had time to match the bid. While driving to the pub, Krystyne began talking to Wally. "I got some money, I'll borrow some money, I can make it work. Just give me a sign that it's gonna work out, Wally," said Krystyne.

Wally, a World War II Air Force veteran, had a number of patches that were placed into an envelope and sealed. When Krystyne reached the pub, Mike was there waiting so he could show her that somehow a patch from the sealed envelope found its way to the floor and sat there, face up. Krystyne knew this was the sign that she had asked for.

She then promised Wally that she'd construct a sign to commemorate him and Anna. The sign, in the shape of a World

War II patch, is posted on
the side of the building and
has been there since 1999.

Wally has only
manifested himself on one
known occasion. A bartender
named Chrissy had a friend
help her wash glasses after
the bar closed late one night.
When the man turned
around, he came face-to-
face with the former owner.
He was described as wearing
an older style of Levi jeans, a white shirt, and a white apron. The
man had no prior knowledge of Wally's ghost.

When running through the list of events that have happened
at the bar, the presence of cold spots are almost overlooked by
the wait staff because it is such a common occurrence. While
paranormal occurrences at most locations are few and far
between, the sensation of a presence and the feeling of cold
spots are nearly continuous. This I can vouch for personally.

As I was exiting the establishment after Krystyne played
the part of a gracious host and answered questions while giving
a tour, I felt something myself. On a hot June afternoon, I was
slowly walking backwards towards the door while talking with
Krystyne, who was sitting at the bar, when I stepped into the
most extreme and foreboding cold spot that I had ever felt.

The basement beneath the bar is curiously partially filled
with dirt. One wonders if objects were buried there during its
time as a speakeasy, but despite speculation, no evidence has
come to light thus far. It is said, however, that those who enter
the basement commonly emerge from it at a quicker pace due
to unsettling feelings and the sensing of a presence.

The bar has since changed ownership once more to Tom
Gorsich, a seasoned bar owner who also owns businesses in the
Rush and Division party district. His daughter Piper manages

the pub. Tom is an adamant nonbeliever in ghosts and claims that nothing unusual has happened since he's taken over. His daughter agrees but notes that friends of hers have been afraid to venture into the kitchen in the apartment due to uneasy feelings.

Theories are many. Perhaps unexplainable events are still ongoing, but the new owners, being closed to the idea of ghosts, either block them out entirely or aren't able to witness such things with closed minds. Perhaps Wally's spirit left when Krystyne did. The two who never met in life did seem to share a connection after death.

The Bucktown Pub is open during the typical operation hours for a bar but serves up an exceptional treat. Mike Johnson's pop culture gallery is now gone, evident by reviews of the bar calling it "no frills," but the atmosphere is still friendly. The Bucktown Pub not being a trendy "it" club frees it from the pretense that such places suffer from. This is a neighborhood bar. Mix in the friendly company in front of and behind the bar and continue the tradition of grabbing a drink at 1658 West Cortland, prohibition or not.

CHAPTER 3

CITY HAUNTS

"Hull House"

First bearing the name Dearborn, Illinois, Chicago is nationally known by many monikers including "The Windy City," "The City of Big Shoulders," "The Second City," and "The Transportation Hub of America." Chicago has seen a lot including a massacre during the War of 1812—at least that massacre was quick. Over six thousand Confederate Civil War prisoners slowly died in the torturous jail, Camp Douglas. Much of the city's noteworthiness comes from "black-eye events" such as Mafia shootouts and the Democratic National Convention of 1968.

By the late 1990s, the nation finally viewed Chicago differently. Instead of thinking of Al Capone, people across America thought of Michael Jordan when the word Chicago was spoken.

Chicago's O'Hare International is the one of the busiest airports in the world, and, until recently, the tallest building was the Sears Tower. The way Chicagoans embraced local hero Mike Ditka and his "Monsters of the Midway" made *Saturday Night Live's* "Super Fans" an immediate success.

Chicago is a place of invention. From early necessities like barbed wire created in DeKalb and windmills created in Aurora to more modern luxuries such as McDonalds, which first opened their doors in Des Plaines.

Chicago is the third largest city in the United States and has been one of the most important forces in American politics and lifestyle even before Illinois earned its statehood. Thousands of troops from the Chicago area fought in every war since the Revolutionary War that America has ever been involved in, even the French-Indian War. Additionally, some movers and shakers of the Civil War including Stephen Douglas, Ulysses S. Grant, and Abraham Lincoln are tied to Illinois.

The devastating Trail of Tears in the early 1830s crossed Illinois along with a mass of wide-eyed prospectors during the great Gold Rush. The railroads and the proximity to both the Great Lakes and the Mississippi River attracted some of the manufacturing giants such as John M. Smyth (furniture),

George Pullman (train cars), Edward Hines (lumber), and Cyrus McCormick (farm machinery). Some of the most important names in retail originated in Chicago including Marshal Field, Montgomery Ward, and Sears, among others.

The English and Dutch established up their settlements in the east, but the French moved inland and quickly viewed the land now called Illinois as an important place for them to establish. For about four hundred years, Chicago has played an important role in the life of Illinois, and for more than half of that time, the Chicago area was the nerve center of the state.

The city of Chicago is a living, breathing museum. It's understandable, but unfortunate, that most people rushing from home to work and back have little knowledge of Chicago's rich history. This is unfortunate because many times Chicago's history had a major impact on American and sometimes even world history.

Some of the unsung Chicagoans are the ones who made the biggest difference in defining the city. In addition to making a difference in the city, some of them did this while having brushes with the paranormal. Others, however, are spending their afterlife creating brushes with the paranormal for other unsuspecting Chicagoans.

Darrow's Getaway

A nearly mythological attorney, Clarence Darrow is just one such case of a prominent Chicagoan who, though deceased for three quarters of a century, still visits the city.

Darrow was quite the enigmatic character in life. He was often heralded as a "champion of the underdog" after he stopped working as a corporate lawyer for the railroad company to defend Eugene V. Debs, who led the American Railway Union, which was striking against the Pullman Palace Car Company. The year was 1893, and America was hit by its largest depression to date. The workers lived in an upscale company town named Pullman that was far more than just housing. More than nine hundred structures from stores, a library, and a school, all owned by the Pullman Company, comprised the town. Rent and items purchased from the stores were instantly deducted from paychecks. When the depression hit, Pullman cut wages but not the rent. The union, against Debs wishes, decided to strike.

After two months in which railway workers refused to handle Pullman cars as well as those cars attached to Pullman cars, the federal government ended the strike. However, the injunction was not honored, and since some of the neglected cars attached to the Pullman cars were mail cars, Debs was charged with interfering with the mail and violating the court injunction.

Darrow seemed on the verge of achieving a very public victory for Debs, but the charge of conspiracy to obstruct the mail was dropped before the trial could come to an end. Debs served six months in a Woodstock, Illinois, prison for violating the federal injunction.

Darrow also defended the MacNamera brothers who bombed the *Los Angeles Times* building, which Darrow spun as a strike for workers against a non-union paper. Twenty workers died in the dynamite explosion. After Darrow was accused of two counts of bribing jurors, he convinced his clients to change their plea to guilty. This move also helped Darrow escape his own subsequent prosecutions. The MacNameras got life in prison but were spared the death penalty.

In truth, Darrow was a lawyer. It's as simple as that. For every instance of his deeds being noble and for the "underdog," there's an instance of him defending a corrupt corporation. Such was the case when the Kankakee Manufacturing Company conned countless investors out of money by creating false documents that overstated the company's value. Darrow defended the company, and the investors, such as Civil War veteran Charles Myerhoff, lost everything.

Darrow was involved in two court cases so major they were each deemed "Trial of the Century" by the media. These two are the Leopold and Loeb murder trial of 1924 (mentioned in a later chapter) and the Scopes Monkey Trial of 1925. His greatest moment, however, came at the defense of Ossian Sweet. Sweet was an African American doctor in an all-white town. After a scuffle with a mob of reportedly one thousand people resulted in one death, all eleven of the people who were in the Sweet home at the time were tried for the murder, even though the shooter identified himself immediately.

In the end, which came after a closing statement from Darrow that lasted seven hours and is now considered one of the greatest speeches ever written, the shooter was acquitted by the all-white jury. The remainder of the cases were dropped. This 1925 case was a landmark moment in civil rights history.

Darrow remained in Chicago and died of heart disease in 1938. The bridge where Darrow often went to contemplate his cases was the site of a ceremony celebrating his life. Poised on the bridge, Darrow's ashes were left to fall from an urn to the water below.

The first of every May at ten o'clock in the morning, admirers come to celebrate this remarkable lawyer. On May 1, 1957, the bridge Darrow loved was officially named Clarence Darrow Memorial Bridge.

Though Darrow had different ideas relating to religion, he also had ideas of an afterlife. According to some, it was his plan to make contact in some way after death. Though he died in 1938, it took until 1991 on Dale Kaczmarek's "Excursions Into the Unknown" tour for Darrow to make his first publicized appearance after his death.

Recently, Darrow has been seen as an elderly man dressed eloquently in a camel hair coat, a suit, and a fedora. Standing on the bridge and looking across the lagoon to the backside of the museum steps is generally how witnesses see him. This appears to be a residual haunting as he does not respond in any way when being called. Sometimes he is only seen by a select few while others present cannot see him.

On at least one occasion, photographs taken from the bridge resulted in a haze hanging over the water, and in another a face appeared in the reflection of the water.

For Darrow, this pond might serve as his heaven. In the busy city of Chicago, finding time to get away can be a difficulty. This was Darrow's safe haven—a place away from phone calls and the many enemies that Darrow likely made by defending the undefendable. Perhaps this is one of the only places Darrow ever felt completely safe and at peace. Perhaps this was his heaven in life just as it appears to be after death.

House Full of History

As has been illustrated, a spirit can be forever linked to a location for any number of reasons. In other cases, a spirit can be linked to an individual rather than a place. This usually happens when someone dies and the deceased continues to look over the person who was important to them. However, spirits can also be attracted to people who present enthusiastic positive energy. These people are said to have white or bright "lights." On rare occasions, spirits have been attached to objects, usually treasured family heirlooms. Some who are particularly sensitive to psychic experiences go to great lengths to avoid being around antiques for this very reason.

This being said, it is possible for an antiques shop to be a hotbed for psychic activity. While there is no confirmation for why the shop, formerly known as Victorian House Antiques, is haunted, the objects within it are a possibility. Or perhaps there are multiple hauntings coming from multiple sources. After all, at least five people have died in the building.

The building, first used as a private residence, was built in 1879. The structure appears to be no different than any other two-flat Chicago-style house of the time. Appearing very menacing, the house stands three stories tall including the attic.

The first family to live in the house suffered a great loss when a female member of the family, and owner of the house, was killed within the house walls. Years later, four more people perished in the attic of the house when it burned.

After its time as a private home, the building became a boarding house, and by the 1970s, nearly one hundred years after the building was created, it was an antiques shop. Known as the Victorian House Antiques Shop, it was connected with a neighboring restaurant predictably named the Victorian House Restaurant.

It was during its time as an antiques shop that it began to take on the reputation of being yet another haunted Chicago location. The sheer number of different types of phenomena and the number of people who unsuspectingly found themselves noticing more than antiques in the store attic is enough to consider this location noteworthy.

As one would assume, the attic seems to have the most activity even though all three floors held antiques at the time. Cold spots seem to occupy the attic staircase on a regular basis, while the mirrors occasionally reflect faces that seem to come from nowhere. In addition, movement has been observed between pieces of furniture while strange sounds, including footsteps, have emanated from the attic when there was no reasonable explanation for them. Lastly, the door of the bedroom, believed to be the location of where the homicide took place, opens and closes on its own.

Several customers, unaware of the haunted reputation of the building, have found themselves very uncomfortable in certain areas; sometimes to the extent of being compelled to leave the room before they have finished browsing.

Perhaps partially due to the ghosts' ability to remove potential buyers, the Victorian House Antiques Shop closed their doors by the summer of 2000. Boldly standing on Belmont Avenue among ultra-chic stores and trendy customers, this vacant building was ignored by passers-by. Those who didn't often had their breath taken away.

As of 2008, the building still stands, now in the form of a property management company. If you look closely at the top of the house, faint burn marks still stain the bricks above the attic windows—a reminder that four lives were lost at one time in that very room.

The Devil Doesn't Just Visit Bridgeport

Inspiration can be found in many places. For Jane Addams that inspiration was found in London. After her father died, Addams spent some of her inheritance touring England with Ellen Gates Starr. It was her visits to Whitechapel in 1883 and 1888 where Addams became impressed with the Toynbee Hall settlement house's mission of social reform.

Addams brought this idea of a neighborhood center back with her to Chicago. She and Starr converted a house first built in 1856 by Charles Hull and opened Hull House in September 18, 1889.

Hull House was incredibly helpful in providing aid to the many disadvantaged immigrants who came to the city. Hull House administrators and supporters also pushed for social reforms, while Addams became a major player in gaining the right to vote for women and establishing the state's first child labor laws. Many programs were made available through Hull House including nurseries and educational courses. A number of sports leagues were also established for the children of the city. In true humanitarian style, no one was turned away. Class, gender, and race were the basis of discrimination nearly everywhere across America except for one place: Hull House.

For this native of Cedarville, Illinois, the Rockford College-educated Addams was awarded the Nobel Peace Prize in 1931. Addams was ambitious and ahead of her time. She pushed for research into the causes of poverty and crime as she also pushed for research into the importance of social workers.

It did not take long at all for Addams and her programs to outgrow Hull House. Additional buildings were purchased and soon over a dozen Chicago buildings belonged to Addams and her program.

Despite all of the help Addams gave, near the turn of the century controversy landed on her doorstep. What might easily be dismissed as an urban legend today, the story of the devil baby enthralled immigrant Chicago for several months.

The story maintained that a pregnant woman placed a picture of the Blessed Virgin upon a wall in her home much to the dismay of her atheist husband who declared something along the lines of, "I would rather have the devil himself in this house than that picture." The man was forced to eat a hefty plate of crow when his wife subsequently gave birth to a child with some spectacular attributes including a full head of hair and a mouth full of teeth. As if this wasn't enough, the child emerged with a colorful vocabulary of curse words. The horns protruding from his head, scale-cloaked skin, and the cloven hooves for feet must have also made for a difficult birth. Some stories go so far to say that the aptly nicknamed Devil Baby even had a tail.

The story continues that the parents of the unusual infant went to have him baptized, but he leapt from their grip before being touched with holy water and danced across the back pews of the church.

Fed up with being laughed at by their child for being poor and without any ability to deal with the situation, the child was taken to Jane Addams at Hull House. The mother and baby stayed at the house in secrecy, and over time, the baby died in the attic.

For a month and a half, crowds approached Hull House with hopes to see the spectacle. Time and time again they were turned away by Addams herself, who was getting very irritated by having to spend so much time down-playing the rumor that had spread like wildfire.

The truth of how the rumor started is still a mystery, but the most realistic lead is that a physically deformed baby was brought to Hull House and the description of it was wildly and unfortunately exaggerated. After the rumors spread and the crowds gathered, the infant was probably sent to another settlement house that Addams formed in Waukegan. Seasoned veterans of folklore, however, may look to another North Shore town for answers.

Lake Forest Cemetery has a grave deep in the back near a ravine for "Damien, Son of the Devil." The story about the location of the grave states that if the son of the devil rises, he will have to cross the water near his grave and therefore be purified before he leaves the cemetery.

Though the stories of the devil baby are erroneous, stories of Hull House being haunted seem more realistic. Even Jane Addams herself respected these tales. She was infamous for keeping a pail of water on the second floor landing at the top of the staircase with hopes that the theory of ghosts not being able to pass over water was true.

She and a number of others who used the upstairs bedroom claim to have seen a woman in white floating across the room. Others have felt uncomfortable and uneasy while there. It was in this room where Charles Hull's wife died.

Addams published a number of books on social issues and two biographies called *Twenty Years at Hull House* and *The Second Twenty Years at Hull House*. It is in these biographies that Addams writes of the story of the devil baby, the hauntings she witnessed, and having to extinguish a number of small fires that seemed to start without reason.

Addams died in 1935, and Hull House closed in 1963 when the University of Illinois-Chicago purchased the land for its Circle Campus. Today, only the original Hull House and the building to its left still stand.

UIC keeps Hull House open to visitors to learn about Jane Addams and the story of Hull House. The people who work there and UIC students know about the allegations of the location being haunted, but few, if any, have seen anything first-hand. Nonetheless, they are quick to admit that being in the house alone after closing is something they choose to avoid if possible. It is usually security guards who are burdened by the occurrences there as they are repeatedly called in to investigate motion detector alarms going off after being tripped by an unseen culprit.

Currently, the second story of Hull House—where the first reporting of hauntings occurred—is closed to the general public and is used primarily as offices. Most visitors to the house peer into the front lobby where an eloquent staircase stands. Dale Kaczmarek took a photograph of the staircase which revealed four monk-like figures holding candles. This is one of the most famous paranormal photographs ever taken and is easily found on the Internet.

The upstairs windows are of interest to ghost hunters ever since people began reporting that a face had been seen staring back at them. Lastly, there are shutters on the interior of the building on the second floor that seem to open and close on their own, much like the shutters at the Country House Restaurant do.

Addams, who is buried at Cedarville Cemetery, gave her life to the people of Chicago and is remembered today as a true daughter of the city. The outpouring from the thousands who clogged the streets around Hull House when her wake was held there showed how many lives this local philanthropist touched. The effects of Addams' work will live on just as the tale of the devil baby will.

An Epidemic Sweeps the City

It starts with a dry but annoyingly persistent cough. The cough leads to fever and chest pains. Eventually, the fever will grow so intense the victim sweats constantly as they cough up blood. The final stage, before modern medicine was able to cure this disease, was mortality.

Near the turn of the century, tuberculosis accounted for ten percent of all deaths in Chicago. This equated to four thousand Chicagoans dying from the sickness each year. From the mid 1850s, Chicago was besieged by sicknesses such as tuberculosis, cholera, small pox, typhoid fever, scarlet fever, and diphtheria, which claimed several thousand lives annually. In 1854 alone, cholera wiped out five-and-a-half percent of the population. In addition, the death rates for diphtheria were over one hundred per every one hundred thousand people in the city for the vast majority of the nineteenth century. Of all of these diseases, tuberculosis was the last one to get under control.

Treatment for tuberculosis was limited until the 1940s. Before modern medicine started saving lives, victims of tuberculosis, which was also called consumption at the time, often endured surgery to collapse the infected lung in order to prevent the bacteria from spreading.

For the most part, medicine and science was without any ideas. The Chicago Municipal Tuberculosis Sanitarium was established in March of 1915 on 160 acres of land donated by Pehr Samuel Peterson on the north side of the city. Until modern medicine made tuberculosis a more treatable disease, the sanitarium stood as a place for victims to rest and try to recuperate. Unfortunately, most of the early patients died.

Since those suffering with the disease basically found themselves quarantined from the healthy, efforts were made to replicate normal everyday life for the patients and make their stay there as pleasant as possible. An underground tunnel still connects the basements of all the buildings for comfortable travel from one building to another during winter. The tunnels run from the main administration building on the west, through the entire length of the sanitarium grounds, and finally to the powerhouse on the east. The tunnels are 1,550 feet long and measure seven feet by nine feet.

In addition to the hospital buildings, there was also a church, movie theater, and parks for people to go to relax. In many ways, the Municipal Tuberculosis Sanitarium of Chicago was a miniature self-contained town with a constantly high population. The first day it opened 650 out of 950 beds were filled with patients.

Through the decades that it was open, hundreds of souls moved on to another world while inside this town of sickness.

While this is true, at least one soul that expired there did not move on to the next phase.

Though tuberculosis has not been eradicated like polio, it is far more under control. The sanitarium closed its doors in 1974 and sat vacant for a number of years. Located at 5801 North Pulaski, it is now called Peterson Woods and is comprised of North Park Village Nature Center and Senate Apartments.

This location is emotionally important for Mary Czerwinski. Her family would routinely frequent the picnic grounds in the time between it being a sanitarium and its current incarnation. Her father still maintains a garden on the premises, and her grandfather died of a heart attack in the parking lot just outside the church building. If this wasn't enough, it was here that she gained her belief in ghosts.

While on a family picnic at the vacated sanitarium in the early 1990s, a young Mary and her brother wandered off from their family to the four-story nurse station. The only thing that had changed over the course of the past twenty years was that the doors and windows were now sealed closed.

"Pretty much everything was left the way it was in 1974," remembers Mary. "There were medicine cabinets with pills still in them, files, records, and even the badges of the workers and nurses."

With no particular agenda other than to waste away a day, Mary and her brother began throwing rocks down the hallowed hallways. After several minutes of this, the two were surprised to hear the same sound repeated on the floor above them.

Bringing their mother's attention to it, the two were puzzled to find nothing at all on that floor other than silence. After their mother returned to the picnic, Mary and her brother continued their investigation. This time their investigation bore fruit. Though the halls were dark from the boarded-up windows, an apparition emanating light was plainly seen by the two at a far end of the hallway.

Mary cannot positively identify the vision as being a nurse, but it was a female shape. "It was a form of some sort of woman, and she didn't seem whole and real. She seemed transparent and brightly glowing because I could still see the wood from a boarded up window that was behind her."

She and her brother made a quick exit and didn't tell anyone about what they saw until recently. When Mary finally mentioned the story to her father nearly a decade later, her father had a confession of his own to make.

During one of the many family picnics to the area, he heard a woman singing. Of the group of people present, he was the only one able to hear it. From his description, the song was some sort of lullaby and possibly not in English. It seemed to be coming from the same building where Mary had her encounter.

By 1997, the nurse's station was finally destroyed to build condos on the land. Most of the other buildings from the time of the sanitarium's existence still stand and were restored when the area became a retirement community.

Knowing that thousands of people died in the immediate area, one might expect to find some sort of monument or plaque commemorating the lives lost to this monstrous disease. For a long while, there was a boulder near the nurse's station bearing a plaque to keep the memory alive, but as of the late 1990s to the present day, the plaque is missing.

With no acknowledgement of the past left, it would be interesting to see how many occupants of the condos know what was there before them. What also remains to be seen is if the hauntings reported in the nurse's station will manifest themselves on the land of the new condos.

There are different schools of thought on each possibility. Some believe the spirit could be attached to the building itself, which would mean that it would leave when the building was demolished, but if the spirit was simply attached to the land or the physical space, the ghost or ghosts could still be around welcoming the new neighbors.

As of yet, there are no known reportings of ghosts, but that doesn't mean that nothing has happened. My Web site,

SlimPictures.com, contains additional information on many of the sites covered in this book. It also provides a forum for people to share their experiences and ask questions. Time will tell if a future story that gets submitted will revolve around the old grounds of Chicago's Municipal Tuberculosis Sanitarium.

Perhaps the city is even unknowingly doing its part to tempt fate as it hosts a "Trails of Terror" Halloween event in twenty-four of the wooded acres on the land.

A Hot Spot Full of Cold Spots

Just as the old-world appearance of the Victorian House Antiques Shop stands out among its trendy neighbors, the Excalibur nightclub, which gained historical status in 1997, looks like it would be more natural in England, or at the very least next to the "Irish Castle" in Beverly, Illinois.

The land where the nightclub stands was first purchased by the Chicago Historical Society in 1865. A building was constructed to display and keep in preserved storage many of the artifacts important to Chicago's history. Unfortunately, the structure and all of its contents were destroyed in the Great Chicago Fire of 1871.

The Chicago Historical Society rebounded and built another building in its place in 1892. This building served as the headquarters of the historical society until 1931 when they moved to their current location in Lincoln Park.

The building went on to serve other businesses like the Illinois Institute of Technology and *Gallery Magazine*, among others. It was even a recording studio for some of the great blues and rock & roll performers to come out of Chicago. It wasn't until it became the Limelight Bar that reports of hauntings began.

The Limelight closed in 1989, and Excalibur opened shortly thereafter. Inexplicable activity started immediately. The first anomaly noticed was that after cleaning up for the night, beer bottles were found opened and emptied the following morning, while serving glasses were also found scattered about the bar in the famous Dome Room. This happened like clockwork every night for a full week. One would hope that living persons trying to steal a drink would be a little sneakier about it.

Phantom sounds were also heard after closing, including sounds of people playing pool in the VIP room, though the room was empty. Perhaps even more disturbing was that when investigating the noise, the pool balls were found to have actually been broken from the rack they were in, providing reason to believe these weren't phantom sounds but sounds resulting from the movement of the billiard balls by an unknown force.

In the basement storage room, employees have heard what they thought was someone in the room dragging cases of beer across the floor. Though the storage room was nearby, there was no discernible source for this sound.

Staircases in the bar have an interesting phenomenon attributed to them as well: blue forms occasionally run up and down them. Those on the staircase at the time testify to feeling a breeze rush past them.

The Dome Room, which is actually a separate bar that shares the same building with the Excalibur, tends to be very active. There is a twelve-inch angel perched near the ceiling on a small ledge. Although this is made of cement and is a mass-produced statue, this one is unique. Glancing at it one moment and looking again a few minutes later results in the odd realization that the facial expression and even the arm positions of the angel have changed.

Cold spots are also commonly felt throughout the basement, women's bathroom, dry storage area, hovering over the bar, and even on a barstool. The exact cause of a cold spot, like most paranormal events, is unknown though many theories exist. One theory is that since spirits need energy to manifest themselves, make noises, move objects, etc., the spirit draws heat energy from the physical space it is inhabiting. Drawing on existing energy sources could possibly have something to do with why some of the most notoriously haunted locations like Bachelor's Grove Cemetery and Archer Avenue are near power stations. Perhaps spirits can even draw their needed energy from the energy generated by moving water. It's still hard not to notice moving water at or very near countless haunted Chicago locations including Bachelor's Grove Cemetery, Archer Avenue, the house on Rainbow Road, Jewish Waldheim Cemetery, and the Sunnybrook Asylum, to name just a few.

The Excalibur nightclub and its adjoining Dome Room were a favorite for WCKG's *Pete McMurray Show*. In 1998, 1999, and 2000, guided by local psychic Denise Guzzardo, they toured a number of haunted locations including the Dome Room as part of their annual Halloween broadcast, which aired live as it happened. It was here where they had the most fun.

Though the angel never changed its position, the second-story landing in the same room kept the radio personalities on their toes. There are several clubs within the Excalibur building with the same general layout. The first floor contains a bar and a dance floor. The walls are lined with tables and booths. The second floor is open in the middle, serving as an elaborate balcony where people can look down onto the dance area. On this second floor there is another bar that takes up one wall, while the three remaining sides provide additional seating. In a scene straight out of *Poltergeist*, after walking through one of the second floor areas featuring tables and chairs, they turned around to notice that the furniture had been completely rearranged in the couple of seconds since they had last seen it.

Making their way up to the dry storage area, which is actually built around the top of the dome in the Dome Room, screams were heard. One of the most extreme events witnessed happened when Denise was standing in the second story women's bathroom when the emergency light began to turn itself on and off. She turned to see what was going on only to find a young girl playing with it. "And the next thing you know," Denise said, "*all* the lights went off." On a subsequent trip to that bathroom in 1999 Denise picked up the little girl's name as being Jane.

In that same bathroom, Mike, a manager for the popular club, said, "In October of 2000, a bartender got trapped in there [one of the stalls]. She couldn't get it open. It was held closed from the outside. There was nobody in here, but she was stuck in there for about five minutes."

The bartender, who came out screaming, returned with a friend so she could collect the belongings she had left behind. As the two women entered the bathroom, the sinks began turning on, on their own. They made another hurried exit.

I was invited to ride along for the 2000 broadcast. Standing in front of the castle-like building, one can see evidence of its life as the Chicago Historical Society. Over the front door, there is a century-old engraved scene from Marquette and Joliet's expedition. The gothic décor of the club is minded by two evil-looking gargoyles, stealthily crawling down the side of the building just above the explorers and traders.

It was Halloween night and the nightclub was rockin' but the Dome Room was closed, thus giving us complete peace in which to explore. We went immediately into the famed Dome Room where I had my breath taken away. An astounding and menacing face of Zeus is painted on the dome itself. I would assume one would have to attend the club many, many times before not being completely impressed by the sight.

Although it's never a good idea to visit a haunted location with the mind set that you are expecting to experience something of a paranormal nature, there isn't enough self discipline in the world to keep one's mind from racing when visiting the Dome Room on Halloween. The night started off with little luck. The angel remained motionless, the furniture did not move, and according to Denise at the time, "Things are pretty quiet," in the previously busy bathroom. Then we went to the dry storage area and things got a little more exciting.

Immediately, Denise picked up on a male presence. She said that his name started with the letter "H" and that he either

died by choking or hanging because she felt pressure on her neck. Our tour guide, the manager named Mike, confirmed that there has been speculation that the builder of the structure hanged himself somewhere on the premises.

Though the name of the architect was Henry Ives Cobb, it likely isn't the famous designer that haunts the site. Cobb also designed Potter Palmer's Lakeshore Drive mansion, the Chicago Post Office, and buildings at Lake Forest College. Cobb died at the age of seventy-one in Massachusetts.

We walked around the storage area and eventually made our way to where the furnace is. Without any light, I led the way with help of a night-vision infrared video camera. I was the first of the group to make it back to where the current managers found a pentagram painted on the wall. This is where screams were heard in years past. As soon as I reached this place, I heard what sounded like two males quietly talking. The conversation was quiet and muffled so the exact words were impossible to hear, but there was no doubt about the sound. A handful of people nearest to myself also heard the sounds.

Though Denise did not make contact with Jane this time, she may have possibly seen her again as she caught a glimpse of someone rushing down a staircase near one of the bars.

By 11:30 the show was coming to and end. Pete McMurray and Denise were closing the show out, so I took the opportunity to wander around on my own for a few minutes. I heard what sounded like the rattling of keys coming from the next room. When I rushed to the doorway, I saw a figure quickly step behind a support column. There was nothing out of the ordinary at the moment. The figure was not transparent and there were no mysterious lights. Nothing seemed odd until the figure did not reemerge from the other side. Upon a closer look, whatever it was I had seen vanished.

After we were off the air, Mike took us to the third floor VIP rooms where many people have felt uncomfortable. The room in which we sat and talked deep into the night had previously been used by the band Tonic as well as for Scottie Pippin's bachelor party.

When we were finally ready to call it a night after one in the morning, we headed down the three floors to the main room. A sidekick for the show, Pinto, who spent most of the evening in various states of fear, led the way home. He walked until reaching a vacant second floor bar. There, he and those near him heard the phantom sound of drinking glasses clinking, as if a toast were in progress. From there he ran the rest of the way.

The Excalibur nightclub has a reputation for hosting celebrities. Cuba Gooding, Jr., has been known to dance the night away, and Prince has even dropped by after concerts to give surprise performances. Legendary Chicago Cub Sammy Sosa has enjoyed evenings there with former Chicago Bull and LA Laker Ron Harper. From Billy Corgan to former owner Dennis Rodman, the Excalibur is as much a link for Chicagoans to have a brush with fame as it is for them to have a brush with someone long since departed.

There are as many theories for the hauntings at the Excalibur as there are stories. Many accidentally attribute the events to victims of the *Eastland* Disaster. Contrary to popular belief, this was never the location of a temporary morgue for victims of the ill-fated ship. The one certainty is that for years to come this slice of Chicago nightlife will attract curiosity-seekers, celebrities, and people just looking for a good time—living or not.

CHAPTER 4

CUBA

"Cuba Road"

A key ingredient which contributes to a person's level of fear in any situation is if they are comfortable with their surroundings. In other words, being in a different environment can put someone even more on edge than they normally would be. Those who have grown up in a small central Indiana town may be intimidated by the masses of people and noise that New York City holds.

A New Yorker traveling the opposite path could easily be spooked by the fact that after sundown in a smaller town, there is quite a bit of darkness. Not every road has the luxury of streetlights. The absence of people reminds them that they are quite alone if help is needed.

For the city dweller looking for a good scare out of their element, Cuba Township in Lake County is the place to go. Without question, it holds the most haunted stretch of road north of Archer Avenue.

In fact, this small road almost serves as a condensed city as far as hauntings are concerned. Some of the most famous hauntings from the most famous Chicago locations appear to have an equal on or near Cuba Road. From intimidating phantom hitchhikers to a disappearing train and a funeral procession to Mafia ghosts, it can all be found on a lonely, hilly, dark, country road in the northern suburbs.

The Archer Avenue of the North Side

Later on you will read about Bachelor's Grove in Midlothian and Archer Avenue in south suburban Justice, Illinois. As far as paranormal investigators are concerned, these are often Chicago's supernatural focal point. However, they are not without comparison. Cuba Road in Barrington Hills and Lake Zurich deserves just as much credit as its South Side counterpart.

The first settlers to the area were the French in 1650, who worked with the Potawatomi and Mascouten Indians. However, these Native Americans were forced to vacate the land over the course of several treaties in the early 1800s.

The area known as Barrington is quite the geographical conundrum. Its borders cross Lake, Cook, Kane, and McHenry Counties as well as six townships including Cuba Township.

Cuba Road in Cuba Township (so named by area sympathizers to Cuba's attempted secession from Spain around 1850) is located between Rand Road and Northwest Highway.

The road is two lanes wide and relatively straight, though it does boast a number of hills. It runs through a primarily residential area, though many of the houses are hidden behind trees. There are a few cross streets but no major intersections. At night, streetlights are few and far between, giving the driver no sense of the world outside the headlight beams.

The flow of traffic along this lonely road between the more major thoroughfares is steady and constant, but if one were to exclude phantom cars, you would find that the road is a little less traveled.

The area has long-standing ties with the Chicago Mafia. Mobsters from the early 1900s up through current times partake in the same practice as many people today: work in the city and vacation in smaller towns and rural areas.

Some attribute the vanishing phantom cars to the luxury cars that the gangsters would most likely have taken on a road trip. This isn't the only possibility though, as cars matching similar descriptions have been seen turning into nearby White Cemetery.

It seems as of late that these luxury cars are not the only vanishing vehicles moving down Cuba Road. Most of the time these phantom automobiles are seen by bewildered drivers who have no prior knowledge of the stories surrounding the famed street.

Julie Dahlquist was traveling back to her home in Wadsworth one evening in 2000 when she decided to try cutting through Cuba Road. Upon turning onto the road she was quickly annoyed by an eighteen-wheeler that was tailgating her. The headlights from the big rig were positioned directly

behind her rear window. The reflection from the lights into her rearview mirror made driving very difficult.

"And then it was just gone," remembers Julie. One moment this large lumbering truck seemed to be just inches behind her, and suddenly she was alone on the road. Since Cuba Road is narrow and mostly isolated, there was nowhere the truck could have turned off without at least slowing down first, which Julie would have noticed.

Since it was night and Julie's vision of the truck was limited due to its extremely bright lights, all she could really see were the lights. The make and age of the truck is still a mystery, but if one were to attempt to link this back to a Mafia presence, one theory could be bootlegging trucks shipping goods to a safe storage area away from the tough Chicago police.

The appearance and disappearance of inanimate objects is under much debate. Most religions claim that only living beings have a soul, so something like a car coming back as a ghost is highly improbable. However, many religions reject the idea of ghosts outright as well. Conversely, there is the Native American belief that every single object has a soul, which they call a Manitu.

Despite having never seen anything of that nature myself, I kept an open mind. All that changed one evening in late July 2001. A friend, Ryan Nally, had dropped by with hopes that I could give him an impromptu tour of a few notably haunted locations. Cuba Road and its surrounding haunts always top my list.

We exited Rand Road and started traveling down Cuba Road. As we went, I pointed out noteworthy landmarks. We finally reached the gates to White Cemetery. We gazed at the cemetery as we slowly drove past. When we faced forward again, Ryan excitedly questioned, "Where's the car?"

Previously, there had been a car traveling about 150 yards in front of us. We were not extremely close to it, but its taillights had been in plain sight. In the time it took us to glance at the cemetery, probably just three or four seconds, the car was gone.

I instructed Ryan to accelerate in an attempt to catch up to the car to see if it was a real automobile. As he sped down Cuba, I looked down the few side roads again in search of a physical vehicle. Before we knew it, we were sitting at the stop sign before Northwest Highway alone; there was no car in sight.

Tales of phantom cars are far from being the only stories swirling around Cuba Road. Later that same evening, we were making additional passes up and down the road. Ahead, near the top of one of the many small hills, we saw what we thought were a series of four or five street reflectors that may have been placed to emphasize an upcoming turn. However, these "reflectors" did not remain illuminated despite the fact that our headlights remained on them. When we got to the top of that incline, we were somewhat surprised to find that the road continued going in a straight line. The area where we thought we saw reflectors along the edge of a curve was actually in the middle of a straight road.

There have long been reports of ghost lights of assorted colors including white, red, blue, and orange that seem to hover over the road. It turns out this is something else I can vouch for.

Getting back to the strong paranormal Mafia presence, there are those who, upon turning on to Cuba Road, have noticed a curiosity in their rearview mirror, a "made man" sitting in their backseat.

This phantom has understandably scared the wits out of several drivers who had no intention to play chauffeur to a cigar-smoking, suit-wearing, wise guy.

Chris Pry is able to empathize with these witnesses. Though he has not seen the mobster on Cuba Road, one evening in early June 2001 he was driving down Route 176 in nearby Wauconda when he checked his rearview mirror only to find a ghostly pale face looking back at him from the backseat. On the second look of his double take, Chris saw the face dart off the right edge of the mirror. Upon turning around to check, he found the backseat empty.

Sporadically throughout the year, but mostly in summer and during the month of November, a couple has been seen in the daylight hours walking hand-in-hand down Cuba Road and then turning down a side street before disappearing. The

most peculiar part about this is that it's not the two people that are seen but their shadows on the ground.

If ghost humans and cars aren't enough, there is also a slew of ghost animals. Most notably is the ghost of a woman and her horse who have been seen riding down the side of the road. Allegedly, at one point in time a woman was killed after taking a fatal fall from her equine. In addition, believe it or not, phantom cows have been noted walking along the road and in front of White Cemetery.

If one were unfazed by the events that have happened thus far on Cuba, for further challenges reach the stop sign before Northwest Highway and cross the road to the other side. No more than just a few yards in, train tracks cross the road. It is here that another form of vanishing transportation is seen. Throughout the years, people about to cross these tracks come to a stop after noticing that there is a train a short distance away. Despite the fact that the warning gates do not acknowledge its presence, some have felt that it's better to be safe than sorry. Those sitting and wondering why the once approaching train has stalled become even more perplexed once they notice that the entire train has vanished off the face of the earth.

Lastly, finally, and more horrifically, we come to the bridge that is just past the railroad tracks. For some still unknown reason, this bridge is the site of a repeated suicide. On numerous occasions, people driving across this tiny bridge on foggy nights have been petrified when a man steps out in front of their car. Since the drivers are caught completely off guard, it is too late to break. They strike the man, actually feeling the impact of hitting his body jolting the car. Exiting the car expecting to see a horrific scene under their wheels, the drivers find nothing but the cold black pavement beneath the still running car dimly lit by headlights and in a veil of drifting fog. It's at this point that some drivers probably wish they had found a body. At least that they could explain.

The most unique thing about these events is that they all occur in the same small area. Why this small stretch of Lake County road is so concentrated with supernatural energy is anyone's guess.

So far we've seen ghost lights, a shadowy couple, phantom cars, trucks, a train, and even a herd of cattle. We've seen the ghost of a woman and her horse, a mobster who likes free rides, and a startlingly suicidal man. Now keep in mind we still haven't gotten out of the car. Our trip to Cuba Road has only just begun as we still have a cemetery and a most haunted of haunted houses yet to visit.

A Cemetery that Compares to Another on the South Side

Most of the noteworthy cemeteries in the city of Chicago, like Rosehill and Graceland, were specifically set up to be cemeteries. However, many cemeteries in the rest of the area simply started as a farmer's back yard. If someone in the family died, a section of the field was cleared for the burial. Additional departed family members were added over time. Neighboring farms that could not afford to stop growing crops in an area of their field might pay to have their loved ones buried on their neighbor's property; thus, a cemetery was born.

These cemeteries usually do not have a church near them and are still relatively small. Some continue to grow while some do not. A prime example of one that did not grow is Swan Cemetery on Winchester Road near Route 60, near the border of Mundelein and Libertyville.

White Cemetery continued. Established in the 1820s, White Cemetery visually appears similar to what one of these small farm-born cemeteries might look like today. This makes the visual apparition of cows wandering near the roadside in front of it all that much more believable.

Simply put, Cuba Road is to Archer Avenue as White Cemetery is to Bachelor's Grove. As you'll read in a future chapter, Bachelor's Grove Cemetery started as farmland before becoming a heavily vandalized cemetery, much like White Cemetery. There are even very rare and unique types of hauntings that one would only find at these two locations.

The vandals at White Cemetery struck in 1968 when eighty gravestones were damaged, including thirty-one that had swastikas spray-painted on them. After this defacement, people kept a closer eye on the cemetery, although it was still very easy to gain access to the graveyard after dark. The gates

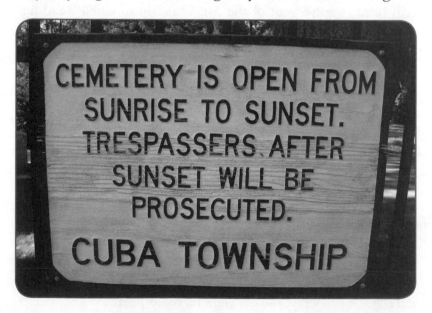

are actually closed only some of the time, and even when they are, they aren't locked, which leads to some smaller-scaled repeated attacks of destruction. More recently, the addition of motion sensors has finally made the cemetery off limits after dark.

Despite efforts to clean the stones from the emotional scar of the Nazi symbol, the remains can still be faintly seen on a few graves more than three decades after it happened.

Ghost lights seem to be the most often sighted paranormal event other than cold spots. Perhaps this is because it takes less energy for a spirit to manifest itself into a singular ball of light than it does anything else.

This being said, it is expected that ghost lights would be seen quite frequently in the one and only cemetery on Cuba Road, and they are. These lights are usually seen floating above the tombstones then floating over Cuba Road and into the back yards of houses across the street.

In addition to the balls of light, luminous apparitions in human form have been reported in the cemetery from time to time.

Not all of the paranormal phenomena can be seen by the naked eye at the time of their occurrences. There are types that do not appear until later when photographs are developed. Frequently, photographs taken on the grounds of the cemetery reveal floating orbs and mists that were not there when the photo was taken.

Lisa Rowe, a Lake Zurich resident, frequents White Cemetery in search of these anomalous photographs. During a span of about one month, from October through November of 2000, her trips yielded around half a dozen of such photographs. Most of the time capturing these images is dumb luck, but sometimes the photographer knows when and where to shoot.

"I was just walking," Lisa starts to explain, "and then I just felt this really strong cold spot, so I turned around right away and took a picture."

This quick reaction picture Lisa speaks of clearly illustrates a large mist occupying the space that Lisa had just walked through. This same trip, which started at sunset and lasted into early nightfall, resulted in a number of other pictures of orbs and mists.

This active, secluded, and downright spooky location has inherited some of the biggest urban legends ever told. While some in the Chicago area claim that Mary Worth is buried at St. Patrick's Cemetery in Wadsworth, the remaining believers point to White Cemetery as the location of Worth's century-and-a-half-old corpse. It would be no surprise at all to learn that the railroad tracks are also linked to the popular urban legend of the phantom children who push stalled cars from the danger of an oncoming train. This legend, though not factual, it usually linked to a town in San Antonio. The story of "The Bloody Hook," (a.k.a. "The Lover's Lane Killer") has also been attached to White Cemetery and Cuba Road.

Over the past ten to twenty years, something that could be viewed as a newer rendition of that legend has surfaced. The new story tells of kids parking on Cuba Road to get a look at the cemetery. They were quickly chased away by a man appearing to be an angry farmer toting a shotgun. In some variations, the man vanishes. Is this a protective former owner of the land possibly protecting his cows from theft? Most likely it's merely another urban legend linked to an area that seems to spawn such legends by the dozens. Then, of course, it could always be a neighbor who believes in protecting the victimized cemetery with a little flair.

Founder of the American Ghost Society, Troy Taylor, writes in his book *Haunted Illinois* about another of the most notorious, but less common, phenomena to happen near the cemetery. Drivers moving down Cuba Road at night near the cemetery have seen an elderly woman walking down the side of the road holding a flashlight, candle, or lantern. Thinking this odd, the driver contemplates asking the woman if she needs help but then notices her turn onto a path that leads to a large house. Nothing seems out of the norm until the next time the driver passes down the same stretch of road during the day. It is under the light of the sun when the driver makes the discovery that there is no house where he had just recently seen one.

This vanishing house has been seen a number of times throughout the years, and recently, it was even seen engulfed in flames. The location where the house is seen now isn't where the house actually stood. Somehow, its ghost image has moved down the street a bit. When it was standing, however, visiting it was quite the macabre adventure for area youths to undertake.

A House Beyond Comparison

Starting at the bridge on Cuba Road, then passing White Cemetery, the next thing to look for is a small, unobtrusive street sign bearing the name "Rainbow Road." Those who have experienced the phenomena on Rainbow Road feel a chill creep across their skin each time the sign comes into their vision.

Rainbow Road seems like any other of the thousands of roads across Chicago's northern, western, and southern suburbs. Houses, new and old, line the road, dotting the trail to one of the more mysterious aspects of Lake County's past.

In the middle of the arc of Rainbow Road sat a driveway marked on either side with a white art deco wall and linked with a locked iron gate. Beyond the gate was another world.

Nearly all remnants of the estate are now gone, lost in the name of progress. However, we will start by seeing the site as it was when the location first earned its haunted reputation.

Stephanie Harlan remembers when she and friend Corey Bauernsmith used to visit this area in the late 1990s during photography trips.

"The gates were always open when we went," recalls Stephanie, who was fortunate enough to have been able to drive down the long and narrow blacktop driveway, past the small white lights that once helped illuminate the drive at night to a small but steep hill. It stands just past the point where the driveway widens to allow for parking. From Rainbow Road there was no sign of any buildings. All of that changed once on top of that hill.

Looking to the right there was a silo, doghouse, and a barn. To the left there was a building simply known by one rather bland and obvious name. The reputation of this structure speaks volumes. Additional hype to emphasize it is not needed. This is "The House on Rainbow Road."

This large house, built in the modernist style like most older buildings in the area, is rumored to be linked to the Mafia. Allegedly when gangsters headed up north to relax and lay low, this is where they went.

The most curious thing is that when the owners moved on, they did so in a hurry. The closets still contained clothes, and the kitchen drawers still held silverware.

By merely hearing first-hand accounts of visits to the house on Rainbow Road, it's apparent the location had an impact on the storyteller. The passion people have when recounting their tales and the intensely detailed description of the location they use as they relive the events is an indication that this is a place that will never be forgotten.

Stephanie visited the location on numerous occasions throughout 1997 and 1998, so one would assume that she would grow comfortable with the site, but that never happened.

Something as distressing as it is mysterious about the location is that the second floor of the barn-like building was always cluttered with baby toys. "But it wasn't just old toys either," Stephanie said. "There were also newer toys on the ground." It seems like, for whatever reason, additional toys have since been added to the mix since the original owners left.

"Then there was the basement of the house," Stephanie continued. "I was there with another friend who was poking around and just looking at everything, and he asked if I had

ever gone into the
cellar. I told him
not to do it, because
I had a bad feeling
about it."

Stephanie has
a family history of
being sensitive to
the spiritual world,
so if she had a bad
feeling, it would've
been wise to pay
attention.

Her friend
opened the cellar
door located on the
outside of the house,
"Then all I heard
is, 'Oh, my God!'
There was a huge
pentagram painted
on the floor, red
stuff on the walls,

and there were half-burnt candles and animal skulls all over
the place." Stephanie did not stick around long enough to find
out whether or not the red that was smeared on the walls was
blood, but the animal bones in the immediate area cause one
to come to a disheartening conclusion.

Mike Pry has had an experience all his own on the second
story of the house. He and some friends went to the property
with the goal of keeping themselves occupied for the night and
to confront their fears.

They started at one end of the top hall and decided to look
into each and every room just to be able to say that they did it.
They devised a plan to leave the door open after looking into it
as reminder that the room had already been checked.

About halfway through their mission, they were interrupted. "Someone whispered my name into my ear from behind me, and I figured it was just one of my friends being a jerk and trying to scare me. Then I realized all my friends were in front of me and I was the last one in the line." Mike turned to see the source of the voice but instead found that all of the doors that they had left open were now closed except for one—the door at the very end of the hallway.

When asked if they went back to the open door to look inside, Mike replied with a very realistic answer, "No way, we got the hell out of there!"

Others have reported similar experiences where doors that they propped open would still find a way to close on their own.

Unfortunately, this house, which still contained so many clues about its previous owners, was burned down as part of a firemen's training exercise. The remainder of the buildings remained behind locked gates for another decade until the entire area was developed into a new subdivision.

This may explain why the phantom house seen near White Cemetery has recently been seen in flames.

Even without the house intact, the area drew curiosity seekers for years. Negotiating over the wall and gate, then walking the long driveway, bordered by new homes on one side and a stagnant pond on the other, past a number of large dead trees that dot the immediate landscape, one would find that the driveway disappears behind a dense cluster of trees. Finally passing the trees, with butterflies in stomach, the remaining buildings are revealed. Where the house once stood was only a foundation filled with bricks and warped metal. There was a pool behind it serving as a breeding ground for all sorts of plant life.

Tiptoeing past the doghouse—just in case—and heading back behind the guest house, another building became visible. This smaller structure was rumored to house hired help in recent years and, prior to that, slaves. Between the house and the barn sat two tennis courts.

Today, the long
and narrow driveway
is a road that services
five lots, only two of
which have since
been developed. The
silo was the last
remaining structure
and remained on the
land until late 2007
or early 2008. There
are, however, still
two pieces of evidence of the site's former existence. Just across
the former driveway is an old mail box bearing the number 92,
and on one of the undeveloped lots, the old flagpole still marks
where the fabled home once stood.

Amazingly, as physical evidence disappeared and structures
were built on top of it, the truth has started to come to light.
The owner of the house was a developer named Robert Krilich.
His name is found in countless court papers but only as a result
of standard real estate business. There are no indications that
he was associated with the Mafia.

There was one confirmed death on the property in 1968.
William Cokenower III was seven years old when he was
climbing on a birdbath on the property. The heavy object
ended up falling on the boy's head, killing him before help
could arrive. William lived in the guesthouse with his family.
His father was the groundskeeper for the Krilich family.

There have been at least two reports of seeing the ghost of a
young boy on Cuba Road wearing a ripped red shirt and overalls.
According to the boy's father, little William did wear overalls and
added, "It does not matter what color Billy's shirt was. It would
have been red from all the blood." Due to the fact that the ghost
of a boy has been seen a considerable distance from Rainbow
Road, I felt it was unlikely this is the ghost of Billy Cokenower.
His sister, Sherry Cokenower-Mitchell, recounts, "My dad did

say to Billy the morning of his death, and these were my father's last words to Billy, he told him to quit lollygagging and get to the bus stop. He could be looking for my father because he did not get to say good-bye."

Regardless whether or not this ghost is Billy's, his playful and restless spirit may well have been the one playing tricks on visitors to the house.

There is another more sinister possibility. Once the element of dark rituals and animal sacrifice was introduced, as we'll also see at the Stickney House, a world of new possibilities was opened.

There is another plot of land that gained notoriety as a haunted abandoned home. This place is located off of Cuba Road, just a third of a mile west of Rainbow Road near a Deer Park sign. The house is gone and the entrance to the area barred, though aerial images show a driveway cutting about one hundred yards into what is now the Cuba Marsh Forest Preserve. With these two similar locations being so near to each other, it's likely that the more prominent and easy to find location, the house on Rainbow Road, ended up absorbing all of the stories, leaving one location lost in time while the other enjoys an inflated reputation.

CHAPTER 5

UNINVITED HOUSE GUESTS

"Grayslake Farmhouse"

SLIMPICTURES.COM/CHAPTER5.HTM

Hauntings at private residences can range from comforting to the most petrifying. The home, in essence, should be the place, more than any other, where one would feel safe. From time to time, unknown forces break through this safety net.

There are cases where a visitation is a welcome occurrence. For example, near Christmastime in 1986, Mary Czerwinski's grandfather collapsed and died of a heart attack in the parking lot of the old tuberculosis sanitarium. At the same exact time, their Christmas tree fell over. Year after year, on the anniversary of his death, their tree falls over once more.

"When I was younger," Czerwinski remembers, "my grandfather would baby-sit me. At night he'd shut the television off and tell me to get to bed. Once in a while when I'm up late, my TV seems to turn itself off. It's like he's still saying, 'It's late, go to bed.'"

Visitation hauntings are, in my opinion, the most common hauntings, and since they are usually very personal, they are also the least reported.

My grandfather had been fighting a long and difficult battle with emphysema. When his health started to deteriorate, he was placed in a hospital. The night he died, my mom was faced with the task of informing Gigi, a caretaker who was a Polish immigrant that spoke very broken English. Since my grandfather had gone into the hospital, she was living in his house alone. My mother spoke very clearly and slowly to her, "My dad died last night."

Gigi nearly interrupted her and stated, "No. Your dad here last night."

According to Gigi, my grandfather paced back and forth in the kitchen the evening he died. It was in the kitchen where he had spent the majority of his last years listening to Cubs games on the radio, talking with relatives, and reading the daily newspaper.

Since the death of her parents, my mother has occasionally been awakened in the middle of the night by an intense smell of cigarette smoke, though no one in our family smokes.

Instead of fearing it or even questioning it, she feels that she is simply being visited by a comforting presence: her parents, both smokers, still checking in on her.

It is one thing to be visited by someone from beyond the grave when the person is loved and missed, but it can be an altogether different situation when it's a stranger who is visiting your house during their afterlife. At times like this, the current owner of the house has to wonder what the motivation is for the haunting.

Egypt in Illinois

Those savvy to Chicago ghost stories remember the mistaken connection between Darius Miller, who is buried at Rosehill Cemetery, and "The Curse of Tut's Tomb." There are also the tales coming from the Field Museum that mummies have been found in locations other than where they were left and phantom screams emanate from the same exhibits.

Egyptian powers, traditions, and maybe even Egyptian Gods seem to have influenced the Chicago area in yet another way.

Known as the Gold Pyramid House, a number of bizarre events have surrounded this private residence in Wadsworth. This architectural marvel is as eye-catching as a private residence can be. To start, it is an exact scale reproduction of the Great Pyramid of Giza where King Tutankhamen was interred over one thousand years ago. It has even been covered with gold leaf twice. Shortly after the six-story structure was first covered with gold leaf, a tornado stripped the structure of the covering. Not caving into Mother Nature, the gold was re-applied, making this the largest 24-karat gold-covered object in existence.

Still, the property is an impressive sight as the huge pyramid stands behind an enormous, sixty-four-foot-tall statue of the Pharaoh Ramses, and dozens of miniature Sphinxes line a walkway to the front of the house. When looking up at the house, it is easy to be humbled knowing that the Pyramid of Giza is actually one hundred times larger than this already impressively large home.

The strange events started even before the house was completed in the early 1980s. Upon digging the foundation, two noteworthy things happened. First, gold was discovered. This was the first time, and still the only time, gold was found in Illinois.

Then, right after the pyramid was finished, a natural spring erupted and formed a moat around the structure. Surveys of the land before building showed no water in the area. Even stranger than that, the water was so pure that the owner was permitted to bottle and sell the water without needing to further purify it. The moat is not visible from the road, but it is when looking at the home with Google Maps. The moat encircling the home measures roughly 180 yards by 90 yards.

The interior of the house is completely Egyptian except for one room, which is reportedly decorated in direct contrast. This rebellious room is the Victorian getaway for the wife of the owner who wanted a break from the Egyptian motif.

Another room is more of a museum than anything else. It contains real Egyptian artifacts found on archeological digs and exact reproductions of the most desired one-of-a-kind pieces. Included is a gold-plated reproduction of King Tut's sarcophagus lid.

It is this room, the Chariot Room, where ravens attack those who enter it from the north entrance. This goes back to the Egyptian tale of black birds that protect the north entrance to the tomb of the boy king.

Understandably, this house is heavily guarded by more than just ravens. Though the owners used to give tours of this museum/house, the tours have been discontinued. As much of a curiosity as this location is, it is still a private home and best appreciated from the road.

The Old Stewart Pig Farm

Driving up to the old Stewart Pig Farm is like stepping back into Lake County's past. Cook County quickly grew into one of the most developed areas in the country with the early establishment of Fort Dearborn and, later, Chicago. The surrounding areas including Lake and Du Page Counties took longer to grow and are now, in fact, two of the fastest growing areas in the world. The addition of Gurnee Mills, one of the largest malls in America, changed the until-then rural landscape of the Wadsworth and Gurnee areas.

The road to the former farm is set off from main road, and the driveway itself is a lonely quarter-mile expanse of blacktop. The hills roll for long stretches uninterrupted by roads, power lines, or other signs of progress. To the right, horses gallop freely on acres of continuous green grass, and directly ahead sits a farmhouse that dates back to the late 1800s. It is along that stretch of pavement where the past meets the present and where the former owners occupy the same house that the current owners call home.

Though most stories involving visitation of a previous resident tend to be innocuous, the story was different for Susan Clark, who came face-to-face with the former owner of the house who had died several years before.

In Wadsworth, Illinois, the land used as the Stewart Pig Farm has a long history that dates back well over a century.

Though it is no longer a pig farm, many of the buildings on the property are original to the Stewart family, including the house and barn. Today the property is split between a number of owners who reside on the land.

Despite the fact that multiple occupants reside on the countryside once owned by the Stewart family, only one seems to have had any bizarre occurrences. Perhaps this is because she is residing in the house the Stewart family used to call home. The house has gone through renovations and an addition; however, the entire original house still exists today.

The first sign that something was awry happened when Susan was standing alone in the basement of the house doing laundry. While preoccupied, she felt something that she thought was a cat rub up against her leg. Curious, she looked down to actually see her pant leg move as if something were brushing up against it.

Not much later, what Susan felt in the basement materialized in front of her and one of her dogs in the upstairs living room. While Susan was relaxing on a chair, a small black animal that looked to be a cat appeared between the couch and a nearby table. Her dog jumped from the couch and took chase. The pursuit of the phantom cat ended abruptly after it disappeared in the middle of the room, leaving the dog quite baffled.

A friend of Susan always has a reoccurring dream when sleeping at the house. The dream is set at the home and features the Stewart family. In this dream, in addition to breeding pigs, the family also raised Miniature Pinscher dogs. Although pure speculation, perhaps the phantom animal that has been seen is actually one of the black Miniature Pinscher dogs refusing to leave its beloved home.

The Stewart family owned the land at least into the 1920s. Later, a man named Galloway, who lived in the city and only retreated to the former Stewart land to ride his horses on the weekend, purchased the land. Since his visits to the house were sparse, it is possible that paranormal events were going on the entire time but he just wasn't there to witness anything.

The animals are not alone in this house. Susan believes that there is at least one man still residing in her home. "The first [phantom] person I ever saw was when I was standing at the kitchen window. I thought I saw my roommate, Michael, walk around the front of the house." She wondered why he was home in the middle of the day but then noticed that his car wasn't there and she was alone after all.

Susan believes that the old rhubarb patch is the most visited location on the property by the former residents. "I usually see Mr. Stewart peripherally, but most of the time he's standing over by the little garden."

Her roommate has had his own run-in with someone actually inside the house. He thought he saw Susan standing at the sink as he passed the kitchen on his way to the computer room. When he reached the computer room, he was shocked to see her sitting at the computer doing work. The form that was seen at the sink was obviously not Susan.

Since Michael only caught a glimpse of a person in the kitchen out of the corner of his eye, there's no telling if the form he saw was female or if he just came to that conclusion figuring that it was Susan, the only other person in the house.

Another encounter occurred within the house walls on Thanksgiving night in 2000. Susan's children were in town and staying at the house in order to celebrate the holiday. Susan awoke in the middle of the night to get herself a drink of water. Upon going through the doorway back into the kitchen, she thought she bumped into one of her kids, but then the figure passed through her body. In her sleepy state, she didn't give any thought to it that night, but by morning she was certain that she had just walked through another entity.

According to Susan, it is really difficult to pick up on what may be several small paranormal events. "The house is always cold and drafty, so I can't really tell if one area is colder than another. Plus, the horses are always making noises, so if I ever hear anything I just figure it's them."

The single most traumatizing event happened when Susan had taken shelter in the barn during a Midwest-style spring-into-summer thunderstorm. "Earlier in the year a tree had fallen on the house, so I took the dogs and went into the barn because of the wind. At one point I turned around, and he was right there. We were face-to-face, and I could see him fully. I just thought 'Oh my God,' and I turned around real quick and tried to be still."

Susan remembers, "The man I saw in the barn was definitely older, but the man I saw from the kitchen was younger."

The other neighbors haven't had any experiences, and the neighbor who lives in the second story of the converted barn where the heart-stopping encounter took place openly admits that he "doesn't even want to know."

A reason for the haunting may have revealed itself as Michael walked through the main horse pasture where he found a granite stone that had an eerie resemblance to a gravestone. "I knocked all of the dirt off of it, and it was perfectly flat," said Michael, who since has been unable to relocate the stone for further examination.

"I always thought they'd have a family burial plot on the land," said Susan, noting that it was not uncommon for families to have plots on their own land for burial up until the early 1900s.

"I don't know why he appears to me," said Susan, "but I'm okay with it; I like it." Despite the initial shock, it seems that the old Stewart Pig Farm is a location where the souls of the living and the dead can coexist.

Where Angels Fear to Tread

Sometimes a haunted site could go unnoticed if the people frequenting it aren't sensitive or simply choose to ignore it. Conversely, a location that some think could possibly be haunted becomes a hotbed of activity once sensitive people join the fray. Such is the case at one century-old house in Grayslake.

Cathy Mahoney comes from a lineage of sensitive family members. Her abilities were further refined when she and her mother started playing telepathy games when she was five. By the time she was twelve, she was able to foresee bad events within her family to the extent that family members would bring over new cars to find out whether or not they would be in an accident in the vehicle. In the early 1980s, three angels sent by her father visited her and informed her of his passing. Since that moment, angels have been a major part of her life.

She is now a designer by trade, assembling floral arrangements and decorating venues for holidays and special events. On at least one occasion, while decorating a building on Milwaukee Avenue in Libertyville, the spirit of a previous owner gave her the final approval.

In 2007, she, her daughter and son-in-law, and their two sons moved into a large and very old brick farmhouse in Grayslake. The house was built in 1909 to house workers at a nearby factory. Cathy actually lived in the house for eighteen months starting in 1982. At the time the house was not haunted. Things have changed.

Within a month of living in the house for the second time, it became apparent that they were not alone. The first apparition, and the most commonly sighted one, is that of a young boy. He has curly blonde hair and seems to be eight to ten years old. He is seen running the length of the first floor of the house and peeking into rooms from doorways. The most characteristic thing about him is his comically wild, flailing and stomping manner in which he runs.

Not only has this apparition been seen by all five people living in the house, but he has also been seen by extended family and visiting friends of the grandchildren.

Another apparition is seen from the house looking out into the backyard. A fully-grown male figure is seen sitting at a picnic table, staring back at the house. Recently, the picnic table has been moved and he has not been seen since.

The third and final spirit seen at this house is unlike anything else written in this book.

This spirit is of a middle-aged man. He is seen wearing blue pants and a red shirt. Cathy has seen him while she is in her bedroom. He is seen leaning into her room, bracing himself by the door jam. After examining the room, he backs away and disappears after taking a few steps into the next room.

This seems fairly innocuous, though creepy enough. What happened next, however, was surprising even for Cathy. She saw this man again, still wearing blue pants and a red shirt, now leaning against an exterior window, looking into the house. The major difference was this time she was not seeing the spirit of a man, but an actual man. Apparently this individual used to live at the house and had some unfinished business with the landlord. According to Cathy, what she witnessed was his soul traveling. This house was on his mind so much that while he slept, his soul repeatedly traveled to revisit the home.

There is no speculation who the man at the picnic table is, but there is one guess at the curly-haired boy. Cathy used to work at Louis Florist in Grayslake. Employees at the flower shop were used to hearing the sounds of a small child running around on the first floor. The story they were told was that the building was at one point a schoolhouse and a child died there after taking a fall. No visual phenomena was ever reported at the site.

Cathy speculates that he may have followed her home. Whatever the case, it does seem that this spirit is attached to Cathy or another family member. Her youngest grandchild living in the house claims that he had talked with the same boy at their previous house.

Based on Mary Ann Winkowski's theory that ghosts survive by feeding on the positive energy of the living, leaving only negative energy behind, Cathy decided to have her house cleansed. In addition, Cathy noted that her guardian angels weren't around as much when the hauntings were active, almost as though they were uncomfortable with what was happening around the house.

In the middle of walking through her house with a burning sage stick, also called a smudge stick, the boy appeared and ran into a bedroom, diving under a bed. He has not been seen since.

Time will tell if the boy has finally successfully crossed over to the other side or will return to the house at a later time. If this spirit is, indeed, the same as the one that was reported at Louis Florist, perhaps he is back there, running through the store once more.

A Vengeful Spirit

Round Lake, Illinois, is another small town in Lake County. When presidential candidates are campaigning for "Everywhere, U.S.A.," they are referring to Round Lake. It is a community comprised of the most purely blue-collar citizens of America. Often times, both parents work in order to earn enough money to cover that night's dinner and their mortgage payments. Luxury can be hard to find in this working-class community where most entertainment either relies on watching Monday night football games between the Chicago Bears and the rival Green Bay Packers with friends and catching up with family.

One of these middle-America houses holds a family much like any other. A tight-knit group, they live in the same house that much of the family grew up in. It is a modest two-story, telltale sign that you're in suburbia. The only difference between this house and those neighboring homes along the street is that not all of the family members in the house are living.

A man we'll simply call "Jake" was something of an antisocial man. He was very particular with whom he spent his time. Often when he was on the second floor of the house and heard people conversing on the first floor living room, he would come partially down the spiral staircase and peek around the edge to decide if he wanted to join the group or not.

This was a man who either got along with people or he didn't. There was no middle ground. Those who ended up on his bad side knew it, as he wasn't a man who hid his emotions.

In the end, Jake was sick. Struck down with disease, he had an oxygen tank and mask follow him wherever he went.

Even after death, Jake is particular with whom he spends his time. The most consistently ongoing event occurs while sitting in the first floor living room. Jake has been seen walking down the stairs, stopping to see who is in the room, and then returning back upstairs where his bedroom was.

The first ever report of seeing Jake came from a neighbor who was walking past the house. She noticed a man walking in the living room when she knew that there wasn't anybody home. The most eye-catching thing about this would-be intruder was that he was wearing an oxygen mask.

When informing the family of what she saw, it became clear that Jake was still around.

There is another neighborhood woman who has had a more confrontational experience with the departed man. The two were openly not terribly fond of each other, despite the fact that she was considered a friend to many other family members. She has only visited the house once after his death. One time was all he needed in order to persuade her to stay away.

While visiting, this person was standing in the kitchen under a display of antique kitchen utensils when a serving spoon from the early 1900s lifted itself off the hook that it was hanging on and dropped right in front of her. Startled, but not really thinking anything of it, she moved to another location in the kitchen. Jake responded to her move by launching a six-pound canister of tomato paste across the kitchen from the counter to her feet.

The spoon falling could've easily been accounted for if the hook it was hanging from had simply lost its grip in the drywall and fallen, but the hook remained in place, which means that the spoon itself had to gain altitude in order to free itself from the hook. The canister of tomato paste is beyond any reasonable explanation. No amount of wind coming through an open window would be able to push this heavy item across a kitchen counter, and then send it airborne to land at the feet of this unsuspecting neighbor.

Jake's point was made clear. The neighbor still remains friends with the family, but she does so at a safe distance.

Death can offer freedom from responsibility whether it be a ghost who steals drinks at a Chicago bar, an old man who grabs the legs of pretty young women at St. Andrew's Inn, or the taunting that this spirit can get away with.

Jake's bedroom is now used as the bedroom for a young boy. Though this child is aware of the reporting of apparitions in other parts of the house, he claims that nothing out of the ordinary happens in the room. Many have claimed, however, that cold spots and even the feeling of wind coming from nowhere are common.

I was invited to check out the house by Lisa Rowe after a speech I gave in Lake Villa in October 2000. Upon entering the domicile, the only thing I picked up on was the family atmosphere. A number of adults were in the family room enjoying a football game on television while their children played in the back yard. Throughout the staircase and kitchen, nothing seemed out of the ordinary. Then we reached the bedroom.

Lisa and I were inspecting the room while listening to the stories that family members had to tell when Lisa mentioned feeling an extreme cold spot pass next to her. An inspection of the vents revealed that no heating or air conditioning was running and a closer look at the windows showed that they were not only sealed tight, but also reinforced for the impending winter with double-pained glass and plastic.

As our conversation in the room continued, I took the seat previously occupied by Lisa. It wasn't long before I too felt as if something had brushed against my right elbow. The feeling of a cool wind passing behind me continued for just under ten seconds. After it stopped, Lisa took a picture with her 35mm camera.

The resulting picture shows a mist immediately to my right. One can only imagine what that picture may have looked like if I had called for her to take the picture immediately as I first felt an unseen object brush past me.

Two Stories: Hard to Believe, Hard to Dismiss

There are two other haunted houses in the Chicago area worth noting. The information is scarce, and one of the houses has since been demolished, so they don't merit their own section, however, these stories are simply too interesting not to share.

Grayslake

Most people would probably continue on with their house hunting if they were to come across a house with a gravestone on the property. Being a logic-minded science teacher at a nearby college, Sue didn't allow for a superstitious fear that would let her pass up a good deal.

The grave was in the back yard, and the only text on it was the word "Baby." The theory is that this grave was placed during America's western expansion, while convoys of covered wagons traversed the country. If an individual died along the journey, it wasn't possible, let alone practical, to transport a body the rest of the way. Casualties were buried where they died. "Baby" was one such victim of the laborious journey.

In between the time Sue closed on the house and actually moved in, someone stole the grave marker.

A while later Sue was doing some gardening when she came across a bone. Afraid she may have disturbed the grave and not remembering its exact location, she went to a neighbor's house. The neighbor reassured her that where she was digging was nowhere near the grave.

Shrugging it off as the remains of a squirrel or other wild animal, she went back to her gardening. As expected, she found more bones. The number of bones she found, however, was alarming.

"It stopped being about gardening and became an archeological dig," she remembers.

When she laid out all of the bones she had unearthed, Sue had the nearly complete skeletons of nine cats. The only bone missing from each of them was their skull.

Sue hypothesizes, "The different spiritualist movements over time went back and forth, cats are good, cats are evil." She speculates that another portion of her yard holds nine feline skulls.

Creepy story, but is this house haunted? Again, this is where Sue differs from "most people." Most people would say yes, though Sue doesn't seem to notice the oddities observed at her home.

She was walking friend and colleague Patrick Gonder through the house, giving a tour, when she glossed over a second floor room. "What's that?" he asked.

"Oh, we don't use that room," she responded, offhandedly. "It's always really cold in that room for some reason, and the dogs won't go into it."

One night, the door leading to the basement started rattling wildly. It remained closed, though it shook violently in place. Sue was on the phone with her husband, who was on a business trip. The sound of the rattling door was so loud, her husband stopped the conversation to ask, "What's that noise?"

"The door's just shaking," was her matter-of-fact answer.

In order to gain some quiet and get to sleep, she had to wedge shoes between the door and the floor. She didn't find the event odd until the next day when she thought about it.

Does this haunting revolve around the spirit of Baby, who no longer has a grave marker? Is it related to a spiritualist who may have lived on the land, much like what is seen at the Stickney House? Lastly, if Sue continues to overlook the paranormal events that seem to be occurring around her house, will they increase in intensity until they can't be ignored?

Orland Park

John Garza is a police officer who has had a few brushes with the paranormal. On one occasion, he was called in with another officer, fire fighters, and an insurance representative to investigate a number of fires reported at a home in Orland Park.

According to the residents of the home, they didn't know why or how the fires started. The insurance company was understandably hesitant to pay the claim before conducting an arson investigation.

The house was examined; however, no faulty wiring or other natural cause for fires were discovered. It was all but confirmed that human hands started the fires.

Minutes after the investigation team dispersed, dispatch alerted them that a call came in reporting another fire at the home.

"Is this a joke?" Garza wondered at the time. These aren't the most savvy arsonists, starting a fire moments after the place was investigated.

When they regrouped, it was immediately evident that this was no joke as smoke was billowing out of a second-story window.

When they reached the room, they found the smoke coming from a bed that was pressed up against a wall. The fire fighters pulled the burning mattress away from the wall, revealing an intense blue flame, a half foot long, shooting out from an electrical outlet.

After the fire was fully extinguished, the investigation team delved into the wall where the fire started. "We wanted to see if something really weird happened, like an electrical line getting crossed with a gas line, but we found nothing," Garza explained.

Not knowing where to turn, the police brought in a psychic to examine the house. "She laid down on the ground in the middle of the basement and said that there was a body buried under the house."

After acknowledging that the house was prone to unpreventable fires, the house was razed. They did not locate a body under the house; however, when examining the area the psychic indicated they should look, a gravestone was found.

Assuming the fires and the gravestone are related, this serves as evidence that the importance of grave markers respecting and remembering the dead cannot be overstated.

CHAPTER 6

EDUCATED SPIRITS

"Antioch High School"

When considering where someone finds who they are, the answer is commonly while in school. It is within the walls of high school buildings that most people first learn to deal with other people, fall in love, handle responsibility, and learn more about their likes and dislikes. This continues through college, where many experience living on their own and taking care of themselves for the first time as well.

This being said, the school experience can be a very important one for students and teachers alike. Therefore, it shouldn't be much of a surprise to find out that a number of area schools have spirits attached to them.

Unfortunately, there are instances where deaths occur within these institutions of learning. Students, teachers, and even visitors have lost their lives during sporting events and day-to-day activities.

There are also the rarer instances where schools share the same land as cemeteries. The time-honored equation will remain the same: after-school parties plus a local cemetery will equal some good ghost stories.

The Sad Past of Antioch High School

Sam Dole attended Antioch High School and graduated in 1999. Her high school experience was just like anyone else's who attended the school. She walked in the building as a wide-eyed freshman, went through school, made dozens of new friends, eventually graduated, and learned a slew of ghost stories along the way.

The ages from fifteen to eighteen are often the most tumultuous time of one's life. There are pressures from school, family, friends, one's own self, social clubs, and work. These pressures may continue throughout life, but for the most part, they are introduced during these high school years. Not fitting in and, on occasion, the introduction of drugs can lead some to irresponsible acts that can put a life in jeopardy.

"It's always kind of weird when someone from Antioch dies," remembers Sam as she thinks about the rash of neck-related deaths of Antioch high schoolers.

A graduate of the school in the early 1990s had a similar recounting, remembering, "While I attended Antioch, many students died in crashes, suicides, and there was also a murder committed by one classmate against another."

She recalls a classmate who seemed sad and mixed up in drugs. Despite this, according to Sam, he never gave the impression that he would do anything harmful to himself. Those thoughts were proved wrong one morning when he was found hanging from a tree within a cemetery near his house. Although it was ruled a suicide, the victim seemed to have second thoughts at the last minute.

Sam recalls talking to the victim's cousin who told her, "The police report showed that he was struggling to get out of it."

Sam also recalls another classmate and next-door neighbor who crashed his motorcycle and broke his neck. The man ended up choking and struggling for his life for half an hour before finally succumbing to his injuries.

"The first story I was told," remembers Sam, "was about the basketball player who stepped on a stray basketball during practice, fell, broke his neck, and died."

The story that's even more well-remembered by students relates to a drama student who was found hanging in the school auditorium. There is some dispute around the death. There are some who believe the activity was one person's "final act," while others feel that it was an accident involving a stunt where a character was supposed to be hanged as part of the play.

The overall recollection of the event is somewhat hazy but appears to have originated from an actual event on October 22, 1990, as reported by the *Chicago Tribune*. Apparently, a Halloween hayride featured actors who were positioned to jump out and scare the visitors. A scare went horribly wrong when a stunt designed to appear like a man hanging from his neck actually did hang himself. According to the article, a tractor and trailer containing forty customers passed the seventeen-year-old victim after he died. The driver of the tractor knew something was wrong when the actor did not make the speech he was supposed to make.

While there are those who might experience a psychological chill while stretching for exercise in the gymnasium or while hanging lights above the stage, there is nothing directly linked to the haunted art hall.

Throughout her time in Antioch, Sam remembers the basement hallway being a point of controversy. After renovations took place, none of the teachers wanted to have their classes along that particular hall. It was the art teachers who eventually had to take the fall and accept that their future lay in that hallway.

Sam had a particular interest in art and, therefore, ended up spending a lot of time in that hall getting to know her teachers. In addition to their roles of authority figure and educator, Sam formed some tight-knit friendships with her art teachers. One such teacher relayed a terrifying experience he had while walking down the hallway.

The teacher was walking towards his classroom after hours one afternoon when the numbered disks on the locks of every locker suddenly began spinning. The locks unlocked, and all of the locker doors swung open.

Searching for someone to rationalize what happened and possibly get an answer, the teacher approached the principal with the story. Far from bring comforted, the teacher was told, "Would you like a psychiatric examination, or do you like your job?"

From the harshness of the principal, it seems apparent that this wasn't an unheard of problem for the school and the principal was hoping to diffuse the situation with the threat of termination in order to preserve the reputation of the school.

As far as Sam is concerned, she doesn't need the approval of the principal to know whether or not her past alma mater is haunted. She remembers one particular afternoon in the

hallway when she was
talking with friends
and was startled by
the sound of a cassette
player playing a tape
in her book bag. What
was the most alarming
to her was that the
player was broken and
incapable of doing
anything. To further

emphasize how strange this was, since the player was broken,
Sam had removed the batteries.

A visitor to the Slim Pictures Web site and class of 1996
graduate of the school added their own story stating, "Very
strange things always happened in that hallway. It also was
always the coldest part of the school. My locker was in that
hallway freshman year. I would find my locker open even
though I had closed it. I switched lockers against the principal's
rules but told him I could not and would not be in that hallway
any longer than I needed to be."

Of all the possible souls that may be present, there doesn't
seem to be any single obvious spirit to blame as there hasn't
been a known sighting. However, as time passes and the secret
continues to leak out of the building, I am sure that more
details will find their way to the surface.

A Failed Cover-up

The administrators at Rosary College in River Forest changed
the name of the school in 1998 to Dominican University. That's
not the only thing that's been altered at the school.

Hard evidence of the paranormal is usually hard to find.
The reasons range from people not wanting that location to
be cast in a bad light, which may be the case at Resurrection
Cemetery and "The Gate," to fear that a known haunted

location will attract undesirables, which is the case at a slew of locations including Bachelor's Grove, St. Patrick's, the Stickney House, and White Cemetery.

Then there are religious reasons. Only in the rarest occasions do churches give any credence to supernatural events. This is evident in how the Archdiocese of Chicago still doesn't acknowledge the somewhat regular miracles that seem to happen at Holy Sepulchre Cemetery.

If churches generally don't recognize supernatural events that are positive in nature, one can assume the hesitation in dealing with supernatural forces and events less than holy.

Typically, any possible evidence of the unexplained is hidden from view. Rosary College, a Catholic college, found itself in an interesting situation several decades ago.

The large and open dining hall has a number of doorways on either side of it. One set of doorways is particularly noteworthy since there is a small concrete arch over the door with a bust of a person engraved on either side of it. The only difference between now and then is that in the past these busts had faces.

The reason for the current negative space above their shoulders is that long ago these faces would reportedly change expressions of their own volition.

Students and other curious parties alike would gather around the faces in question. Rumors and speculation ran rampant around the school. The way the administrators decided to handle it was by removing the focal point of the stories.

They couldn't very well tear down the entire cement piece without a costly bill. So they did the next best thing—scrape off the faces.

To this day, no more paranormal events surround these doorways, but the strange blank faces act as a constant reminder of what happened there and how the threatened school administration handled the situation.

However, that's not the story the school administration tells. They claim that one face was created and then for whatever

reason the project could not be finished, so that face was removed to resemble the other faceless heads and shoulders. They then added the scrape marks to the other faces.

It is apparent where some of the facial features once were as there seem to be remnants of noses and eyebrows on a few of the heads.

In addition to this most famous case at Dominican University, there are also a few other tales of hauntings at the building.

Allegedly, there is a dorm room without a door where paranormal events happen. It is in this vacant room where supposedly there was a suicide of, depending on the story, either a student or a nun.

The real explanation for the vacant room is that it was intended to be a dorm room, but structural beams go through the room, thus making it too cramped.

There is a chapel on the second floor of Lewis Hall. Immediately next to an open library, it is large and breath taking. The story around it is that a ghost who plays the organ haunts the area. The sound coming from the massive pipe organ is so loud that it is heard from neighboring rooms.

According to former student Jenny Hutzenlaub, in the music hall people feel as if they're being watched, and objects are heard moving when it is empty. Apparently, the sounds are similar to the dragging sounds heard at the Red Lion Pub.

The reasons for the hauntings at Dominican University are unknown, but even those who aren't believers have to take a second look at the mysterious blank faces in the dining hall.

Lake Forest College

Looking at the history of Lake Forest College is like looking at a thick slice of Chicago's history. Located thirty miles north of Chicago, ten miles south of Waukegan, and just a half mile from the coast of Lake Michigan, Lake Forest was established along with the university in 1855. Presbyterian pastor Robert Patterson founded the location with the hopes of creating a town with the principal purpose of educating Presbyterian ministers. At the time, Northwestern University in Evanston served a similar purpose for Methodists.

Almerin Hotchkiss created the design of the city with the campus as the center. By 1860, the school was set to open with college-level courses, but plans were put on hold with the beginning of the Civil War. By the time the Civil War ended and Reconstruction was in progress, the college seemed ready to finally open, but then the Great Chicago Fire of 1871 put plans on hold once again as residents struggled to rebuild physically and economically. In 1876, the doors to the university finally opened, thanks largely to Mary Farwell, who started Lake Forest College as a branch of the university.

The rich inhabitants of the city looked to find safety in the suburbs after the 1886 Haymarket Riot. This is when Lake Forest initially became the home of upper-upper-class residents, which it still is today.

The year 1897 saw Reverend James C.K. McClure take over as president of the university, and it was then that the school experienced much of its physical growth, including the construction of Holt Chapel in 1900.

By World War II, Lake Forest was a well-established town. Its location between Fort Sheridan in Highwood and the Great Lakes Naval Training Center near North Chicago made it a logical choice to serve as a military training center where four hundred young men prepared for the war. Of those four hundred people, seventy-five died.

Lake Forest and Lake Forest College experienced the same population boom that the rest of the county did after the war.

Today, rather than being based on educating ministers, Lake Forest College is a liberal arts school that boasts an annual enrollment of nearly twelve hundred students.

Of those students, it's probably safe to assume that over half pass the century-old Holt Chapel with caution on their mind. It is in this large religious building that organ music emanates from within the thick brick walls without cause. The music has actually lasted for long periods of time and, on occasion, even lasts throughout the night. From time to time, the flash of a white ghostly light has been seen within the chapel during the music.

The mysterious odor of cigar smoke is also commonplace. Though there are no real leads regarding the source of any of these hauntings, the most famous event to take place was witnessed by a night watchman. While making sure Holt Chapel was secure, he set down his cigar in an ashtray just outside the front door. Now inside, a misty, pulsating, light blue form confronted him. The form then faced the security guard before passing through a nearby brick wall.

Unfortunately, all reports of hauntings at Lake Forest College are fairly sketchy, and there haven't been any additional known sightings, though the phantom organ music tends to be sporadic but much more repetitious.

Perhaps the institution of higher learning with the most stories and the dreariest past is just a few minutes away at…

Lake Forest's Other Haunted College

Most of the time when speaking with a religious figure about ghosts and the paranormal, ghosts are blown off as something that doesn't really happen. It's a different story at the Catholic Barat College.

"The nuns tell us that they're just other nuns trying to protect us," states Laura Callahan of the many spirits active on the grounds and within the halls of Barat College.

The evidence seems to be all around, especially on the tongues of the students who routinely go around the campus in search of the more famous spirits. As would be expected, Halloween is the most popular night.

"My boyfriend tells me to not even go out then because there's too much voodoo (as he calls it) out there," says Sara Rendall, a third-year student of Barat College who has yet to go exploring on Halloween.

That's not to say she's never gone exploring at all. One evening, she and a group of friends decided that it was their mission to seek out the little boy in the art wing.

This is probably the most popular story; however, it is mostly unknown outside of the college. Like most of the ghost stories, this takes place in the building known as Old Main, which is the heart of the school.

Barat College was founded in Chicago in 1858 but moved to Lake Forest in 1904. Knowing that the move was coming, forty-five acres of land were purchased and developed. Old Main was actually finished in 1901, though it wasn't used as a school until 1904.

The story of the little boy, according to those who are constantly in search of him, is that a few decades ago a maintenance worker for the school was forced to bring his son to work rather than leave him at home alone. It turns out the child would have been better off at home because when the father was preoccupied with whatever project he was working on, the child wandered off. The next time he was seen was in the basement of the elevator shaft. Apparently, he had walked through the opened doors to the elevator on the third floor where his dad was working. Without checking first to see if the elevator had arrived, the child stepped into open air and fell four stories to his death.

Though the child has been seen in the basement hallway near the elevator doors, the area where he primarily makes his presence known is in the art rooms on the floor from which he fell.

He has been quite burdensome to art students who put their paintings away at night only to find a blue handprint on them the next time they see them. Apparently, the boy is fond of dipping his hand into blue paint and adding his own personal touch.

There is one room he is particularly fond of, perhaps because it was the last place he saw his father. As the legend of this room goes, after dark when the school is mostly shut down other than for the hallways, those who go to the room have the opportunity of seeing him if he so allows them.

The tall, wooden double-doors to the room are locked tight each night, but if the boy wants to meet you, he will make it clear.

"He won't open the door if you're scared or if anyone in the group is scared," warns Sara, who has apparently been on the boy's good side. Sara visited the room with a group of friends to find the door locked and then walked down the hall a little ways and returned to test the door again. Somehow, and without any reasonable cause, the door was unlocked. Upon entering, Sara and her friends found nothing more than an empty and dark art room, but they took it as a sign from beyond the grave.

The third floor of Old Main, also the top floor, has one particular window of interest. It is from outside looking in that people have claimed to see a nun sitting near the window. That in itself wouldn't be much of an odd occurrence at this Catholic school, but the window is of particular interest. The specific room in question was formerly used as living quarters for the nuns. That is not the case anymore.

According to students, the nun in question is linked to a guilt-stricken nun that hanged herself in the hallway just outside her room as a result of the intense guilt over becoming pregnant. As one would suspect, the former room occupied by the nun is the one where she is seen today.

One can find the window in question by standing in the art hallway and looking out a window, and to the left. The very last window to the right is the window. From this singular vantage point one can keep tabs on both the phantom nun and the mischievous child.

Downstairs, on the first floor of the building, is the Sacred Heart Chapel. St. Madeleine Sophie Barat established the Society of the Sacred Heart in France in 1800. It made its way to America by 1818, and now the Society of the Sacred Heart can be found in forty-four countries on six continents.

The chapel bearing the name of the society was built in 1924 and holds the most commonly reported of the paranormal phenomena: the psychic scent of flowers. The scent has been noted throughout the chapel, down the hallway immediately outside of it, and on the nearby staircase. No visual or other phenomena accompany the smell. It is similar to the cigar smell coming from the chapel at Lake Forest College in the aspect that both are scents from somewhat unknown sources and they take place in a chapel around one hundred years old on a college campus in Lake Forest.

Today, the chapel is still in daily use for masses and prayer services. It is also the location of graduation ceremonies.

While most of the paranormal events take place within the building known as Old Main, there is also an outdoor location very uncommon to most colleges—a cemetery.

The cemetery is hard to locate for those who don't already know about it. Many students who attend the small school don't even know it exists. In the parking lot nearest to Sheridan Road, there is a building with a very unique and bizarre piece of art in front of it. Looking to the left of that, there is a row of very tall and dense evergreen trees. Walking towards those trees, a small path becomes visible. Eventually, tombstones come into view. This is where the nuns who gave their lives to God and Barat College are buried.

There is one particular point in the cemetery that reportedly draws people within the cemetery to it, the eight-foot-tall statue of Jesus' crucifixion. In the daylight hours, this could simply be attributed to the fact that it is a large and striking monument, but the school seems to want to mask the presence of the cemetery, so at night there is no light in the area. Even without actually seeing the monument, people continue to be drawn to it as if they were in a trance-like state.

DePaul University took over operation of Barat College in 2001, but the college only survived another three years. In 2004, after one hundred years of education, Barat College was sold off, from the land and buildings to the books in the library.

Most of Old Main will continue to survive, only now as condominium housing. The chapel, however, was demolished. If any physical act perpetuated today could further incite some already active spirits, one would think that demolishing a much loved and already haunted eighty-year-old chapel would do it.

CHAPTER 7

SOUTH & WEST SIDE CEMETERIES

"Bachelor's Grove"

SLIMPICTURES.COM/CHAPTER7.HTM

Unfortunately, the stigma of the South Side of Chicago as being one of the most dangerous parts of the nation has not passed. The thought of the South Side being a constant danger to one and all is a misnomer. For the most part, the western portion of the city has quietly assumed this title.

However, the South Side hasn't been able to shake this image. It is an unfortunate victim of bad press sticking around long after the fact. This is even more deplorable when noticing all of the diamonds in the rough throughout the South Side. These diamonds include great museums, hotels, restaurants, hang outs, haunted locations, and respectable suburbs filled with some of the hardest workers in the city.

The fact that there isn't a glamorous stretch of elite suburbs in the west or south suburbs, such as the North Shore in the northern suburbs, makes it easy to overlook the positive aspects of the area.

When walking through the many huge cemeteries on the South and West Sides, there is almost a comical symbolism of why the South Side is still fighting with its reputation. While the cemeteries within the city have grave stones bearing the names Marshall Field, Montgomery Ward, Edith Rockefeller McCormick, and Potter Palmer, the famous names on grave stones in the South Side include Sam Giancana, "Machine Gun Jack" McGurn, Tony "Big Tuna" Accardo, and "Scar Face" himself—Al Capone. However, cultural greats like Alexander Robinson and Cardinal Joseph Bernardin also call these burial sites their final resting place.

Though the South and West Sides are mostly overlooked, there's one thing that can't be disputed: the haunted locations around these areas are among the most incredible and inspiring in the City of Chicago.

There are a number of events that have transpired at these cemeteries that many view as modern-day miracles. Perhaps in those bleak moments filled with crime and disparity, the residents of these towns looked for a sign from a higher being. Amazingly their requests were answered. Repeatedly.

A Saint Among the Sinners

Mount Carmel is one of two enormous and noteworthy cemeteries on South Wolf Road in Hillside, Illinois. This is one of the more popular cemeteries as far as tourists are concerned. Each year, literally thousands of people visit the cemetery to visit the graves of total strangers.

The Bishop's Mausoleum is located directly in the center of the cemetery. Here, several of the most revered religious leaders in American history are interred. Most recently, this large building was the destination of a pilgrimage in 1996 for people from across the country who came to pay their final respects to the recently departed Cardinal Joseph Bernardin.

In the eyes of many, it is understandably unfortunate that the graves of these leaders are not visited as much as the leaders of a far less noble cause. One doesn't have to go far to find them either.

On the cemetery's main road, between Julia Buccola Petta's monument and the Bishop's Mausoleum, is the mausoleum of Mike Merlo, a noted gangster who was the head of Unione Siciliane. After Merlo's death due to cancer, "Bloody Angelo" Genna took over operations until he was eventually killed by Vincent Drucci, Earl Weiss, and Bugs Moran. Angelo is interred in Section 17. His killers are in the same cemetery. Drucci is buried in Section 12 (in a $10,000 silver casket), and "Hymie" Weiss is buried in Section K.

Along with Angelo in the Section 17 mausoleum are his brothers. Among them are "Tony the Gentleman," who was killed less than two months later by the same gang and "Mike the Devil," who was also claimed by gunmen. Their three remaining brothers, Pete, Jim, and Sam, fled to Sicily after the deaths but are now also interred with their brothers.

The killers, Drucci, Weiss, and Moran, all worked for Charles Dion O'Banion, who is buried in a prominent grave in nearby Section L. The leader of his own gang and a former altar boy, Charles was killed in a flower shop by Capone's gunmen.

"Machine Gun Jack" McGurn started out as a boxer but ended up being one of Capone's top gunmen. The reason he became involved in the Mafia was because his father, Angelo DeMora, was killed in a Mafia hit. He and Jack are buried in Section O.

Also buried in Mount Carmel is Roger Touhy, who was framed for kidnapping, finally won parole, and was assassinated immediately after his release at the age of sixty-one.

Some of the most important people in the history of the Chicago Mafia are represented with grave markers at this cemetery including Frank "The Enforcer" Nitti, who assumed control after Capone and killed himself before being arrested. Nitti is buried in Section 32 under the name Nitto in view of Capone's grave. Section M holds the remains of Antonio "The Scourge" Lombardo, who also briefly controlled the Unione Siciliane before being assassinated in the middle of the day on a crowded Madison Avenue. Sam Giancana, the ruler of the Chicago scene for nine years until 1966 is here, as is John May. May, buried in Section 22, was simply a car mechanic for the gang controlled by Bugs Moran. He was the innocent bystander who was caught in Capone's crosshairs along with six others during the St. Valentine's Day Massacre. The most famous Mafioso ever, and the man responsible for May's death, Al Capone, is buried in Section 35 just off Wolf Road.

There is an element of irony and poetic justice that the man who ordered the hit, Capone, and the man who planned it, McGurn, are forever interred with one of their victims.

There is also poetry in Capone, in many senses an embodiment of evil and greed, being buried at the exact opposite end of the cemetery from Julia Buccola Petta, who is considered a modern-day saint.

Despite the fact that dozens of famous people are buried at Mount Carmel Cemetery, many believe that the one grave to visit is Julia's.

The ghost world allows for many strange things to be true including the allowance of someone to become far more

famous and popular long after their death than they ever were while alive. Julia is one such case.

Julia's life was tragically taken at the young age of twenty-nine while giving birth to a stillborn infant. She was buried in her wedding dress under a nondescript grave, sharing her coffin with her baby. At the time, she was remembered by her surviving family and a newly widowed husband. Now she is remembered by a whole city.

After her death, Julia's mother began having nightmares. These nightmares consisted of her daughter begging and pleading to be removed from the earth from where she had recently been buried.

This started a six-year battle by her mother to have the body of Julia Buccola exhumed. Finally, the church and cemetery agreed to go through with the task to appease the elder Buccola. Their findings were remarkable.

Decomposition of the human body begins almost immediately, and it tends to be a rapid process wherein obvious physical changes begin in the body within the first week. Therefore, all present at the site of the excavation expected to see nothing recognizable other than bones. To their complete surprise, Julia's body looked as if she were still living.

According to first-hand witnesses, her skin was still fresh and soft, and she actually appeared as though she was simply sleeping. While Julia appeared completely unchanged, her infant was in the expected condition: nonexistent other than skeletal remains.

A monument was erected on Julia's grave depicting Julia standing on her wedding day. There are two photographs attached to the base of the monument. One is Julia on her wedding day while the other was taken the day her body was exhumed, just before reburial.

Those who knew the story immediately considered Julia a saint. She died while giving birth to her first child, and her body was proven to be incorruptible. She was an instant heroine for Chicago's Italian-American women.

Julia has been seen outside of her grave without the help of an exhumation. She has been seen walking the grounds of the cemetery in the area nearest to her Harrison Street grave site.

For the most part, she has been seen at night, but there is at least one notable daylight encounter where a lost little boy was eventually found holding Julia's hand. When the worried parents finally found their child, Julia vanished.

Julia's memory and inspirational past continues to live on throughout Chicago and, in particular, in the neighborhood around the cemetery.

We've only started to scratch the surface on religious miracles in a number of South Side cemeteries.

Truly Holy Happenings at Holy Sepulchre Cemetery

There is nothing that equals the innocence and purity of a child. Without having lived in the "real world," the child isn't jaded, corrupted, or tempted by sin. Therefore, when young Mary Alice Quinn confessed to her family that she had been visited by a religious figure, it was taken as truth. Over time, she became known as "Chicago's Miracle Child."

From that day forth, Mary Alice decided to devote the rest of her young life to religion and, in particular, to Saint Theresa. It was soon apparent Mary Alice had the power to heal, and she used this power on sick people throughout the South Side of the city. She made it known that even after death she wanted to be able to continue helping people from beyond the grave.

Unfortunately, she was able to put her will power to the test very soon. Tragically, Mary Alice died at the tender age of fourteen.

Word spread quickly that Mary Alice was determined to keep her promise. She appeared to people across the South Side and even across the world immediately after her death and throughout the 1940s.

Holy Sepulchre Cemetery holds the bodies of famous Chicago murder victims Barbara and Patricia Grimes. The sadness and positive energy form a balance as Mary Alice was also buried here with the Reilly family in Section 7. The reason she was buried with the Reilly family was to keep away curiosity-seekers and her many followers. Considering that you're reading about it here shows that it didn't work all that well. In truth, at the time of her death, Mary Alice was so revered that no secrets about her would keep.

Soon, people were visiting her grave on a daily basis. Many went to the grave to leave religious items like rosary beads and

crosses in thanks to all of the help and hope that she gave to Chicagoans. Others went to pray for Mary's help concerning sick and dying loved ones, while others walked away from the site with dirt from the grave site, believing it was some sort of holy relic symbolizing the healing powers Mary Alice had demonstrated.

Though rare, there have been documented cases of miracles occurring at the site of the grave. The stories involve people attending the grave with loved ones very near death. After praying for some time at the grave site, they are overwhelmed with the smell of roses. From that point on, their sickness goes into remission or completely disappears.

Even without the desperate prayer sessions, people have reported the smell of roses around the grave site during all months of the year. The scent seems to serve as a reminder that there is a higher power looking over us. Mary Alice appears to be part of that higher power now.

The smell can be overwhelming and is reportedly most common in January. While leading a small tour on January

11, 2001, a few members of our group including Mary Czerwinski, Molly Lo Mastro, and Lisa Rowe smelled the scent just off to the right of the grave for a brief period before it disappeared.

It may be noteworthy to point out that a row away from Mary Alice's grave is a nine-foot tall Reilly family plot marker that depicts St. Thérèse of Lisieux holding a cross and a number of roses. It is framed by the words, "I will let fall a shower of roses."

Holy Sepulchre Cemetery isn't that old of a burial ground compared to other prestigious city cemeteries. Until 1911, this is where the Worth Racetrack stood. The location finally became a cemetery in 1919. In addition to Mary Alice's grave, the cemetery also holds politicians Lar Daly, Dan Ryan, and Richard J. Daley, who was Chicago's mayor for longer than any other person, twenty-one years.

The cemetery also holds a monument commemorating Saint Oliver Plunkett Ashley. He was executed several hundred years ago in England and is buried in Ireland. A piece of his skull is currently on display in Dublin, but before it ended up there, this first-class holy relic passed through Chicago's South Side. While in the city, it was passed on from ill person to ill person, healing whomever it touched.

For a time, Chicago had two signs from above that they were not alone, but no one could have suspected what was to come next at Queen of Heaven Cemetery.

Heaven Comes to Queen of Heaven

Like Mount Carmel Cemetery, which is located immediately across Roosevelt Road, the occupants of Queen of Heaven Cemetery reflect the best and the worst Chicago has to offer. While Hill Number 7 holds the body of Father Martin Jenco, who survived 564 days as a Beirut hostage, another portion of the cemetery holds Tony "Big Tuna" Accardo, who was a high-ranking member of the Chicago Mafia from 1941 until his death in 1992. Entertainer George Kirby, frozen pizza magnate Mama Celeste, Chicago Bear William Wightkin, and Chicago Blackhawk Elmer Vasko are all buried here. However, the stories behind this cemetery do not revolve around who is buried here. They revolve around who is represented here: Jesus Christ.

South suburban Hillside resident Joseph Reinholtz was losing a battle against blindness. He made a trip to Medjugorje in Bosnia, Herzogovina. It is in this location where the Blessed Virgin Mother has visited many people. Immediately following the trip, Joseph's eyesight began to slowly improve. The first thing he was able to see again was a small statuette of the Virgin Mary he had purchased for less than a dollar years before. The statue was weeping.

Two years later, in 1989, he again visited Medjugorje. While there, he contacted a noted visionary named Vicka who told him to seek out a cross near a three-branched tree. After returning home, he found the cross the visionary described in his own neighborhood. Set back and surrounded by the graves of veterans at Queen of Heaven Cemetery stands a twelve-foot

cross very similar to the one located at the small cemetery behind Barat College.

After praying at the cross for over a year, on August 15, 1990, at the age of eighty, the Blessed Mother appeared to him for the first time. She appeared again on All Saints Day less than three months later with Saint Michael and three other angels.

This day was important because from this day on Joseph was visited by the Virgin Mary and Saint Michael six days a week until the day he died. The two were accompanied, on occasion, by Saint Joseph, other angels, and even Jesus Christ. For some unknown reason, Joseph was never visited by a holy figure on Tuesdays.

Observing the absence of Tuesday apparitions, the Archdiocese of Chicago declared that Joseph refrain from visiting the cemetery on Tuesdays.

By this time, Joseph's small group of friends that joined him for his prayer sessions began to grow. The reason Joseph revealed the secret was that he believed it was time for people to come back to the church. Word quickly spread throughout Chicago. The cross at Queen of Heaven became a phenomenon that nearly every resident living nearby and others from across the country attended.

This happening changed many lives, especially that of Joseph Reinholtz and Peggy Montalbano. Peggy, who described herself in a *Chicago Tribune* article as someone who hadn't prayed in nearly twenty years, was mysteriously drawn halfway around the world to Medjugorje where she met Joseph. It was also here where she began to pray once more. Returning to her home in nearby Mount Prospect, she ended up hearing about Joseph's visions and began visiting the cemetery on a regular basis.

When Joseph began telling his story, it served several purposes for people across the country. They were reassured that they were not alone in the large and intimidating world. They were reassured that there is a higher being and that their blind faith wasn't all for naught. They were also reassured that there are literally thousands of people near them, their own neighbors, who may have been feeling the same fears and were now at each other's side, sharing in the astonishing phenomena. During bad personal days and days of national horror, they could find peace in knowing that there is a little heaven left on earth.

This wonderful story helped ease the blow of distressing news on July 24, 1991, when the *Chicago Tribune* ran the story of the Hillside miracles next to an article aptly titled "Horror in Milwaukee Apartment." Jeffrey Dahmer's horrible secret was now in the open, as the daily prayer sessions continued in Hillside with the number of people regularly reaching over one hundred.

Christmas of that year was particularly noteworthy as over five hundred people braved the cold and crowded around the miraculous crucifix. Though the apparitions of religious figures continued to appear only to Joseph, the rest of those gathered close enough to see were treated to another miracle: seeing the statue bleed. Many of those nearest were brought to tears by the powerful image.

One curiosity is that while there were those who saw blood slowly trickling down the statue of Jesus placed upon the cross, others merely saw a clear water-like liquid.

As is the case regarding events of a supernatural nature, different members of a group may see and experience different things. While normally applied to stories of ghosts and hauntings, apparently this characteristic can be extended to other supernatural events.

On the twenty-fifth of each month, Joseph was given a message, which he would relate to others in attendance. The messages highly emphasized the importance of prayer and regular attendance at mass. In particular, Joseph made clear the message given to him by the Blessed Mother regarding prayer for the tortured souls in Purgatory for prayers alone hold the power to free souls from that wretched state.

The crowds only continued to gather. Eventually, the crowds grew too large and the foot traffic was damaging the plant life around nearby graves. In the summer of 1992, the cross was moved to its own location near the back of the cemetery. The new location is more secluded and surrounded by trees. There is also a large parking lot designed to accommodate the many daily visitors. Though some were concerned, the apparitions also moved to this new location.

On August 15, 1993, exactly three years after Joseph's first sighting, the Blessed Mother escorted Joseph into Purgatory. She did this so he could see the pain and suffering these souls were experiencing in order to inform everyone of what he saw.

The Blessed Mother also emphasized the teachings and practices that are among the most revered in the Catholic Church, including receiving the sacrament and saying the rosary. For leading this religious life, the Blessed Mother promised those who followed her that she would be present as they passed from life into the afterlife.

One particularly heartwarming story at the cross happened when Joseph was leading prayers but suddenly stopped and began laughing. He then explained that one of the angels had wandered off and was playing with a child in a stroller. The Virgin Mary then called him back to her side and instructed him to straighten up and pay attention. At the time, the baby was seen reaching up from the stroller towards the sky.

Eventually, Joseph suffered a debilitating stroke in February of 1995 and was unable to continue his daily visits to the site, which he had been able to keep up every day of the year (minus Tuesdays) for nearly six years.

Though he was not able to reach the crucifix, Joseph was still visited in the hospital by the Virgin Mary everyday until the day of his death.

Though Joseph has passed on, there are still occurrences at the crucifix. There are those who have since seen blood on the cross, while photographs of the monument are said to have shown the shape of halos, angel-like forms, and even large bright golden lights that some view as doorways. In addition, sweet smells including the scent of lilacs, roses, and honeysuckle have filled the air in the vicinity of the cross. Most inexplicably, some who have prayed at the site were amazed to find that the rosary beads they were holding had turned to gold.

Time has passed, and the cross is no longer visited by hundreds of people each day. However, the large parking lot serves as a reminder that, for a number of years, this was one of the most sought-after locations for religious pilgrims.

Even now, nearing twenty years since fist contact was made and about a decade since the death of Joseph Reinholtz, the cross is never alone. Throughout the day, visitors still come to sit, appreciate, and pray. The cross is located in the southeast portion of the cemetery, near Wolf Road and the Fresh Meadows Country Club, across from Section 6 of the cemetery. As of press time, there is a lot of landscaping around the cross. Also, visitors to the cross have created a makeshift shrine to the Virgin Mary, which is apropos considering the nature of the visions that have been reported at the site.

Something Far Less Holy at St. Casimir's

When first investigating an alleged haunting, one has to consider many possibilities. Among them are the motives of the storyteller, the possible rational causes for such an event, and if a prankster is the ultimate culprit.

The first report of a phantom at St. Casimir's Cemetery, originally a Lithuanian cemetery located near Alsip on 111th Street, was first assumed by many to be a practical joker or a simple lunatic. However, as the events continued over three decades and additional details were learned, there became a need for another possible cause.

The first sighting of an apparition at St. Casimir's Cemetery, which occurred in broad daylight, was of a tall and frail man standing just within the cemetery past the front gates. He was reportedly wearing a long black cape.

St. Casimir's Cemetery is a large Catholic cemetery located on 111th Street not far from Holy Sepulchre Cemetery and Mount Olivet Cemetery. The cemetery was founded in 1909 for Lithuanian descendants. There aren't many notable names buried in this cemetery except for Anna Marija Norkus, who, in recent years, has been linked to the most famous ghost in Chicago, Resurrection Mary.

This location is known as the home of the "Vampire of St. Casimir's."

Drivers along Kostner Avenue eventually come to St. Casimir's Cemetery, as it ends at the cemetery and forms a T-intersection with 111th Street. While sitting at that street light at night, the headlights of the car illuminate the front gate. Unsuspecting drivers have been able to see a ghostly figure standing behind the gate disappear just as quickly as he appeared. This figure doesn't stay in one position, as he has been seen near 111th Street, 115th Street, and even in backyards of nearby houses.

The descriptions are always the same: a ghostly white, disturbingly thin male over six feet tall. He is always wearing all black or possibly very dark blue. Some accounts have the man wearing a cape, while at other times the light is too dark to definitively tell whether or not he is. As if these characteristics didn't stand out enough, the one thing that remains etched in the minds of those who have seen him firsthand is his large and broken teeth. Some have gone so far as to compare the large teeth to canine teeth, further emphasizing the vampire similarities.

Dogs in nearby houses frequently see the man while he is in their backyard and react by wildly barking at him. While making his getaway, witnesses have seen the man leap over very tall obstacles with ease before vanishing.

In recent years, this ghost has been linked to a mentally handicapped man who died while jogging in the area one evening. He was wearing dark clothing, which a motorist did not see until it was too late.

The story of the so-called "Vampire of St. Casimir's" is a mysterious one, most notably due his activity. This appears to be a legitimate classic haunting since the phantom is aware of his surroundings. This is apparent as he avoids objects in his way rather than unknowingly walking through them, as would be the case in a residual haunting.

Conversely, one of the most famous sightings occurred on 115th Street near Restvale Cemetery on October 10, 1979, when the "vampire" showed characteristics of a residual haunting. That evening near midnight, he walked out into traffic as if he was not aware of the cars on the road. At least one car had to swerve out of the way to avoid hitting what the driver thought was a pedestrian.

In cases of residual hauntings, it's not as if a person or soul is trapped on earth like a classic haunting. Residual hauntings revolve around an event rather than a person. The apparitions in a residual haunting are unaware of what is going on around them because it is an event is replaying itself. Viewing a residual haunting is literally looking back in time as all of the actions have already happened. In another sense, it is a memory repeating over and over again for new witnesses. It is in these cases when dates, such as an anniversary of the event, can play a major role.

This would provide a cause for the actions this phantom performed on the night of October 10, 1979. Perhaps in reality this person died at that exact location in a car versus pedestrian accident several years ago to the minute.

In Dale Kaczmarek's *Windy City Ghosts*, an interesting theory is brought forth about the three most visited locations by this spirit. Kaczmarek theorizes that this man died near Restvale Cemetery, is buried at St. Casimir's Cemetery, and may have lived near the intersection of 118th Street and Joalyce Drive.

Perhaps you could provide the next lead on this story. It would be interesting to search the gravestones nearest where most of the sightings took place to search for the grave of a man who died on October 10 or 11 in the mid 1970s or before.

The Many Specters in Naperville's Cemetery

Though frequently overlooked by the headline-grabbing ghost stories of Archer Avenue and downtown Chicago to the east, Naperville has quite a few ghost stories associated with it.

In fact, Naperville contains so many stories that it can support two different ghost tours of Naperville groups. Lifetime resident and folklore enthusiast Diane Ladley started the original tour group. Ladley considers Naperville, "The most phantom-friendly town in the Midwest."

Naperville, which now boasts a population nearing 150,000, started in 1831 as Naper's Settlement, named for Captain Joseph Naper and his family. Naper's family had a history in the shipping business throughout the Great Lakes. However, when he reached the Chicago area, this is where he stayed. He was a state politician serving alongside Abraham Lincoln. He also fought in the Black Hawk War of 1832 and later in the Mexican War of 1846.

His final resting place is Naperville Cemetery. Naperville Cemetery is a sprawling flat piece of land along South Washington Street. In this affluent and friendly community, fences aren't needed to keep out vandals after hours, giving the cemetery a friendlier feel.

In fact, this cemetery is so friendly that children play here day and night under the watchful eye of a nanny. By the way, the children and the nanny are permanent residents of the cemetery, having passed away some time ago.

"Ever since I was a little girl, people have reported seeing lights moving around in the cemetery late at night," Ladley recalls. Ghost lights of various colors moving through the cemetery, particularly in the northeast portion of the cemetery. This portion of the cemetery is reserved for the graves of children.

Ladley's tour group came across a red ghost light in the area floating and swooping in between the gravestones. It even vanished only to reappear and continue its "cemetery dance." Ladly's group stood in flat-footed amazement watching the spectacle unfold before their eyes.

Whimsical speculation, perhaps more hope than anything else, is that these children who've had their lives cut short are enjoying their afterlives in the form of one long recess where they play hide and seek.

According to Ladley, one day in broad daylight a man walking on a path near this section of the cemetery came across a woman who was "dressed like Mary Poppins." Not only did she stand out because of her clothing from a different era but also because it was a hot summer morning and she was wearing a very heavy dress and hat.

The two even traded pleasantries in the form of "good mornings" as they passed each other. After he passed, he turned to get another look at her bizarre dress, but she had vanished.

The ghost lights aren't the only sighting Ladley's tour groups have come across. On home video footage, a large shadow was seen moving around in the distance. "You could see it actually move in front of the street lights in the distance." Ladley continues, "Suddenly you see it [at] half the distance… It just seemed to jump and move and blur so quickly."

The shadow appeared behind Ladley while she was telling her stories, but she does remember seeing a shadowy form out of the corner of her eye. At the time, she thought it was a member of the group examining gravestones in the area. It wasn't until an observer looked at the tape they recorded before they noticed that something unexplainable was going on.

Unlike many others, the administrators at this cemetery are open to talk of the supernatural. They are so accepting of their visitors from the other side, in fact, that they have requested paranormal investigations of their offices. They even hold an annual tour of the cemetery where visitors learn the history and importance of the monuments while interacting with costumed actors portraying the notable citizens of the cemetery.

Despite the cemetery having no gates to prevent entry, the typical rules do apply: visiting the cemetery after dark is trespassing.

There are hundreds of head-turning grave markers across Chicagoland. From a rotating monument depicting the Di Salvo family at Mount Carmel Cemetery to the striking Rod V. Pikas monument and other anchor-clad graves of victims of the *Eastland* Disaster at Bohemian National Cemetery, Naperville Cemetery also boasts an eye-catching stone.

Otto Klein's grave includes carvings of a horseshoe, flowers, a lasso, and a cowboy hat. The grave is remarkable enough on its own without a colorful story. However, it certainly has one of those too.

It seems one day in the early 1990s a cemetery worker was cleaning up the area around Otto's grave. She placed a hand on it for support, and her vision was instantly filled with another image. She was suddenly transported to another place and another time—Otto's final moments as experienced by

Otto. She could smell saw dust, she could see that she was in some sort of arena, she could hear a crowd cheering, and, most amazingly, she heard Otto's final conscious thought, "Why me? Why now?" She heard these questions in her head as if she was asking this herself.

Not knowing the story of Otto's demise, the cemetery worker started researching. She discovered that Otto performed as a trick rider with the Barnum and Bailey Circus. One of his many death-defying feats situates him riding at top speed on his little mare, Kitty. Gripping the saddle's pommel, he dismounted, landing on the ground just long enough to use the extreme speed to his advantage and propel himself over Kitty, landing on the other side of his horse. He continued leaping back and forth over his horse for two laps before again mounting the mare and safely coming to a stop.

During a performance at Madison Square Garden on April 21, 1915, there was a horrific accident near the end of his second lap. He lost his grip on the pommel and fell face first against a box. The young man lost consciousness and died a few hours later in a hospital. He was the second Barnum and Bailey performer to die in as many years; both died at Madison Square Garden.

The phrase, "the show must go on," can't possibly have a stronger impact than when noting that after the disaster of the Hagenback-Wallace train wreck, they only missed one show before being up-and-running for a Madison, Wisconsin, performance. Barnum and Bailey put on another show the very day of Otto's death. Arthur Maywood took over for Otto, performing the same tricks—including the one that took Otto's life. It was likely the biggest challenge in Maywood's professional career. The *New York Times* noted, "his face was very pale and his lips drawn as he raced around the Garden." He completed his run without incident.

Otto met a most untimely death. Though only twenty-eight years old, he had already established himself as one of the best trick riders in the country. His personal life, however, was just getting started. He was a newlywed, and his young wife was half a country away, back in Naperville. This is likely the inspiration for the final thought of, "Why me? Why now?"

The cemetery worker had never experienced anything like this before or since. Perhaps this performer wasn't fond of spending the last eighty to ninety years in obscurity, blending into the cemetery background. He reached out in spectacular fashion to get one woman's attention. In the process, he got a lot of attention and continues to do so from people who have started visiting his grave site.

This is part of the beauty of these ghost stories. A person that could potentially be forgotten after death is celebrated today for activities in life as much as for activities after death. Otto will not be forgotten.

The Natives Are Restless

Alexander Robinson was one of the most influential and important people during the settling of the area now known as Chicago. In addition, he is one of the most overlooked heroes in American history.

His ancestry was a strange one, especially for the time. His father was a Scottish trader while his mother was an Ottawa Indian. The Ottawa had a history of occupation of Mackinaw that dated to the late 1600s. Different groups within the Ottawa community settled throughout the Great Lakes, notably Lakes Huron, Michigan, Erie, and reaching as far south as the St. Joseph River, which dips into Indiana from Michigan.

One of the clans that ventured to the southeast returned to Mackinaw around 1706. This is where Alexander Robinson's journey began. The sketchy records of the day date Robinson's birth anywhere from 1763 to 1772.

He arrived in Chicago prior to the Fort Dearborn Massacre of 1812. It was August 15 and the War of 1812 was not even a month into its nearly three-year life. Native Americans allied with the British. The alliance largely began with a British victory at the Mackinac Island trading post and was fueled by their desire to prevent further westward expansion by the Americans.

After evaluating the vulnerability of Fort Dearborn, located on the banks of the Chicago River at what is now Michigan Avenue, it was ordered abandoned. The march, reinforced with support from Fort Wayne, Indiana, did not last long. An ambush by Potawatomi warriors led to a one-sided battle that left an estimated eighty-one dead; all but fifteen were Americans fleeing the Fort. Additional prisoners were taken with the intent to sell them to the British as slaves. These individuals were purchased and immediately released.

Robinson had actually met with the would-be attackers and participated in efforts to dissuade the warriors from attacking. Though unsuccessful, he came to the aid of John Kinzie and his family, the Fort's Commanding Captain Nathan Heald and his wife, and Captain Griffith. Robinson initially wanted to take them across Lake Michigan, closer to Fort Wayne but, fearing for their safety, ended up taking them via canoe all the way up to Mackinaw Island, a trip of over three hundred miles.

"After the battle, Robinson tried to talk to the newspapers to give his story, but they wouldn't listen. They already wrote the history they wanted to remember," said Buzz Spreeman, a descendant from Robinson's first marriage.

Robinson returned two years later, becoming a permanent resident of the city in 1814, and his presence was felt immediately. His relationship with both the white settlers and Native Americans made it possible for him to act as a mediator and interpreter.

Through his actions as a mediator, he was able to help Chicago get settled more peacefully. In 1843, in appreciation for his good deeds, Robinson was awarded 1,280 acres of land in two 640-acre plots in a sheepskin deed signed by President John Tyler. The two surveyors, who started setting aside land from opposite ends, did not meet in the middle as expected. In reality, there was a gap of 160 acres remaining that was awarded to Robinson as well. In addition, Robinson received a lifetime gift of $200 a year (around $3,700 today), which was later increased.

John Kinzie stayed away from Chicago until 1816, waiting out the War of 1812. He performed the September 1826 wedding ceremony of Robinson and Potawatomi's Catherine Chevalier. In the second Treaty of Prairie du Chien, signed on July 29, 1829, Robinson became chief of the Potawatomi, Chippewa, and Ottawa tribes.

Robinson now went by the name Chief Che-Che-Pin-Qua (meaning 'Blinking Eye' or 'The Squinter'). The final syllable in his native name is commonly misspelled "Quay," which is actually feminine in nature. Rather than "Qua" or the equally acceptable "Guay," the "Quay" error is so pervasive that it even found its way onto his monument.

Robinson lived on the land awarded to him; however, where he lived is not the area currently known as Robinson Woods. He first lived in a two-story farmhouse on 4406 River Road. The house stood for nearly 150 years before being demolished in the mid 1990s.

Except for a brief stint in Iowa, Robinson remained a Chicagoan until his death in 1872. Depending on the birth records, Robinson either lived until he was 100 or 110 years of age.

Alexander, Catherine, and other descendants were placed in the family burial plot on their land. In 1955, the final cabin on the land, which was first occupied by Alexander and Catherine's daughter Mary Rager, burned to the ground, never to be rebuilt. Though ancestors of the Robinson family are still in the area, the Forest Preserve District of Cook County has taken over the land. No descendants of Alexander Robinson have lived on the site since 1955.

Soon after the cabin burned down, another heartbreaking event took place nearby. The cold, nude bodies of Robert Peterson, 14; Anton Schuessler, 14; and his brother John Schuessler, 13 were found at Robinson Woods. The mysterious murder of these boys was the most heinous act to take place in Norridge until John Wayne Gacy's exploits were revealed to the world in the 1970s.

This high-profile crime was "solved" under suspicious circumstances in 1994. The heinousness of the crime, coupled with the possibility that the wrong man took the fall for the murders, leaving the deaths un-avenged, has left many thinking it was these murders that has led to the hauntings at Robinson Woods. What is usually not reported, however, is that the bodies were found at Robinson Woods South, located about a mile away.

The numerous types of visual, auditory, tactile, and even olfactory paranormal phenomena that plagues Robinson Woods appears to be linked to the Robinson family. There may also be unrest because the burial of Robinson descendants is no longer permitted on their family's former land. The year 1973 marked the first time a descendent, one of Robinson's great grandsons, was refused burial on the grounds by the city, specifically, the Chicago Board of Health.

Mary Czerwinski and I visited Robinson Woods for the first time in July of 2000. It was over a year before I went back; however, it has become the haunted site I frequent the most.

It was nearing the end of the day—one of our most productive days when first researching the book as we visited and photographed nearly a dozen sites throughout the northern portion of Chicago. On our way back, Mary noted that we were close to Robinson Woods. Despite being tired and hungry, we decided to make a short stop at the family burial grounds, shoot a few pictures, and leave. What ended up happening was one of our most exciting encounters with the unexplained.

Mary and I both have journalistic roots. We made the decision to cover all of these stories in a straightforward manner and without sensationalizing them. In no way did we ever expect to experience anything ourselves.

We are generally lacking in the sixth sense as we very rarely pick up on impressions from the past or from spirits with whom

we arc sharing the same space. That's why we knew something special was happening instantly.

Our initial plans dictated that this would be a short visit, but as we walked into the woods we both felt very welcome and had the desire to settle in and relax.

We walked down the path to a large boulder that has some historical information about Alexander Robinson engraved on it. As we lingered, groups of deer started to wander towards us. They were going about their business and paying no attention to us. They almost seemed to welcome us as equals as opposed to being a source of intimidation they should fear.

The boulder is at the foot of a paved path less than one hundred yards long. On either side of the path are benches. Standing on these benches can elevate one to a height over eight feet, which is the area where lilacs are inexplicably smelled throughout the year, even in the dead of winter.

We started to walk past the boulder deeper into the woods when Mary walked into a cold spot. I ran back to the car to get a still photo camera, hoping that we might be able to capture a form or mist on camera that we couldn't see with the naked eye. Walking back towards Mary, I stopped and noticed that my digital camera, which I charged the night before, was completely drained. A number of mechanical malfunctions such as this are common at haunted locations.

I was still a few hundred feet away when I heard a singular, but very clear beat of a tom-tom drum. This is a commonly heard sound that has also been recorded by Northern Illinois parapsychology students.

I finished my walk back to Mary and started to explain that the camera wasn't working when I was interrupted by a second beat of a tom-tom drum. Mary and I looked at each other instinctively. Then she asked, "Did you hear the first one?"

While all of this was going on, another group of deer, unphased, started to wander in towards us from our right side as the other group began to get closer from our left. In addition to how cavalier the deer acted towards us, I was surprised at how they had adjusted to their surroundings. The forest preserve is directly under a main flight path for O'Hare International Airport. Large airliners buzzed over the tree tops and eighteen-wheelers rumbled down the nearby four-lane River Road. The deer didn't care; they were numb to the distractions.

At this point, our conversation was cut short by a strange sound just over our heads. The sound lasted two seconds at the most but was so loud and strange that we both jumped. The best description we've been able to compile thus far is the sound of a strangely fluctuating static or suction-like sound with the sound of a snapping whip interspersed.

The greatest thing about working with Mary is she keeps a very level head. She does not jump to conclusions, and she always looks for a rational explanation, no matter how far-fetched, to explain things before calling it a paranormal experience. After hearing that strange sound, she looked at me dead in the eyes and declared, "I can't even begin to explain that!"

A few minutes later the sound happened again. This time it lasted considerably longer. Since it continued for a prolonged period, we were able to pinpoint a specific point on a tree branch above our heads where it seemed the sound was originating. Visually, there was nothing out of the ordinary there. Most disturbing to us, the hardened deer, seemingly beyond getting spooked, fled the area as fast as they could. Simultaneously, dogs in the houses across the street began barking wildly.

Animals are believed to possess a higher consciousness of nature, including the supernatural. The animals in the area seemed to know something was happening.

With the deer now gone and the sun setting, the woods became a different place. It was now very quiet, the silence being broken only by the occasional air traffic and the mysterious sound that happened once more.

Mary and I were now on high alert. For the first time, we were tense and nervous, but we did not want to leave. We walked around for a while, but nothing was happening. Still, there were no animals in the area.

Mary decided that we should sit and relax. We took a seat on one of the benches and began talking about an unrelated topic. The way we were positioned, I was facing the path and the road while Mary faced the boulder and the woods.

Mid way through the conversation, a third tom-tom beat rang out. A short time later Mary froze and sternly said, "There's a deer."

A massive buck was standing no more than twenty feet from us. The animal was large and imposing with a huge set of antlers. Mary and I stood up quickly. I placed her directly in front of me, and we headed down the path back to the car. As we walked away, the buck escorted us out. At the front of the path, he stopped and stood in a defensive position, barring us from reentering.

Mary and I drove down the road a short way and reviewed our research material. We wanted to see if there was any prior mention of animals or the odd sounds we heard. There was not.

We returned to the shoulder of River Road, which doubles as a very small parking area for the forest preserve. By this time, the sun was nearly down. While it was darker outside, it was completely dark within the woods.

I grabbed the infrared video camera and boldly started to head into the blackened woods when Mary shouted for me to stop. Apparently, I nearly walked into a deer that was holding its defensive position at the entrance. Since the deer was no more than three feet into the shadows, I hadn't seen it. It wasn't the large buck but rather another deer that assumed the exact same position near the entrance of the woods.

At the time, the trees around the path were densely wooded. In recent years, the underbrush has been cleared away while some trees were removed, creating a very open entrance. Before being cleared, the entrance appeared as a hole in the foliage.

After making a lot of noise and walking towards the deer, it slowly and reluctantly retreated. While my vision through the camera was choppy due to the slow shutter speed needed to see in the darkness, Mary had almost no vision at all.

After cautiously looking around for a few minutes, we started slowly back towards the street. Then, Mary grabbed my shoulder and said, "Scott, shoot over there! I think I saw something move."

As I turned to my right, the strange sounds buzzed over our heads again. Mary summed up the excitement of the night by saying, "That's it, I can't take anymore of this," before heading out of the woods.

We initially thought that we were treading too close to the deer's home, leading to its confrontational behavior. After learning of Native American beliefs regarding reincarnation, however, we came to the conclusion that perhaps the deer were protecting us from the negative spirits in the area.

I asked Buzz Spreeman about the belief that a chief would be reincarnated as a buck. He acknowledge the belief of returning in other forms but hadn't heard anything regarding deer or, specifically, a buck. He then went on to tell of a vivid dream he had in which he, in full traditional buckskin attire, defended himself against wild animals before being approached by a buck who instructed him to live a good and positive life, to live the "right" way. The buck then retreated through an archway, morphing into an Indian before disappearing.

"Maybe grandpa's looking out, making sure I don't mess up," Buzz said with a joking but still serious laugh.

In addition to the previously mentioned phenomena and our own experiences, people have reported ghost lights, seeing Indian faces on trees in developed photographs, and even an apparition of a Native American ghost.

Possibly resulting from the denied burial of Robinson's descendants or the city's retaking of the family land, this is one of the more actively haunted locations in Chicago.

I visited the site in October of 2006 with Marcus LeShock to shoot a segment on haunted Chicago for CLTV's *Metromix: the TV Show*. Like clockwork, as soon as the recording was over and the camera was put away, we heard the mysterious sound. It was the first time I heard it outside of the woods. We were on the shoulder of the road near the head of the path.

Later that same month, Mary and I led a group on a trolley tour of haunted sites. The night started at Robinson Woods. After visiting the monument, we were making our way out when a series of six phantom tom-tom beats created a rhythm. Roughly half a dozen people heard this. This was especially exciting since, in the past, I had only heard singular beats whereas this was a series and had a tempo.

Dan Melone, archeologist for the Forest Preserve District of Cook County, who contributed mountains of information to this chapter along with Buzz Spreeman, had his own unique run-in with the paranormal. In the early 1990s, he and a friend were test driving a new car. "Let's go to Robinson Woods. There are ghosts there!" he urged his friend. Melone had been visiting Robinson Woods for years intrigued by stories of ghosts that had persisted, though he hadn't encountered anything himself.

He and his friend entered the darkened woods, making their way past the monument, reaching the same area where I had heard the series of six tom-tom beats, when three figures came into view in front of them. Currently, a Shagbark tree marks the site where the figures were standing. "They were faint white, and their faces were completely blacked out, vacant," remembers Melone. When he asked his friend what she thought of what they were looking at, he found that she had already run back to the car. He followed suit. To this day, he isn't completely certain what he saw, but he certainly wasn't going to stick around to find out.

Those expecting a conventional cemetery will be disappointed as the Robinson family members are in unmarked graves. As late as the 1970s, though, there were possibly as many as twenty individual gravestones on the land.

Scars from pervious visitors who, for whatever reason, feel compelled to destroy are apparent on the boulder. The site was vandalized significantly in 1931 when Catherine Chevalier's gravestone was broken into three pieces. A chain-link fence has surrounded the grave site since 1926, but curiosity-seekers, rather than people who legitimately wanted to pay their respects, continued to visit this site.

The state even pushed to make it a tourist attraction. There was a sign on the highway [I-294] that said, "Come see a real Indian Cemetery.'"

Aside from the boulder, visitors today can enjoy the accomplishments of a Boy Scout Troop headed by Chris Heck. They did a commendable job erecting a sign displaying photographs and telling more of Robinson's history. The opposite side of the sign gives botanical and wildlife-related information on the woods.

Several of Robinson's descendants, who now number between 5,000 and 6,000, are actively involved with the woods. Spreeman was one of many who attended a sacred drum and pipe ceremony in June of 2008. Part of the reason for the ceremony was to allow for the spirits of those buried on the land to rest peacefully. Time will tell if the spirits on the land were receptive to the message, but there is speculation that the event will take place every year regardless.

Robinson Woods is a fantastic place to honor a Chicago hero and do some "ghost hunting;" however, keep in mind this is Forest Preserve District land and is closed at sunset.

The Most Haunted Cemetery in Chicago

Simply put, Bachelor's Grove Cemetery is one of the most haunted cemeteries in the entire world. The number of officially reported hauntings are in the triple digits, while unreported sightings are far more numerous.

For starters, on the Midlothian Turnpike just outside of the cemetery and on the path to the cemetery, people have observed phantom cars. Much like at White Cemetery, the cars are described as being large black luxury sedans, usually identified as being from the 1940s or before.

Most of these sightings began around the 1960s when the cemetery became isolated. The Midlothian Turnpike used to meet up with the front gates of the cemetery, but the road had to be moved when plans called for its widening. The old part of the turnpike was left untouched. Now it is used only for foot traffic into the cemetery.

More importantly, as far as hauntings are concerned, the cemetery became more secluded due to the road change. Rather than being a place of quiet mourning, Bachelor's Grove Cemetery became a constant victim of vandalism, and, for the past thirty years, the site of satanic worship. Much of the rituals take place within the questionable foundation of a house. More on that later.

In addition to these changes, the path to Bachelor's Grove Cemetery became something of a lover's lane. This is the reason Bachelor's Grove has sometimes been linked to the urban legend of "The Bloody Hook," which is based on the Texarkana Lovers Lane killings.

The history of Bachelor's Grove Cemetery is about as colorful as the mountain of hauntings that continue on this single acre of wooded land all year, day and night. The number of spirits and types of activity witnessed at the cemetery continue to grow, and nearly all of them have interesting stories behind them.

For example, at one point before the land was used as a cemetery, it was a farmer's field. One day while tilling the land, the farmer's horse inexplicably bolted into the murky pond which now stands between the cemetery and the new turnpike. The weight of the metal plow pulled the horse and the farmer to the bottom where they both drowned. The plow horse and farmer continue to visit the site of their demise. They were first seen by baffled police officers who saw an ethereal farmer and horse running down the four-lane road outside of the cemetery in the late 1970s.

During the 1920s and 1930s, while Chicago was ruled by Al Capone, that same pond was used as a dumping ground for illegal firearms and victims of Mafia hits. This is often linked to reports of phantom men wearing 1920's and 1930's era suits.

Crystal Warren, a Midlothian resident who frequents the cemetery in search of ghosts and a good scare, remembers that upon entering the cemetery one day she felt as if someone was

behind her. Looking back, she saw two men. Startled and scared, she ran through the cemetery, around the small pond, and across the street where she looked back to see the two men standing at the guardrail along the Midlothian Turnpike. According to Crystal, the men were wearing clothing that fit the time period of the 1920s. Without prior knowledge of the stories of the pond, Crystal even compared the men she saw to gangsters.

This is particularly interesting since Crystal didn't know the history of the site, making her story more believable because she wasn't just embellishing stories she may have already heard.

Crystal often visits the cemetery with Holly Smith, another Midlothian resident. They come to this place to tell ghost stories and "freak themselves out." Though usually the only ghosts they encounter are the ones in their tall tales, sometimes they get more than they bargain for. On one occasion while entering the cemetery alone, a young, pig-tailed girl in an old-fashioned pink dress confronted Crystal. Crystal stopped dead in her tracks with her eyes wide-open and fixed on the phantom. The apparition smiled at her and sent Crystal running into the cemetery for safety.

Crystal, Holly, and other friends witnessed another event. They entered the cemetery near dusk and took a seat just to the right of the front entrance. They sat in a circle and told ghost stories for hours. Nothing out of the ordinary happened until they verbally stated that it was late and time to leave. As this was said, a strand of barbed wire, near to where they were sitting which had been hanging lifelessly from atop the gate, suddenly flew straight up in the air. At the time this happened there was nothing around it that could have caused such a commotion. Maybe there were eavesdroppers on the conversation who felt like contributing another ghost story of their own.

Another apparition, and the one that is least easily explained, is the sighting of a two-headed man again in the area of the pond. Few attempts have been made to even try to explain this phenomenon. However, Dale Kaczmarek, president of

Chicago's Ghost Research Society, has made the speculation, "Perhaps this apparition is actually the ghost of the farmer and his horse in a state of perpetual materialization."

Adam R. Rotsch visited the cemetery in the late 1990s with friends. He was startled to see what appeared to be a disfigured man walking over the pond. In his description of the man, Adam alluded to the man having a large bulge of some sort protruding from his shoulder. This appears to be similar to the sighting of the two-headed man. The only real difference was the interpretation of what the second lump was. While some assumed it was another head, Adam merely thought the man had a hunchback.

Adam had no prior knowledge of the stories of the two-headed man and was very hesitant to think that is what he had seen.

Bachelor's Grove Cemetery is similar to White Cemetery in that there are disappearing cars patrolling the road outside of it. The two cemeteries are also similar in another very unique way: they each have a vanishing house.

Many people have observed the house since at least the mid 1960s. All claim it to be a two-story Victorian house with a porch swing and a light shining from the inside. The light coming from the house even illuminates the surrounding woods. The house seems to move around a lot, as it is not seen in the same location every time. It has been seen within the cemetery, just outside the cemetery gates, along the path, and even floating over the pond. When the house is seen floating over the pond, it is most visible from the Midlothian Turnpike by passing motorists, who often aren't aware that the house isn't supposed to be there. Those who have seen it are unable to approach it because it gets smaller as the person walks closer until it finally disappears.

The most mysterious aspect of the vanishing house is that there is no record of there ever having been a building on this land. However, just a few hundred yards from the cemetery sits the foundation of a structure. This is where much of the satanic activity takes place.

We're still not done with this small site. In addition, there are at least three types of ghost lights that reside in the area. One is a blue orb frequently seen floating about the cemetery throughout the 1970s and 1980s. Currently, flashing white balls and red streaks above the path towards the cemetery can be observed.

On the same night Adam may have encountered the two-headed man, it was also a particularly active night for ghost lights. He said that red lights were flashing throughout the cemetery in a way that it looked like they were "dancing" with the green light periodically given off by fireflies.

Probably the most famous phantom of Bachelor's Grove Cemetery is the Madonna of Bachelor's Grove (sometimes called Mrs. Rogers). This is a woman in white who wanders around the cemetery while holding her infant baby in her arms. Some believe that the best time to see the Madonna of Bachelor's Grove is on nights with a full moon.

Though not regularly occurring, one of the most seldom-reported phantoms is a man in a suit who gives off a modest yellow glow. Someone first saw the man while they were spending the night in the cemetery as part of an experiment.

Pete Crapia, who also organizes the Grove Restoration Project at Bachelorsgrove.com, can vouch for the validity of this tale. While taking a photograph, Pete saw something yellow out of the corner of his eye. Looking at the developed picture revealed a yellow blur. Though Pete never actually saw the shape of a man, he can attest to an energy source of some sort that gives off a yellow glow.

Apparitions don't just happen within the cemetery. The wooded pathway away from civilization and into the dark unknown is also the site of disappearing men wearing black overcoats. While some of these visions can be attributed to actual cultists, a case is easily made regarding those who disappear in front of surprised witnesses.

In addition, phantom dogs have been known to patrol the area near the beginning of the path all the way to the cemetery entrance. Bob Jensen of the Ghostland Society and an active debunker of haunted sites was one such witness who had no knowledge of the phantom animals until he encountered one in the path near the cemetery entrance. He was completely taken by their piercing eyes.

Amateur ghost photographers might want to start at Bachelor's Grove Cemetery. It is said that if one goes through a full roll of film in the cemetery and the surrounding woods the chance of capturing an anomaly is greater than the chances of not.

Everything from strange mists and floating orbs to full human figures have been captured on photographs. Other sounds and voices have also been recorded on audio tape, including a voice calling out to the deceased of the cemetery by name.

Mari Huff of the Ghost Research Society captured the most famous paranormal photograph ever taken at the cemetery. Her random infrared panoramic picture of the cemetery, when developed, showed a woman clearly sitting upon a gravestone. To see this picture, visit GRS.com.

Also noted are the common characteristics of cold spots, but at this special location, even they are taken to extremes. Measurements from within the cold spots, or sometimes within certain rings of gravestones, show temperature dips ranging from twenty-five to forty-eight degrees Fahrenheit during warm weather (warm weather being defined as temperatures of sixty degrees Fahrenheit or higher).

The first trip I made to the cemetery happened in the summer of 1999 with Jeff Lord and Jason Jacobs for the video documentary *Voices from the Grave*. No paranormal activity was noted other than a cold spot experienced by Jason. Pictures that he took of the area showed no anomalies. However, those pictures would become very important later.

The most curious thing we found was just outside of the cemetery fence. There, in the woods, was a camouflage blanket, a shovel, some sort of carving tool, a bottle used for huffing drugs, and an animal skull of either a deer or a large dog.

Though we can't say for sure there had been a satanic ritual performed there, signs would point to "yes." Perhaps the answer to that question comes from a Midlothian native who told us, "If you ever come here at night... well, just don't."

A second trip was quickly planned for a few months later with a small group of people. Sometimes it is good to go out with a group because some people may be able to pick up on things that others can't. Conversely, large groups are never a good idea because there can be just too much personality getting in the way of making paranormal contact. One person jumping to a conclusion can also accidentally influence people to think that they see something as well. Soon there is mass hysteria over nothing at all happening.

Thus, we made our way south of Chicago again. Finding the cemetery this time would prove to be much easier than the first time. The Rubio Woods Forest Preserve sits directly across the street from the cemetery, but still, the entrance to the cemetery is barely visible as it is covered by trees. The best way to find it is to look across the street from the Rubio Woods parking lot for a chain in front of a path with a sign suggesting "closed" hanging from it.

That is the path to the cemetery. Walking around the chain that serves little purpose and continuing down the path, the old Midlothian Turnpike is barely visible under foot due to the overgrowth of weeds. Continuing down the path for about two hundred yards into the woods, eventually a chain link fence and then grave stones become discernible to the right.

The gates to the cemetery have been broken open. Chains had been attached to the gates to keep them closed, but then tears were made in the fence for use as another entrance.

Stepping inside the cemetery, it is obvious that the past half-century has not treated the cemetery well. Several bodies were removed and placed in different cemeteries after the cemetery started its downward spiral, but other bodies reportedly have been removed since by perpetrators of a pointless crime.

Gravestones have been stolen, while some have turned up in backyards at nearby houses. Countless others have been unearthed and thrown into the murky pond. Of the estimated one hundred people still buried there, only a little more than a dozen of those are yet represented by grave markers. Of those, one hundred percent have been vandalized to some extent.

Visiting Bachelor's Grove is a surreal experience due entirely to its reputation. It is sadly too easy to overlook that part of Chicago's history is buried here and is being insulted by repeated acts of vandalism. One of those buried here actually worked on the construction of Chicago's famous Water Tower.

By sunset of our second outing, the action started. What was first seen was a bank of fog that began to develop. Considering that we were near a pond, this would make sense, but the fog was in the opposite end of the cemetery away from the pond. It was near the front entrance, just outside of the gates. Something else that was curious was that out of the eight people that were there, only seven people could see the fog. I was the one who could not.

Not too long after, several people claimed they saw a person walking near the area where the pond was. Only about half of the group was able to see this, which means either only half of the people were capable of seeing it, or half of the people were fooling themselves into believing that they were seeing something. Again, I did not see anything.

The next hour or so of that night went by without much activity until I suggested to the group that we take one last walk around the perimeter of the cemetery before leaving. On this walk, Dianne Markus, who was alone walking behind the group, had the small finger on her right hand squeezed by an unseen hand. She didn't mention anything at the time but told me the following day.

After our little walk, Adam (the same Adam who had seen the red ghost lights on a previous trip) and I walked down the center of the cemetery. It was there that I saw what appeared to be a face illuminated in the leaves of a distant tree near the pond. I handed the camera to Adam as my blood began to run cold.

After looking at what I had pointed out, Adam panned to his right, looking into the woods. "There are eyes," was all he could say.

He handed me the camera, and I could immediately see what he was referring to. It appeared to be two sets of glowing eyes looking out at us from the woods, about twelve feet above the ground. They were not visible to the naked eye but rather through the lens of an infrared video camera.

We headed back towards the entrance of the cemetery where Adam requested that I take video footage of a nearby tree. It was at that tree that Adam had experienced strange feelings in the past, and it is at that tree where Jason felt a cold spot on our previous trip. During filming of the tree, nothing appeared out of the ordinary, but upon playback of the footage, the outline of a boy wearing shoes and black shorts is plainly visible. When comparing the footage to the pictures of the tree that Jason took, it is apparent that there is no object or strange coloring of the tree that could give it such an appearance.

In addition to photographs with orbs in them, other interesting things were found after the fact. The most exciting was finding more sets of eyes. While we first saw the glowing eyes at night through an infrared video camera, the same eyes were photographed during the day in a different part of the cemetery. On both occasions, the unaided eye could not see the sets of eyes. When comparing the two times we caught the eyes on tape or film, it is apparent that the eyes are the same based on size, distance between the eyes, and between the sets of eyes.

A particularly interesting thing happened when we first arrived. I advised everyone to spread out and look around the entire area. Dianne went off with Jamie Lemm. At one point they thought they felt a cold spot, so they starting walking

back to tell me about it. At the time, I was standing next to Dave LaPorta who took a picture of them. Upon development of the film, a large mist is seen floating in the air in the area where they thought they felt the cold spot.

Since our first visits in 2000, a number of massive trees have fallen into the cemetery, crushing the surrounding fences, making it impossible to lock the cemetery. However, the forest preserve and the local police keep an eye on the land, regularly chasing away visitors in an attempt to protect what's left of the cemetery. A visit in the summer of 2008 revealed a welcome sight. Several of the graves had flowers placed on them. The most visited grave at the cemetery, a grave at the Fulton monument that simply states "Infant Daughter," was covered with toys. The small trinkets served as gifts to commemorate the young, lost girl.

The damage to the cemetery cannot be undone; however, it seems that the visitors are shifting from vandals and cultists to more respectful ghost hunters and historians. Perhaps this will be enough to help the spirits at this cemetery find peace.

CHAPTER 8

CHICAGO'S DARKEST HOURS

"The *Eastland* Disaster"

Chicago is a city not unfamiliar with tragedy. There are several dates that will live in infamy in Chicago, and most of those will be covered in this chapter. Every city in the world has their claims to tragic car accidents, fires, floods, and other disasters of near Biblical proportions, but almost from the moment the first settlers established Dearborn, later renamed Chicago, it seemed death was in the cards for this lake-side village.

The first mass loss of life was the Fort Dearborn Massacre when the blood of white settlers and natives mixed on the banks of the Chicago River. Since then, Chicago has laid claim to some of the most grisly incidents in America.

For example, the Iroquois Theater fire claimed six hundred lives, primarily women and children, just five days after Christmas 1903. This was the worst theater fire in America's history and the third worst in the world.

There is also the tale of the *Eastland* Disaster of 1915, which claimed nearly nine hundred lives and is the greatest maritime disaster in America during peacetime.

The small town of Des Planes, in 1979, was the site of the single worst plane crash ever to take place on American soil; 273 killed.

In addition to the Iroquois Theater fire and the Great Chicago Fire of 1871, which killed another three hundred Chicagoans, fire was also the culprit in the ninety deaths of school children in the Our Lady of the Angels School. Chicago appears to be cursed land.

There is one interesting point to observe; though thousands of people died in these events, hundreds of those who died still remain at the spot of their demise. All of these locations are purportedly haunted.

The Great Chicago Fire

October 8, 1871, will forever be remembered as a day of fire. The deadliest single fire in the history of America claimed an incredible fifteen hundred lives in the Northern Wisconsin town of Peshtigo near Green Bay. However, a much smaller but still greatly destructive one in Chicago often overshadows this massive fire. Estimations of lives lost range from two hundred to three hundred, but there is only one active haunting associated with it. This is somewhat lower than what could be expected considering the massive loss of life, the horror of their last moments, and the unexpected nature of their deaths. Though it is a little strange that there is only one haunting out of the possible three hundred deaths, it almost makes complete sense that it's in Streeterville.

Since the fire followed the lead of the wind, which was coming from the southwest, identifying the location where the fire started was quite easy. All one had to do was find the southwest most part of the "burnt district." The property owned in that area belonged to the O'Leary family. The woman of the house, Catherine, operated a neighborhood milk business out of her barn, which was now a pile of ash. However, the small house she lived in with her husband and their five children was left untouched just a few yards away. It just happened to be in the right direction.

What wasn't in the right direction was the heart of the City of Chicago, which was just over a mile away.

The fire was later blamed on a cow in the O'Leary barn kicking over a lantern. The cause was of little concern to the hundred thousand people who lost their homes as a result of the fire. Also lost to the flames were 28 miles of wood-paved streets, 120 of the roughly 560 miles of wooden sidewalks, 18,000 buildings, and a third of the value of the city; $200 million.

The disaster seemed inevitable. Chicago was in the middle of a warm Indian Summer and had only received a little more than one inch of rain since the Fourth of July. On top of that, nearly everything in the city was made of wood. Wood that was now completely dry and served as good kindling. The *Chicago Tribune*, who repeatedly published editorials about the lack of safety precautions after seeing similar incidents around the country, warned the city that Chicago's doom was pending. In fact, the city fire department already had their hands full as they put out twenty fires alone in the week before the Great Fire. It didn't help that the largest of these fires occurred the day before the Great Chicago Fire, which went on to be known widely and aptly as the Great Conflagration.

By midnight, the flames jumped across the south branch of the Chicago River and continued on their path of destruction. An hour and a half later, it claimed the City Courthouse Tower. The mayor, Roswell B. Mason, had to flee. Prisoners held in the basement of the building were released just before the enormous bell from the tower came crashing through the building and into the basement. The last blow came at 3:30 in the morning when the roof of the pumping station caved in and put an end to any fire fighting efforts. The fire had the city.

The fire reached as far north as Fullerton, leveling over ninety-six percent of the 13,800 buildings on Division, before a miraculous rain came down to save what was left of the city.

The city was so hot that it took over a day for it to cool down enough for people to be able to reenter it. What they found was devastating. Grease in the Chicago River ignited and caught several boats on fire. Shop and business owners who were able to find their safes intact often had the contents of it burst into flames upon opening it by feeding flammable oxygen to the intensely hot contents. The Tribune Building, which had warned of fire danger, was gone along with the new Palmer House. William Ogden had a very bad day as he lost both his home in Chicago and his lumber company in Green Bay to two massive fires within the span of a few hours.

Possibly the greatest historical losses were the destruction of both the first Chicago Historical Society and the house of I. N. Arnold. The Arnold home contained a massive art collection, library, and collection of Civil War and Abraham Lincoln memorabilia. Arnold had been a friend of the great president.

After all was said and done, the damage path was three-quarters of a mile wide and four miles long. Around two thousand acres of land was decimated.

On the other hand, there was the Water Tower. William W. Boyington, the same architect who created the front entrance to Rosehill Cemetery, designed the Water Tower. It was completed in 1867 and opened in 1869, just two years before the Great Fire. The Lemont, Illinois, limestone from which it was made was one of the only materials able to stand up against the intense heat.

The fire was unique in the sense that it allowed the growing metropolis of Chicago to start over and organize the city in a manner that would better suit future growth. However, Mayor Mason was not around to see it. Joseph Medill, managing editor of the *Chicago Tribune*, was elected mayor of the city in November on a platform of stricter fire codes. Understanding public relations like a seasoned newsman, Medill did not run as a member of the Republican or Democratic Party but as a member of the Fireproof Party.

As the city of Chicago would never be the same again, neither would the Water Tower. On rare occasions, a pedestrian walking around the area of the Magnificent Mile between the Water Tower and the Hancock Tower has seen the figure of a man hanging himself in one of the upper windows.

Though no one can positively claim they know the identity of this person, several have ventured the guess that this was someone who worked at the young Water Tower when the Chicago Fire took place. While he manned his position, flames gathered around him, and other buildings fell to the ground. By 3:30 in the morning, the roof of the pumping station across the street fell in, but by this time, there was no escape for the man who was working fearlessly to save his city.

At this point, he had two options: die in the fire or kill himself before the fire could make his final moments even more torturous. The man apparently decided to take his life rather than die from the intense heat.

His death is reenacted from time to time, leading one to believe this is a residual, or retrocognitive, haunting. Therefore, realistically, the ideal time to see this is between two and four in the morning on October 10. However, this is true only if the theory behind the haunting is true. It is still not certain that the person who died in the Water Tower died as a result of the impending doom of the Great Fire.

Other theories suggest that a mass of looters fled to the burned out Chicago in hopes of taking whatever was left behind, and that the hanging man was actually a looter who was paying a harsh price for his sin.

However, looting did not occur in Chicago. This story rings untrue because Mayor Mason entrusted Lieutenant-General Philip Sheridan with, "The preservation of the good order and peace of the city."

Sheridan, who is also the namesake of Fort Sheridan and Sheridan Road, manned a militia-like force to oversee the security of the entire Burnt District. There was, however, widespread fear of looting based on published editorials in city newspapers that theorized that Chicago would have to deal with lawlessness based on what had been observed other large-scale fires. Fortunately, the fears never came to fruition.

While the story of the Great Chicago Conflagration is mostly centered around property damage rather than lives lost, the other disasters Chicago has suffered through produced more personal traumas.

The Day the Angels Wept

Though there were other disastrous events in Chicago's past that claimed more lives, this event has had a lasting impression on those who know of the story. This is for two reasons. First, the event happened in 1958, so there are still people around who remember seeing the reports on the news or even going to the gutted shell of a building the following day. The other reason relates to the victims. In this case, three nuns died along with ninety-two grade school children.

The Our Lady of the Angels School did not break any fire codes that led to the horrible outcome. Largely, this is because, at the time, the fire codes were very poor. This school was just like any other across the country, and December 1, 1958, started just like any other day. By the end of the day, however, America knew that this would be a day that should never be forgotten.

Though two people separately confessed that they started the fire, they both also recanted their statements. To date, no one has been found guilty of setting the fire in the basement of the school on 909 North Avers.

The fire was set in a refuse drum, where it sat smoldering for a long period of time. Near the end of the school day, sometime after two o'clock in the afternoon, the nearby glass window exploded from the heat and fed the nearly suffocated fire with a new dose of fuel in the form of oxygen. The fire rapidly spread up the staircase, feeding on rubberized paint and filling the halls with thick, black smoke.

Teachers who had classes on the first floor were able to evacuate their classes safely at the first smell of smoke; however, the classrooms on higher floors didn't have the luxury of an early warning. They also didn't have the luxury of sprinkler systems or an alarm system linked to the fire department. In fact, there was only one fire escape for the fourteen hundred students enrolled. Also, the door to that fire escape was stuck closed for several vital minutes.

The fire moved up to the second floor by moving within the walls. Soon, fires started erupting, and glass objects, like light fixtures, started exploding throughout the building as a result of the intensely hot air.

By this time, the thick black smoke made exiting through interior stairwells and hallways impossible. Some resorted to jumping out of classroom windows to escape the heat. In this case, the odds of survival actually increased by taking this risk.

The call was made to the fire department at 2:40, nearly half an hour after the small fire had started. The fire department promptly arrived at its given destination some four minutes later. Unfortunately, it was given the address 3808 West Iowa rather than 909 North Avers. Fire Department Engine Number 85 went to the Our Lady of the Angels Church, which was located within the same block of the school, but precious minutes were still lost. Once they made their way to the school, they came across another time-killing obstacle: a locked gate that the fire department had to break through.

Almost as soon as the fire fighters were able to make visual contact, a request for all available ambulances was made. Once on the scene, the presence of the Chicago Fire Department was immediately felt. Several men caught children who were jumping from windows. In under an hour, the blaze that seemed unstoppable was entirely extinguished.

The grim task of recovering bodies for identification was set to begin. Some of the remains were so unrecognizable that identifications were made based on jewelry or other objects the child possessed at the time of the fire.

As a direct and immediate result of this tragedy, there were several changes in the fire code. Among them were mandatory sprinkler systems and automatic fire alarms linked to the fire department.

The story of the Our Lady of the Angels fire contained paranormal events before, after, and even during the fateful afternoon. In the days leading up to the fire, a number of events some may link to extra-sensory perceptive visions (ESP) acted as warning signs of the tragedy. One of the most notable occurred the night before when a woman entered her son's room only to see an image of her son in a casket.

During the fire, as people were escaping, children were seen safely waiting outside for the rest of their classmates. It was later found that some of those seen outside of the school had actually died within the building.

Some accounts maintain that there is still a psychic residue based around the school. Included are screams that fill the hallways and phantom floating faces. Witnesses speculate that these are victims of the fire.

Many wonder why there is no plaque or monument commemorating the ninety-five lives lost at the site of the school, which has since been rebuilt. As it stands, the only memorial to the victims of the third worst school fire in American history is in the same location as the cross where Joseph Reinholtz had his daily meetings with the Virgin Mary, at Queen of Heaven Cemetery.

Of the ninety-five deaths attributed to the fire, forty-two of them are buried at Queen of Heaven Cemetery. Twenty-five of those are buried in a section dedicated specifically to the victims of the fire. Section 18, in the absolute center of the cemetery, holds the Our Lady of the Angels Monument.

The monument is comprised of two small walls bearing the names of all ninety-five fatalities of the fire. Between the walls is a large angel poised to look down over the graves for eternity. Also on the wall is a key identifying in which cemetery each victim is located.

Visitors to the cemetery who are in the general vicinity of the monument have felt something of a burning sensation. Sometimes this feeling is accompanied by the smell of smoke.

Rather than think that those buried here are haunting the grounds and sharing with others some of the feeling of being in a horrible fire, there is probably something altogether different going on here.

A popular example in modern days is a fatal automobile accident. It is common for bereaved friends and family of the recently deceased to gather at the side of the road where the accident occurred to grieve. People gather to create shrines, leave flowers, candles, religious icons, and personal letters to the deceased. In addition, people come to reflect and cry with one another. It is quite common for this to continue for upwards of a week and then repeat on the anniversary of the death with the same emotions. The area where this happens is not at all haunted by any means, but the area still holds the strong emotional and sorrowful energy. Subsequent visitors to the area might be able to feel this emotion despite not knowing the history or relevance of the area.

This very well may be the case at Queen of Heaven Cemetery. Indeed, the amount of grieving in this section is disproportionate to the remainder of the cemetery as this is a section specifically for children, much like the one found at Naperville Cemetery.

In addition to friends and family coming to the site to grieve, a number of survivors have probably visited the site to grieve and relive the experience. It was only they who knew exactly what the smoke smelled like and what the details of the scene were.

In all actuality, there weren't just ninety-five victims of the fire. The fire department saved an estimated 160, but as they were lucky to be alive, they were still scarred by their memories.

Michelle McBride was one such case. She survived a jump from an upper window of the school while on fire. She suffered burns on seventy-five percent of her body. She went on to write a book about the event titled *The Fire that Would Not Die*. She also went on to create a makeup company that created products to hide scars on burn victims. The company, The Phoenix Program, was poetically named after the mythological creature famous for rising from its ashes.

Michelle was never able to entirely move beyond the fire that she suffered through when she was thirteen years of age. In early July of 2001 she passed on but without fanfare and without her name on the monument. Ninety-five lives came to an end, but countless more were damaged. Michelle, a hero who deserves to be celebrated, is buried at All Saints Cemetery.

Unfortunately, Chicago's list of massive tragedies is only beginning.

A Disaster in the Sky

The estimated time of flight was three and a half hours. Unfortunately, the airplane came to a rest on the ground three hours, twenty-nine minutes, and twenty-nine seconds early. The smoke generated by the plane rose to an elevation far higher than the airplane ever did.

Being an eyewitness to an airplane crash can be very traumatizing, but seeing the accident everyday for ten days before it even happened is incredible. That's what happened to David Booth from May 15 through May 25, 1979 as he slept.

Nightly, this twenty-three-year-old Cincinnati office manager watched in horror as an American Airlines aircraft crashed immediately after take off. After a week of enduring this dream, David was sure that the crash was gong to happen, but the biggest details were still missing. On May 22 he contacted FAA officials in Ohio. They took his story seriously and began working hard to identify exactly where and when this would take place.

Together, they decided that the plane in David's dream was a DC-10. They studied the manner in which the plane crashed in the dream. Unfortunately, they came to dead ends when it came to which exact flight it was, and even what city they should monitor.

Unfortunately, on Friday, May 25, all of their questions were answered. An American Airlines DC-10 flying out of Chicago's O'Hare International Airport and destined for Los Angeles crashed, killing 273.

Everything down to the way the plane crashed was accurate to David's dream. Immediately, he was overcome with grief for not being able to gather enough information to prevent the catastrophe.

Thanks to a camera mounted in the cockpit, the take off of the flight was broadcast live on a closed-circuit television station within the airport to help time pass by faster for passengers waiting for their flights. All seemed to be going well at first. A team in the cockpit that had a combined 47,000 flight-hours manned Flight 191. The captain alone, Walter Lux, had 22,000 hours of flight experience, most of which was in DC-10 airplanes.

It soon became evident that things would go very wrong very quickly. Immediately after takeoff, the engine on the left wing separated. It flew straight up into the air and then slammed into the end of the runway.

When the engine came off of the wing, it took about a meter off the leading edge of the wing with it. This disabled all of the important hydraulic lines located in that portion of the wing. It also crippled the captain's control panel. There was nothing anyone could do.

With warning systems not functioning properly and vital parts of the plane not being represented correctly on the control panel, the first sign that there was a problem to the cockpit occurred when the plane began a sharp bank to the left.

Questions posed by the control tower went unanswered as the flight team was too preoccupied with saving the craft. Then, just thirty-one seconds after take off, Flight 191 crashed very near to a trailer park in Des Plaines. The final descent showed the plane falling 400 feet at a bank of 112 degrees at nearly 180 mph.

Immediately following the accident, nearby residents heard frantic knocking on their front doors. They would open them expecting to find someone in a hurry or some sort of emergency but ended up finding no one at all. This event still plays itself out on occasion with rare stories of people coming across a frantic or disoriented stranger who is in search of a telephone. These strangers often disappear in front of shocked witnesses.

Even at the O'Hare Airport gate from which Flight 191 left, a man has been seen using a pay phone and then vanishing immediately after hanging it up.

In the area where the plane crashed, which is very near to a retention pond that the residents of the trailer park have come to call Devil's Ditch, people have seen white ghost lights. Some have mistaken these lights for flashlights of people who might be looking for souvenirs from the wreck.

At the time of the crash, according to unconfirmed reports, some went to the accident site to steal jewelry and other belongings off of the bodies of the very recently deceased and dying. This is unlikely, however, since even rescuers had difficulty reaching the site due to the extreme heat.

Still, many cannot help but remember the flight. For some it was a flight they couldn't get tickets for, thus accidentally saving their lives. For some, like Bionic Woman Lindsay Wagner, it was a last minute feeling of impending doom that ended up extending their lives.

Some residents are frequently reminded of the disaster on rainy days. Since the tragedy, the Des Plaines Mobile Home Park has expanded. Some of the new lots overlap the crash area. When the ground is so saturated that it cannot absorb anymore rainwater, bits of glass and even personal effects of the travelers come to the surface.

I visited the mobile home park with Mary Czerwinski on the twenty-first anniversary of the crash. There is an eerie feeling in the area. This isn't linked to paranormal activity but rather knowing what once happened exactly where you are standing. The air traffic is constant. Looking closely, it is evident which runway Flight 191 must have taken off from. Standing there, it's easy to be lost in the horror, imagining what the scene looked like first hand.

Sometimes imagining isn't necessary as screams and moans are still heard emanating from the location where 258 passengers, 13 crew members, and 2 pedestrians on the ground met their maker. It is in this area as well where a dog training center is. Here, even very highly trained dogs act strangely.

The constant sounds of winding jet turbine engines flying over the treetops remain a constant reminder of the horror that took the neighborhood by surprise in May of 1979.

While most children grow up telling tales of 'true' ghost stories like "The Man with the Hook" and "Bloody Mary," the children growing up in this neighborhood tend to tell stories of "The Man Who Died in Front of Trailer 6" and "The Ghost in My House."

For the children of the Des Plaines Mobile Home Park, ghosts are just as much as part of life as school and recess. That's just how it is. Surprisingly, not all of the ghost stories of this location revolve around Flight 191.

One resident of the park recalls lights flashing on and off by themselves and even the switches in the fuse box routinely turning to the off position immediately after being rectified. Even the toys were fair game for this phantom. "We had a train set that would start and stop on its own." Eventually, her family had to go so far as to have a priest come over and bless the house. Apparently, the culprit of all the goings on was a former resident who remained at the house in search of his wife. The hauntings stopped after the priest blessed the house.

Residents living near the front of the community point to a vacant trailer and tell the story of the man who died of natural causes directly in front of it. For an unknown reason, since his death, the man has been seen on a regular basis in the trailer across the street.

There is also the eccentric who made a habit of firing his gun into the air for completely random reasons. As the story goes, the neighbors had enough of his antics and called the police. Attempting to make a getaway, he drove to the only entrance of the park, but the police had it blocked. At the showdown, the man saw that he was trapped and decided to fire his gun one last time, pulling the trigger, ending his life, and hitting the ground all while members of the trailer park community watched. Though this happened years ago, the trailer where he lived alone is still vacant. People residing on either side of the empty trailer claim that it isn't really that empty after all. Movement has been witnessed inside, and sounds have emanated from within.

There seems to be no real rhyme or reason why this location seems to be so conducive to hauntings. Of course the sudden and traumatic death of hundreds would be an obvious answer, but the fact that there are so many other hauntings on the land that are completely unrelated is quite the mystery.

In addition to the hauntings and exhibitions of ESP, there are also coincidences linked with Flight 191, the worst air disaster in American history until September 11. In Los Angeles that Memorial Day weekend, there was a Book Sellers Association convention. Heading to the convention on Flight 191 were several representatives of Chicago writers. Judith Wax, who was the managing editor of "Playboy Magazine" and one of the 273 lost, had just finished an autobiographical book titled *Starting in the Middle*. In the book she confesses that she is deathly afraid of flying in airplanes. This excerpt can be found on page 191.

Christmastime Tragedy

Three days after Christmas in 1903, mothers with their children and even children's groups from out of state filled the eloquent Iroquois Theater for an afternoon presentation of *Mr. Bluebeard*. Partway through the second act, the atmosphere changed from a light-hearted afternoon to one of the darkest days in Chicago history. It ended up being the most fatal theater fire in American history and the third greatest theater fire ever.

Man seems to have trouble challenging the elements. The creators of the *Titanic* deemed the massive vessel "unsinkable." The result was the most famous shipwreck ever. The owners of the *Tribune* called their tower "fire-proof," yet it was no match for the Great Conflagration of 1871. Like the first Tribune Tower, the owners of the Iroquois Theater appeared to invite disaster by calling their grand theater "fire-proof."

In 1904, the year after the great theater fire, a book was published called *Chicago's Awful Theater Horror*. It was written by the survivors and rescuers present, creating the most immensely comprehensive book on the topic. It also includes pictures taken at the time of the event. This very hard-to-find publication is the most detailed, significant, accurate, and important writing of the fire ever.

The introduction, written by Bishop Sammuel Fellows, discusses how many lost their faith after the tragedy. He also discusses the claim that the theater was fireproof:

> "The unusual number of exits were boasted of. Most of them were unseen or actually bolted and locked. The alleged fireproof curtain was a flimsy sham... The scenery was of the most combustible material, loaded down with paint and oil. Not a bucket of water was on the stage... There had never been a fire apparatus of any kind on the balcony or the gallery... At no time had there been a fire drill by the employees of the theater. There were no notices posted to tell what to do in case of fire. There was no fire alarm box anywhere in the structure. Common prudence and common sense were completely set aside."

The coroner, John E. Traeger, told the jury at the trial, "Instead of being the safest theater in Chicago, the Iroquois was the unsafest."

As the Great Chicago Fire would be known as the Great Conflagration, the Iroquois Theater fire went on to be referred to as the Iroquois Holocaust and rightfully so as, at the time, it was the greatest fire tragedy ever. Only acts of nature such as volcano eruptions had claimed more lives at once.

The advertisements declared, "Don't fail to have your children see *Mr. Bluebeard!*" The advice was followed, and three days after Christmas and three days before New Years, the theater was packed with women and children. There was an estimated two thousand-plus in attendance. It was so overcrowded that people were forced to occupy the aisles during the show.

Not long after three o'clock in the afternoon, a moonlit scene began. Most of the lights were dimmed, and a spotlight was brought to life to highlight the action on stage. One of the lights shining from on stage sparked, igniting the curtain on stage right. This was a somewhat regular occurrence for a production at the time. The flame was noticed by many nearest to the stage, but a second thought was not given.

The flame quickly climbed the curtain and started to fan out near the ceiling. The production continued. Though more alarming, it was something that veteran stage performers had seen numerous times in the past.

No danger was felt until a number of choirgirls were on stage dancing. It was at this point in the performance, at 3:15, when glowing and flaming embers started to fall on the dancers below. The dancers fell back to a safer position and continued. Audience members with the clearest view of the spreading fire stood but froze, unsure if they should run or continue watching the production.

It was at this point when the star of the production, Eddie Foy, came to the front of the stage to inform the audience there was no danger and to remain calm. His request was short-lived.

They attempted to drop an asbestos curtain in order to keep the fire in the backstage area, but it snagged. There were several feet of space between the stage and bottom of the curtain. By this time, backstage was a raging inferno. A number of performers ran for their lives by going through a backstage door. Opening the door, however, caused a strong draft of wind. The wind pushed the fire through the small opening between stage and asbestos curtain, shooting a literal wall of fire over the audience. Pandemonium broke out.

Quickly, the balconies and the upper gallery, which held a combined one thousand people, caught fire. Those in the top gallery rushed towards the only exit and staircase. It is thought that this is one of the areas of the greatest loss of life. People fell on the staircase and were quickly joined by others who fell on top of them. A wall of people, many dead from being smothered, filled the only exit.

Some were able to escape before the corridor became impassable but only by accidentally crushing those who had fallen underfoot. A number of victims were later found bearing footprints about their bodies and faces.

Charlotte Plamondon survived the fire and remembered, "I saw children lying in heaps under our feet. Their little lives were ended, and rough feet were bruising their flesh."

On the eastern side of the top floor, a number of people found a small hallway that they mistook for an emergency exit. Many rushed through the hallway only to find that it led to a private staircase. In front of the staircase was yet another locked door. Another fifty to sixty people died at that spot.

As mentioned, a number of doors were locked and hidden. The reason was to keep out nonpaying theatergoers and to maintain the visual beauty of the theater. Even the doors that functioned properly did so backwards; they opened inwards. When there was a rush of hundreds of people to the door, they couldn't find enough space to pull the doors open.

This was the area of some of the most agonizing moments for both visitors and potential rescuers. Firemen could hear the screams of people being burned alive from the other side. All that separated help from death was a few inches of metal in the form of a door that could not be opened.

For those who were trapped in the upper portions of the theater, they searched for doors leading to fire escapes. They found the doors, but most of the fire escapes weren't yet erected. The theater was only about one month old at the time of the fire, so the safety precautions that were planned were still not yet realized.

Some found relief from the suffocating smoke thanks to an open door in the rear of the building but then stepped into the light expecting a fire escape only to fall to their deaths. Some were fortunate enough to find

a functional fire escape but were still victimized when another doorway exploded and shot thick flames up the fire escape, thus burning those on it.

The smoke was as deadly as the fire. Even after the fire was extinguished, dozens of lives came to an end due to smoke inhalation. Many others died in the theater as a direct result of suffocation because the fire consumed all of the oxygen. Simple skylights would have made a measurable difference because smoke would have been free to leave the building. There were a number of skylights in place on the ceiling of the theater, but they were all nailed shut—yet another task left on the "To Do List" of the theater owners.

Other lives still came to an end by falling from a makeshift bridge of ladders and planks over the back alley constructed by students at nearby Northwestern University and some painters who were working in a nearby classroom at the time of the fire.

Many of those who survived by way of the back alley simply lived because falling onto the bodies of those already deceased cushioned their fall.

This back alley was used for a short while to store bodies that were cleared out of the way for rescuers to enter. At one point, the number of bodies in the alley exceeded 125. This is why the alley was dubbed and will forever be known as "Death's Alley."

Thompson's restaurant adjoined the theater. It was written that at three o'clock it was a restaurant, at three-twenty it was a hospital, and at four o'clock it was a morgue. The task of recovering the bodies was grim. Adding to the pain of finding so many dead was that it was rare that any were found living. Those who were found with faint vital signs would surely die over the next few days.

Entering the theater, firemen first had to remove a pile of corpses measuring seven feet in height. Emphasis was placed on speed of removal of the bodies in case there was still a person clinging to life in the middle of the heap somewhere. Occasionally, a light moan would emanate from the lifeless mass, giving the rescuers incredible motivation. This scene is described further in *Chicago's Awful Theater Horror*:

> "There was hardly any need to ask the men to work harder, for they were pulling and hauling as though their own lives depended on their

efforts. Everybody worked. The reporters, the
only ones in the theater besides the police and
firemen, laid aside their pencils and notebooks
and struggled down the wet, slippery stairs,
carrying the dead. Newspaper artists threw
their sketch books on the floor to jump forward
and pick up the feet or head of a body that a
fireman or policeman found too heavy to carry
alone."

When all was said and done, over 570 people died in the
span of fifteen minutes from burning, suffocation, falling, or
being trampled. Over the next few days, dozens more died,
bringing the final death count to 602. All of the country took
notice as the victims of the fire were from thirteen states and
eighty-six cities or towns.

The Iroquois Theater died with its victims that day. The
owners of the theater were put on trial for their disregard for
human life. Among those alleged to be ultimately responsible
were the general manager William J. Davis, Mayor Carter
H. Harrison, Building Commissioner George Williams, Fire
Marshal William H. Musham, and a number of other city
officials and theater employees.

Today, another grand theater stands on the land. It is
referred to as the Oriental Theater or the Ford Center for the
Performing Arts. Under new management and ownership,
this theater has been able to accomplish what the Iroquois
Theater only aspired to. There is a monument at Montrose
Cemetery, but unfortunately, there is not a plaque or other
marker to commemorate the lives lost at the site of the
Iroquois Theater.

Some can testify that the plaque is not needed to serve as
a reminder as there are forces at work do the job. Many have
claimed to feel cold spots and the feeling of a presence in the
alley. Others have heard faint screams filling the otherwise
empty alley, and unseen hands have even grabbed some.

On December 30, 2000, on the ninety-seventh anniversary of the fire, I made my second trip to Death's Alley. For whatever reason, this seemed to be a story I was drawn to. I had visited Death's Alley in the past and noted nothing supernatural other than a sudden and oppressive feeling of sadness after walking though the length of the alleyway. The time was shortly after three in the afternoon when I set up the camera in front of the doors that had been sealed shut. I began to tell of the horrors of the incident on video when I was interrupted by loud banging sounds coming from overhead.

At the time, there were no performances going on and the theater appeared mostly, if not entirely, vacant. I stepped back to get a better read on the location of the sounds and identified it to be coming from the general direction of one of the upper doors.

I will never know for sure if there was a rational, physical reason for the sounds, but if one were to make links to a paranormal occurrence, one possibility is that the area is where a sealed door once stood. People trapped inside could have found some heavy object to strike the door repeatedly in a desperate attempt to open it. The sounds happened on the anniversary of the fire during the same minutes that such an event would have happened, indicating it could be a residual haunting. In the name of being levelheaded, we'll just assume there was a worker doing some construction, but in the end, both options are real possibilities.

Another Lapse in Safety

The day should have been one without cares or worries. After all, this wasn't just a day without work at the Western Electric Company; it was a day for their employees highlighted by a free cruise across Lake Michigan to Michigan City, Indiana where they would be treated to a relaxing picnic.

The Iroquois Theater passed the safety inspection in a very questionable manner. On the other hand, the steamship the

Eastland passed its safety inspection just two months prior to the outing with flying colors. Unfortunately, the results would be very similar.

Several ships were chartered to transport over five thousand people across the great lake on July 24, 1915. The scheduled time of departure was 7:30 in the morning, but as early as 6:30 there were already five thousand people gathered.

The *Eastland*, which was the first ship set to depart, began boarding. It was docked along Wacker Drive between Clark and LaSalle Streets. As is usual, the ship began to tilt towards the wharf because passengers gathered near the entrance. Within ten minutes, the ship was righted again thanks to admitting water into some empty ballast tanks.

Soon, the ship began to list towards the center of the river.

By seven o'clock, the tugboat *Kenosha* was poised and ready to escort the ship out to sea. At this point, there were over one thousand people on board, and the ship was tilted at an angle of about seven degrees.

With the addition of E. W. Sladkey, the final passenger took his place aboard the ship at quarter after seven. There were about two thousand five hundred people aboard the ship.

Many of them were on the top, but some were below deck due to damp morning drizzle. On the promenade, the musical stylings of Bradford's Orchestra attracted many young dancers.

By now, the list had grown to an estimated ten to fifteen degrees. Chief Engineer Joseph Erickson gave the command to correct this by filling the opposite ballast tanks. Seven minutes passed before his command was followed.

The *Eastland* again stabilized, but the balance of weight and ballast tanks were in an unstable configuration. The *Kenosha* readied itself to help maneuver the ship into Lake Michigan while a worker on Clark Street prepared to raise the bridge.

Quickly, the *Eastland* began to tilt to port again despite the fact that the passengers were all on the starboard side nearest the wharf.

At 7:20, just two minutes after the last passenger boarded the ship, water began to fill the main deck. At this point, unsecured objects began to fall from tables. Two minutes later, warning whistles were blown. Still, Captain Harry Pedersen planned to shove off despite the current list being between twenty and twenty-five degrees.

Once the lines were released and the ship floated away from the wharf, passengers began to wander toward the sinking half of the ship, greatly increasing the probability of the ship tipping over completely. There is some speculation that another vessel passed by the side of the *Eastland* blowing its horns in an apparent bid of "Bon voyage."

In a last ditch effort, they turned on bilge pumps to pump out the water that had come onto the ship. Workers below deck had the best handle on the situation and already knew that the ship was doomed. With water rushing in and the list surpassing twenty-five degrees, they abandoned their posts.

Passengers were next asked to try to find a place to stand on the starboard side of the ship (the side which they boarded from). However, the angle was so great the passengers on the top deck were unable to get their footing due to the floor being wet from the morning mist. The orchestra then made the switch to ragtime music now that dancing had become impossible.

When the list had reached an incredible forty-five degrees, even the largest objects like pianos and refrigerators started sliding across the ship. This was the first time passengers realized they were in danger. The band finally stopped playing.

With water pouring into the ship, nothing short of the most fantastic of miracles could save the *Eastland*. Finally, it lazily rolled on to its side, throwing those on top into the Chicago River and trapping those below deck.

At 7:30 in the morning, the exact time the ship was set to sail, it lay on its side in twenty feet of water. The space of time between when the passengers knew the ship was doomed and when the ship actually rolled over was only two minutes. Not a single lifeboat was released. Those below deck had almost no time to rush all the way back above deck.

The *Kenosha* positioned itself between the *Eastland* and the wharf. Here, hundreds were able to pull themselves up on the starboard side of the *Eastland*, which now sat looking up to the sky, and walk along the side of the *Kenosha* to safety.

What they heard however must have been horrible. All around them were people in the water struggling for life and accidentally killing each other by pulling those who could swim underwater. Below their feet was even worse. Many were trapped in the ship with the only factor that determined how long they would live being how much oxygen was available. They did anything possible to draw attention to their location. The frantic banging on the steel wall of the ship, which was now under foot of the survivors, would be impossible for even the most cold-hearted to ignore.

Recovery of bodies and the search for the living was immediate. A net was stretched across the Chicago River at West 12th Street to bring to an end the constant parade of floating corpses of men, women and children.

The death toll climbed fast, and rescuers on the scene were quickly able to see that this would become the worst disaster in Chicago's long history of plight. If there was enough sympathy to spare, a good portion belonged to the fire department. The same team that had the awful task of reporting to the Iroquois Holocaust that claimed 602 lives was also the first to report to the sinking of the *Eastland*. Though an official count was never made, estimates range from 850 to over 900 lives lost.

While the Iroquois Holocaust claimed the lives of an entire family, the *Eastland* Disaster claimed the lives of twenty-two whole families. It still stands today as the worst American maritime disaster during peacetime.

Commonwealth Edison Workers reported to both disasters as well. They supplied high-powered lights to see through the smoke in the theater, and now they cut through the side of the ship with blowtorches to reach survivors.

The fact that the *Eastland* passed a safety inspection just weeks before it sunk leads one to wonder if any money illegally passed hands. There was never an investigation or speculation at the time. In truth, the *Eastland* had a history of close calls. The ship would never make it past the design stages today. It was tall, long, and thin. It was top heavy with very little ballast. The captain and crew have to be heralded for simply keeping the ship afloat as long as they did.

Of the hundreds of bodies pulled from the Chicago River that day, most were placed in temporary morgues including the 2nd Regiment Armory, the J.P. Galvin Funeral Home, and the Reid Murdoch Building. Contrary to popular belief, the second Chicago Historical Society building, now the Excalibur Night Club, was not used as a temporary morgue.

The 2nd Regiment Armory held over two hundred bodies that were laid out in rows. Scared friends, relatives, and neighbors of those who had planned to take the picnic trip arrived to identify their loved ones. The last of the bodies was finally identified nearly a week after the disaster.

Time went by and the *Eastland* was nothing more than another painful memory in the life of Chicago. Then, in 1989, two things happened. A plaque was finally erected at the site of the disaster to pay homage to those who died, and the 2nd Regiment Armory, which had been owned by many other businesses in the past decades, was bought by Oprah Winfrey. Harpo Studios, as it was named, and became the site of the most popular daytime talk show in television history.

The stretch of Wacker Drive between Clark and LaSalle Streets is considered haunted. The first reports of paranormal activity were reported just days after the disaster. People heard screams and cries for help echoing up from the water below. Usually, there was nothing visible in the water, but on some occasions visual apparitions, in the form of faces on the water, accompanied the sounds.

Looking into wavy water under poor light isn't the ideal way to view something clearly. The imagination can run wild when lighting conditions are poor. After hearing phantom cries for help, there's no telling what kind of tricks the mind can play on the eye.

This has the characteristics of a retrocognitive haunting. Apparently, whatever is happening is merely a replay of the events from the morning of July 24, 1915.

The happenings at Harpo Studios, however, may be different. No one from the *Eastland* Disaster died at what is now Harpo Studios. It would make sense that if one were going to get lost on the way to the other side, it would happen at the site of the demise. This makes the Harpo Studios haunting more difficult to explain. With the rush to identify bodies, it is very likely that paperwork became mixed up and identities were accidentally switched after the loved ones were gone, thus leading to bodies being buried in incorrect graves away from their families.

Perhaps some of the ghosts, in particular a "Grey Lady" donning a dress, a hat, and violet perfume, have returned to set the record straight. The "Grey Lady," as she has become known to show staff, has occasionally been seen in person but is usually seen on security monitors.

Many have also heard the sounds of laughing, crying, conversation, music, crashes, and even the glass-on-glass clink of a toast. All of these sounds are very possibly the last sounds a number of people heard before their death.

In addition, objects are moved from office to office without explanation, and doors slam shut on their own. Many of the previously mentioned phenomena might be linked to a spirit on the premises who is attempting to gain attention. However, it seems that there is also a retrocognitive haunting at this location in addition to the classic haunting.

Sometimes the sound of crowds walking up and down the lobby staircase is heard. The sound couldn't possibly come from just one or two people but rather from a very large group. The sound is apparently quite overwhelming and impressive.

This sound could be a psychic replay of the hundreds of people who walked through this building, hoping not to find a deceased loved one. The anticipation and worry over the state of their friends and family could probably only be matched by the emotional charge of actually finding them there. The sounds of these very emotional memories might be continuously replaying.

While there was the possibility that the happenings at the site of the disaster would decrease or stop completely due to the creation of the monument commemorating the importance of the site, it did not happen. Also, the plaque remained there for just over a decade before being stolen in spring of 2000. A spike of reports following the stealing of the marker would make sense and follow trends, but alas, the world of the paranormal is an unpredictable one.

By 2007, not only was there a plaque but also a museum-like display explaining and illustrating the historical significance. This is the treatment and respect that should be given to many other sites in this chapter.

CHAPTER 9

PLACES OF WORSHIP

"Holy Family Church"

Churches are meant to be sanctuaries. They are places to go to be closer to love. They provide unbiased security and safety against the outside world. Couples are united, people are purified, and infants are baptized in this safe haven. What happens when the safety and stability of this sacred place is upset?

Most religious figures have great trepidation about the paranormal. The Archdiocese of Chicago even stated that they could find no events that could be classified as supernatural going on at the cross at Queen of Heaven Cemetery. There is a lack of consistency considering how the same organization barred Joseph from going to the cross on Tuesdays when he said that he was not visited by heavenly beings on that day.

We have already seen three chapels with claims to paranormal events at Lake Forest College, Barat College, and Dominican University. Though they wouldn't officially go on record, religious figures have acknowledged their otherworldly acquaintances. Conversely, the Beverly Unitarian Church has accepted spirits that share their church with them so much so that there is mention of them in the written church history.

A most petrifying event happened at St. Rita's Church on All Saints Day in the mid 1960s. Perhaps these souls confined to religious establishments are tired of being fully rejected. Their only option left is to clear their throats and do their best to make their presence unquestionably known.

The Haunted History of Holy Family Church

This massive church just outside the southwest reaches of the Loop was constructed in 1857. All was going well during the first fourteen years of existence for this structure. The church was establishing itself, and new members of the congregation were being added, but then disaster seemed imminent when the Great Conflagration broke out from the O'Leary residence. The following morning the city was in ruins, except for Holy Family Church.

The church faced the Great Chicago Fire that destroyed and killed with reckless abandon full-on. However, the fire ended up going around the building like an obstacle it didn't want to touch. The church's survival of the fire was accredited by members of the church to Our Lady of Perpetual Help.

To give thanks, the church lit seven lights in the east end of the church and added a statue of Our Lady of Perpetual Help. It is at this site where a crack began to form. Progression of the crack would have surely compromised the structural stability of the church. Then, for some reason, it simply stopped at the statue. The crack, which had been slowly progressing from floor to ceiling hasn't moved at all for over one hundred years. Credit is given to the Our Lady of Perpetual Help statue.

Another statue within the church came under the public eye in 1973. A photograph was taken of a hundred-plus-year-old statue of the Virgin Mary standing in front of an exposed church wall. The photograph, when developed, revealed faces on the wall behind the statue that were not visible when the photo was shot. The faces were plainly seen on parts of the wall behind the statue where the wallpaper had peeled away.

A simulacrum, or the tendency of the mind to accept a superficial semblance as reality, is the rational, physical world explanation. The same explanation could potentially be applied to seeing faces in water, like at Clarence Darrow's Bridge and at the site of the *Eastland* Disaster, in photographs where distant trees and branches might coincidentally arrange themselves in such a way to represent the outline of a human form, or how shading on a gravestone might resemble a face.

On a couple of occasions, the individual leading mass has looked out in to the congregation to see something distressing. Standing on the second story organ loft overlooking the church stood a man in black. After services were over, the presence of the intruder was often investigated; however, not only had nothing been moved, but the door hadn't even been unlocked.

The last noteworthy statues at this church are the two striking wooden statues of altar boys, each holding a candle.

According to legend, these statues represent two brothers who were altar boys for the church until they both drowned in a tragic accident. These statues may not be modeled after specific individuals, simply symbolizing young members of the church willing to give their time and love to the church. However, the young brothers certainly deserve to have monuments erected in their name. They have been responsible for a number of fantastical paranormal events after and even before their deaths in 1874.

People throughout Chicago saw forms of the two boys in the days just before the Chicago Fire. This was three years before they died. They apparently warned people of their deaths yet to happen.

There are many different schools of thought on what type of phenomenon this is. One idea posed by Patricia DiPrima in her booklet *Apparitions Good and Evil* states that a doppelganger may be this form of apparition. Some believe that, "the 'double' or ghost-like version of someone still alive, was a manifestation of the soul." This lesser-known type of phenomena has been noted around the world by names such as "fetch" and "co-walker."

One late evening in 1890, years after the death of the boys, Father Arnold Damen was awakened in the middle of the night by two altar boys who had been sent to him by a woman on her deathbed so that he could administer her last rites.

After he arrived at her house, she graciously thanked him for coming to her but could not understand how he knew to come. When Father Damen told her of the two boys she had sent, he noticed the two boys were nowhere in sight. The woman hadn't sent anyone for him, though she desperately did want him to be there for her. Some accounts dictate that the woman was the mother of the deceased boys.

Today, a large statue in front of Holy Family Church immortalizes Father Damen, who founded the church. He is still remembered in Chicago by a street bearing his name, which forms a T-intersection at Rosehill Cemetery. His presence is felt more directly at St. Ignatious High School, which adjoins Holy Family Church.

On more than one occasion, and mostly during times of construction and renovation, Father Damen has been seen wandering the halls at all hours of the night. Apparently, he's still keeping tabs on the latest changes within the institution he helped create.

One Incredible Day at St. Rita's

Without question, the most dramatic, isolated, single paranormal event in Chicago's long and storied past happened at St. Rita's of Cascia on far South Fairfield. While most encounters with the paranormal are brief and fleeting, those who were in St. Rita's Church on November 2, All Souls' Day, in the 1960s were privy to a scene as intense as, if not more than, any horror movie.

Over a dozen people were at the church praying when the organ, located on a second floor balcony, began to play on its own. The parishioners stopped praying to see who was at the organ. What they saw was far from expected. Instead of the familiar face of a church member, they saw six hooded figures. They were dressed in either all black or all white. Those dressed in black were positioned on one side of the organ while those in white stood on the other side.

As strange and possibly even distressing as this was, St. Rita's faithful were even more petrified when the figures came forth and began drifting to the ground. The parishioners rushed to the front door, but despite being unlocked, it was held shut by an unknown force.

The organ continued to create loud and piercing sounds while the monk-like figures were drifting through the pews toward the parishioners, who were pushing on the doors with all their might. Finally, a voice came from nowhere with the demand, "Pray for us!"

At this, a cold breeze rushed the doors, flinging them open and freeing the petrified witnesses. The fifteen traumatized people emerged through the doors and tumbled down the staircase outside.

According to some of those who attended mass the following Sunday, the statue of an angel moved on its own during the service.

Instantly, the story became a legend throughout the south side of the city. This was an isolated event; there hadn't been any paranormal events reported at the church before or since.

The church instantly down-played and denied the validity of the story. As far-fetched as the story can seem, the reasons for discounting the witnesses seem even more far-fetched.

The most popular and reasonable cause is mass hallucination. This is always a possibility in cases where multiple people who are on the same wavelength witness a paranormal event. In this case, everyone had been praying fervently for souls on this Catholic holiday, so it's reasonable that all of the witnesses had a vision related to All Souls' Day, which is evidenced in the demand of, "Pray for us!" However, the large number of people, the detail of the event, and the length of the event leads many to discount this possibility.

The other theories are discredited much more easily. Some claim this was a prank, but this prank could be pulled off by nothing less than George Lucas's Industrial Light and Magic special effects team.

Other claims state that strong winds kept the doors shut, the sound of the organ playing was caused by a door rubbing against the floor, and that one or two altar boys standing in the balcony were the inspiration behind the six hooded figures. Sound like a stretch to you, too?

Those who visit the church immediately forget the horror story that surrounds it. It is easy to get lost in the total beauty of the building. The massive cross, the stained glass windows, and the larger than life Shroud of Turin are more than enough to overwhelm.

On the other hand, when viewing the organ loft, it's hard *not* to think about the horror felt by those fifteen people on All Souls' Day in the 1960s. It is a story that is altogether original and beyond comparison.

The Irish Castle

The far south suburb of Beverly holds one of the most interesting and noteworthy of Chicago's many architecturally unique buildings.

The structure was built under the supervision of Robert C. Givins in 1886 after visiting Ireland, where he was particularly interested in their castles. Givins reportedly constructed the building, since nicknamed "The Irish Castle," as a surprise for his wife.

Givens was the Bill Veck of his day. A wealthy real estate promoter, he once sent a man up in a hot air balloon to drop free deeds to his land in order to get it quickly settled. After he retired, he started writing novels, seven of which were actually published.

The property changed hands in 1908, in 1920, and again in 1942. The owner from 1920 to 1942 was Dr. Miroslaw Siemans. While there, his family used the third floor tower room as a chapel. This was a sign of things to come, as the next owner was the Beverly Unitarian Fellowship, which eventually merged in 1959 with the People's Liberal Church in Englewood to form the Beverly Unitarian Church.

The ghost stories around the location have come to light only since the structure has been used as a church. It seems that a handful of the many past tenants have enjoyed their stay so much they've decided not to leave.

One of the first instances that proved the church was inhabited by more than Unitarian faithful occurred when a man was having a conversation with a young girl. This young girl spoke with an Irish brogue as she remembered what the Irish Castle was like when she had lived in it while it was a home

rather than a church.
Eventually, the man
excused himself. Soon
after leaving the room,
he realized that the girl
he had been talking
with was far too young
to have lived in the
building before it was a
church. Upon reentering
the room where the two
talked, the girl was not
there. A search of the
remainder of the fifteen
rooms revealed no
trace of the girl. It also
revealed that no doors or
windows were unlocked.
In addition, the freshly
fallen snow outside had
not been disturbed by footprints.

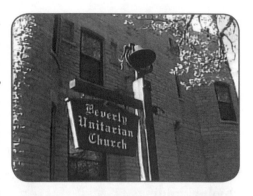

Most guesses at the origin of this female phantom point
to a young woman named Clara who died in the Irish Castle
during an influenza outbreak while it was a school for girls in
the 1890s.

Before the first owner, Robert Givins, sold the location in
1908, he rented it out to other interested parties including the
Chicago Female College.

This girl, and possibly some spirits who have gone unseen,
seem to enjoy the many festivities that regularly happen at
the church. One New Year's Eve, the young woman was seen
donning a beautifully striking red outfit. She came down the
staircase and walked to the nearby doors, which opened for
her. As she walked outside, party-goers gathered at the open
doorway to see her continue to walk away from the building,
again without creating footprints in the snow.

She has been seen at other celebrations including weddings and the installation of the new pastor, Reverend Leonetta Bugleisi. During the celebration, she looked towards her husband as someone came up behind him and hugged him around his waist. Quickly, Reverend Bugleisi approached him to see who had put their arms around her husband, but he didn't know what she was talking about. He didn't feel anything and whoever it was never walked away from behind him. All that was seen was a pair of arms.

Again attributed to parties, guests enjoying a beverage sometimes find their drink has been finished for them, much like the beer-drinking ghosts found at the Excalibur night club.

Phantom sounds are also very much a common occurrence at the church. Like the sounds at Harpo Studios as a result of the *Eastland* Disaster, the sounds heard are often similar to sounds commonly heard at parties such as muffled conversations and sounds from around a dinner table.

According to the informational flyer about the history of the building that is distributed by the church, these party-like sounds can be controlled. The wife of a custodian, who was given the third floor of the castle as an apartment, would shout out that it was time for bed. At this point, the noise abruptly stopped.

Surprisingly, half of the literature about the history of the church is about the known ghosts at the property. In addition, the regulars and workers at the Beverly Unitarian Church are very loose-lipped about the stories around the building.

Much like Hull House and the Country House Restaurant, this church has its strange events seen in windows. Movement is seen late at night through windows from outside. Figures holding candles have been seen moving from one window to another.

In addition to Clara and the originators of the random sounds that fill the three-story suburban castle, the ghost of Eleanor Veil is thought to still tend to the gardens behind the castle.

Another of the spirits is apparently talented, as unseen hands have played the piano in the main room of the church. The sounds are usually heard by people in other parts of the building, but they can't find anyone near the piano when they go to see who the musician is. The room is always found empty and silent.

It seems that the winter months tend to be the best time to view paranormal activity, but the candle-lit apparitions in the windows are seen throughout the year between one and two A.M.

An Overlooked Recent Hotbed of Activity

The northwest suburban town of Libertyville boasts beautiful homes, a number of quaint shops, a vintage movie theater, and, oddly enough, the final resting place for a king of Yugoslavia.

The Saint Sava Serbian Monastery is located on Milwaukee Avenue not far from the border of Libertyville and Gurnee near U.S. Highway 120. At first glance, it is more than obvious that the building and surrounding cemetery represent a culture far different than most represented in the northern suburbs.

The monastery itself is different than the typical Christian church, as there are two large rugs in the place of pews. Guests during events such as weddings stand rather than sit. The building is naturally dark as there are no lights, and the windows are all constructed of darkly colored stained glass. There are two impressive crown-like chandeliers and other interesting objects within the building. To the left there is the grave of Peter II (Karadjordjevich) of Yugoslavia.

Lately there have been a lot of changes. While an empty lot to the left of the cemetery is under development, the as-yet unused land in the right portion of the cemetery was also the site of a lot of construction equipment. In 2000 it appeared to be the site of a landscaping project. This was when a flare-up of encounters with the paranormal started to be reported.

As someone who worked for JPM Productions Gurnee for five years, I often found myself driving down Milwaukee Avenue near midnight. Time and time again the Serbian Orthodox Monastery caught my attention. Whether it was the unique architecture or the glow of red eternal flames on a number of gravestones, I always kept one eye on the cemetery.

Until recently, there weren't any stories revolving around the cemetery, and until now, there was never a published report of paranormal activity centered on this site. That is, until former Libertyville resident Ali Baldwin came to me in the fall of 2000.

Sometime around August of 2000, she and boyfriend Kirk Stattler were coming home from a visit to Kirk's parents. After their visit, they found themselves on their way home between one and two in the morning. Passing through Gurnee on Route 21 (Milwaukee Avenue) at this hour left them quite alone on the road.

After passing through Gurnee, Ali, with Kirk asleep in the front passenger seat, entered Libertyville. This stretch of road is strikingly similar to Cuba Road and the road that leads to another Libertyville landmark, "The Gate." This stretch of Milwaukee Avenue is narrow, straight, long, ill-lit, and is often draped with fog.

This night, however, was clear. Almost back to their apartment now, all seemed well until Ali saw the dark figure of a person illuminated in her headlights several hundred yards in the distance. The figure seemed to stand still at first. Though it would be strange for someone to be out for a walk so late at night, Ali thought nothing of it since this nocturnal person was so far away. Suddenly, it wasn't so far away.

As if approaching the figure at a rate of speed near fifty miles per hour wasn't enough, the figure began running directly at her car. Fearing for the stranger's safety, Ali slammed on her breaks, but the momentum of the car was too great.

The momentum shift and sound of screeching tires woke up Kirk from his slumber to witness the car striking the individual.

To Ali's surprise, the figure continued running towards the car and then drifted through the hood, through the windshield, and eventually through Ali before they finally came to a rest.

Ali's blood turned cold as soon as the figure made contact with her. The two sat in the car stunned. Kirk, now fully conscience, turned to Ali with a nervous panic and frantically asked, "Did we hit him?"

The event was so real and fast that he still had no time to process what he just saw. It was at this point that Ali noticed where her car came to rest—immediately across the street from the Serbian monastery and cemetery.

This was an honest statement from two friends who still don't know what to think of their experience. For a while it went by as a one-time event that could possibly, but probably not, repeat itself. With great hesitation, another witness, Sam Dole, had a confession to make.

In late June of 2000, I was interviewing Sam regarding her experiences at Antioch High School and the reportedly haunted Abbey Woods. She hesitated to start a story and even considered hiding it altogether because it sounded so incredible. With a little urging, she told her story.

Sam worked the front desk at one of the nearby hotels on Milwaukee Avenue in Libertyville. Frequently, she has to work the latest shift, which runs from midnight through the early morning hours when most people are getting to work.

"A couple of nights ago," she started, "I was working the late shift and this woman staggered in. I thought she was drunk at first. She asked me how much a taxi would cost from here to somewhere on Diversey. I asked her if she was staying at the hotel, and she didn't really say anything. She just wanted to know about the cab."

Sam was initially reluctant to help this person, who she figured was intoxicated and had been roaming the streets aimlessly for the past few hours. Eventually, Sam gave in and decided to call a taxi service just to get rid of the woman.

Once Sam got on the phone, the woman saw that she was

being helped and smiled. "I don't know what it was, but it looked like she had dirt smeared all over her teeth," said Sam, still somewhat nervous from her bizarre encounter from just days before.

Coincidentally, a taxi pulled up to the front door to drop off a couple customers of the hotel. Sam watched through the glass doors as the hotel guests exited the car. The strange woman walked outside and got into the back seat of the cab. At this point Sam turned away, back toward the phone, to tell the taxi service that they probably would not be needed, but if they were needed, she would call back. She hung up the phone and faced front again. What she found was of some surprise to her. The driver of the taxicab was now looking around the hotel lobby.

"Can I help you?" Sam asked.

The cab driver then asked her if she had seen the woman who got into his car. He then went on to say that she got in the back seat and asked him how much it would cost to get to a specific location on Diversey in Chicago. He then looked down at his rate book for a moment. The next thing he knew, his car was empty. He did not hear any sounds of the woman exiting his car nor did he feel the car move as if someone had exited it.

"The only place she could've gone is back into the hotel," the man reasoned. As logical as it sounded, Sam was positioned at the front of the hotel lobby, and she would have heard the doors open and the sound of someone walking on the hard tile floor. This strange woman apparently vanished from the back seat from this man's car.

Vanishing hitchhiker stories like this are somewhat regular but never before with such intimacy and with multiple people who had separate conversations with the alleged phantom woman.

It will be very interesting to see if the hauntings continue throughout the construction and afterwards. Frequently, the phrase "rest in peace" is taken quite literally. As seen at

White Cemetery and Bachelor's Grove Cemetery, when there is change to a resting-place, it tends to lead to flare-ups of paranormal activity.

It doesn't necessarily have to be a negative change, and it doesn't have to be a cemetery for such things to happen. It is quite common for dormant spirits to find new reasons to show themselves when a location important to them undergoes a change. Often, this is a way for them to show that they have negative feelings about the changes.

If both spirits seen near the monastery are the same, one can guess that this person lived or worked somewhere on Diversey in Chicago, is buried at the cemetery, and died in a car-pedestrian accident. Since both events happened around 2:00 AM, this is very possibly the time of her death.

In addition to the already interesting aspects of this haunting, it is also noteworthy that a short walk through the back of the cemetery and through a wooded area will place you at "The Gate." Also, many of the very first roads were Native American paths. Sometimes the Native Americans who used them considered the paths to be sacred ground. As it turns out, Milwaukee Avenue was among the very first plank (wood-paved) roads in Lake County and, therefore, quite possibly a Native American path.

CHAPTER 10

OUR MAFIA TOWN

"Frank Nitti's Suicide"

SLIMPICTURES.COM/CHAPTER10.HTM

When prohibition was passed, the rule of the city was passed from politicians to the Mafia. New York was famous for its five families, but Chicago was always different. It was, and still is, ruled by street gangs that answer to a higher force. Like New York's families, there still is a hierarchy of power, but the lines tend to be more blurred and, therefore, more difficult for law enforcement to decode.

Carlo Gambino, Lucky Luciano, and John Gotti are some of the few Mafia figures who aren't Chicagoans. Bugs Moran, Tony Accardo, Sam Giancana, Charles O'Banion, Tony Lombardo, and Al Capone are among the immortals forever attached to the city. There are also non-Mafia criminals like John Dillinger and "Babyface" Nelson who lived and died in Chicago, living on their own brand of organized crime.

Mayor Richard J. Daley must have been extremely happy to see the Bulls win six NBA Championships in the 1990s. In addition to bringing in a lot of revenue for the city, the championship wins made Michael Jordan Chicago's icon rather than Al Capone. Chicago has fought against its notorious gangland image for the better part of a century.

Attempts to create bus tours of famous Mafia sites always tend to come up against opposition from the city while many historical Mafia locations have since been destroyed. Try as they might, the Mafia's history will always be interwoven with Chicago's past. Also, it seems that the Mafia will always have an active place within every major city in America, including Chicago.

The Single Most Famous Event in the History of the American Mafia

Haunted locations with links to the Mafia dot our Illinois landscape, from city sites like the Congress Hotel's Florentine Ballroom to the Minneola Resort in Fox Lake. However, no place has as much historical significance as the site of the St. Valentine's Day Massacre.

While St. Valentine's Day is revered as a day of love and affection, it also set an ironic stage for two rival gangsters with no love lost between them. It was the date of the most lethal and famous single act of vengeance in the world of the Mafia.

The S-M-C Garage located on the north side of the city was not well known. That changed instantly.

Al Capone's life almost ended well before he was a gangster. At a New York bar, where he worked as a bartender and bouncer, Capone welcomed a couple into the eatery. His greeting to the woman was perhaps a little too direct by saying, "Honey, you have a nice ass, and I mean that as a compliment."

The woman was with her brother Frank Gallucio. Gallucio punched Capone in the face. Capone started to go after him, but Gallucio pulled out a knife and slashed Capone across the face three times. This led to his nickname "Scarface."

Capone was not in the clear yet; Gallucio approached Charles "Lucky" Luciano about the situation. Luciano was the most powerful mobster in New York and is often credited with creating the Mafia as we know it today. Fortunately for Capone, all he had to do was apologize to Gallucio about his remarks.

Al, along with his more violent brother Frank, left New York for Chicago at the beckoning of his Godfather Johnny Torrio in 1921. Torrio was a high-ranking and highly feared contract killer. Torrio was also the nephew of "Big Jim" Colosimo, who ran one of the bigger gangs in Chicago. Capone was connected.

According to the National Crime Library, in the early 1920s, "Political corruption was a tradition in this vast prairie city, creating an atmosphere of two-fisted lawlessness in which crime flourished. The city became known for its wealth and sexual promiscuity."

At the time of Capone's arrival, Colosimo and his wife Victoria Moresco were at the top of the "skin game." Together they brought in over $50,000 a month through prostitution, which is equivalent to over half a million dollars today. In this era where crime was commonplace, notable Chicagoans such as Enrico Caruso and Clarence Darrow were regular customers. To further illustrate how embraced Colosimo was by the city of Chicago, his pallbearers almost exclusively included political figures: one congressman, an assistant state's attorney, three judges, and at least nine Chicago aldermen. In today's era, if a political figure was even at the funeral of someone of such ill-repute, it could very well end their political career.

New York gangster Frankie Yale, killed Colosimo. He was later arrested but was released in New York. Torrio took over Chicago with Capone at his side.

Capone oversaw the Four Deuces, which had been Torrio's headquarters. The Four Deuces was an explosion of vice. The one building was a whorehouse, speakeasy, and casino. Capone, enjoying his riches, bought a house on Prairie Avenue where Chicago's elite used to live (many already moved to the Gold Coast).

Torrio and Capone moved most of their operations out of the city because it was becoming more difficult to pay off everyone they needed. Cicero was their destination. Here they were able to buy the city government and police department. It was at this time that Capone took control of Hawthorne Racetrack.

Torrio made many trips to Italy and New York, including a visit to New York where he developed the National Crime Syndicate with Lucky Luciano and Meyer Lansky. While Torrio was gone, Capone took charge of the largest gang in Chicago.

Despite leaving Chicago, the Chicago police followed the Capones to Cicero as deputy sheriffs under the authority of Cook County Judge Edmund J. Jareki after word spread of voting fraud. Seventy-nine plain-clothed policemen bearing shotguns patrolled the city of Cicero in unmarked cars.

Seeing Al Capone's brother Frank walking down the street, the police stopped their car and started rushing him with their guns drawn. Fearing for his life, Frank, not knowing if the men were police or assassins, went for a gun but was quickly shot to death. Since Frank reached for a gun, they were able to claim self defense. To add even more insult, the police who killed Frank Capone were also assigned to watch over his funeral.

In addition, Dion O'Banion, one of the most prominent bootleggers in the city, was beginning to cause trouble for Capone. He was stirring things up with the Genna brothers, who were allies with Capone and Torrio, and he shot and killed a man who he had met at Capone's Four Deuces. This ended up bringing a murder investigation against Capone.

Despite the fact that O'Banion supplied flowers valued at $20,000 at the funeral for Frank Capone, something had to be done. Three assassins killed O'Banion in his flower shop while he was preparing the flower arrangement for Mike Merlo's funeral. Though no one was ever brought to trial, those within the Mafia knew that Capone and Torrio were behind it.

This gangland slaying further deepened lines between gangs. Capone won and lost with the killing. The uncontrollable O'Banion was gone, and Capone took over his bootlegging empire, but Hymie Weiss and George "Bugs" Moran, close friends of O'Banion, made Capone a target.

Capone survived over a dozen assassination attempts without injury over the next two months, but Torrio wasn't as lucky. He was shot four times by Moran and some of his men. Despite suffering multiple gunshot wounds that nearly took his life, he was quite fortunate.

The gunmen opened fire on Torrio's car, showering it with bullets. The problem for them was that Torrio was not yet in the car. Still, four bullets ripped through the car and struck Torrio, sending him to the ground. Bugs Moran himself walked up to Torrio, rested his gun against Torrio's head, and pulled the trigger. They had wasted one too many bullets on the car. Moran was out of ammunition.

Just days later, Torrio plead guilty to a charge involving bootlegging, keeping him safe within the walls of a Waukegan jail. While in jail, Torrio retired and named Al Capone as his successor. Capone's first act of duty was a large one. He wanted to get back at the man who almost took the life of his mentor.

Capone had a man approach Moran with an offer of good whiskey at what turned out to be a too-good-to-be-true price. Moran agreed to receive the shipment at the S-M-C Cartage Company Garage at 10:30 in the morning on February 14th.

The stage for the ambush was set. Al Capone was in Florida and "Machine Gun Jack" McGurn, who organized the entire event, was checked in at a hotel with his girlfriend that the press dubbed "The Blond Alibi." From a building across the street, the assassins waited to see Bugs Moran enter the garage to wait for the whiskey shipment.

Seeing a man they thought was Moran, some assassins put on stolen police uniforms while others wore trench coats. The four men armed themselves with two machine guns, a .45, and a shotgun, each fully loaded with garlic-soaked bullets. They then got in their stolen police car and went to the garage. Inside, they acted as if it was a raid.

The seven men awaiting the shipment of whiskey lined up against the wall as they were instructed. Instead of being placed in handcuffs, the sound of machine gun fire filled the air. The assassins first shot at the head, then the chest, and finally the stomach.

In order to make a safe and inconspicuous getaway despite the audible gunfire, the men in police uniforms carried the guns while the men in trench coats marched to the police car with their hands up. To the unknowing observer, it appeared as though there was a shootout between crooks and police where two men were brought to justice.

It was far from the truth. After seventy machine gun rounds were fired, four men lay dead while the three others writhed in pain from their soon-to-be fatal injuries. Only one remained living long enough to make it to a hospital. The Gusenberg brothers, who had previously tried to kill McGurn, were among the victims. It was actually Frank Gusenberg who survived at first. By the time police arrived on the scene, Frank had crawled over twenty feet towards the door. With twenty-two bullets in Frank's body, Police Sergeant Sweeney asked him who had shot him. His answer was, "No one. Nobody shot me."

Moran, however, was not on the list of those who died. He was approaching the garage when he saw a police car enter the parking lot. Thinking it was a raid, he left the scene immediately. When later asked about the crime, he uttered the famous words, "Only Capone kills like that."

Later, McGurn had the presence of mind to marry his girlfriend so she did not have to testify against him as stated in the Fifth Amendment. While the world knew that Capone and his men were behind the killing, no one was ever put on trial.

In Chicago's attempts to put their Mafia connections in the past, the Four Deuces was demolished along with the S-M-C garage in a 1967 urban renewal project. The exact area where the garage was is now a small park with five trees arranged as if they were clubs on a number five playing card. The tree in the center is the exact spot where six of the seven men died. That is where the back wall of the garage once stood.

Neighbors passing by with dogs often find that their canine friends act strangely there. Often even the best trained dogs try to run away from the park or start growling at something unseen. Strange photographs captured at this site reveal mists and orbs.

Phantom sounds are also commonplace there. Included in the list of sounds are screams, moans, shotgun blasts, and the sound of machine gun rounds.

The bricks themselves, which were splattered with blood and bullet holes, became souvenirs after its destruction. A man named George Patey of Vancouver, British Columbia, made the biggest purchase when he bought over four hundred bricks. These bricks, carefully numbered, were put back together at a restaurant he owned.

Many believe that these bricks are bad luck. People that stole bricks from the demolition site have reportedly suffered bad luck in the form of illness, family crisis, and bankruptcy. Such was the case for Patey's bar.

Today there is some dispute over where the actual bricks are. Most likely they are scattered throughout the U.S. in the possession of collectors.

The hauntings and strange events around the St. Valentine's Day Massacre don't stop there. James Clark, who was one of Moran's top triggermen until the time of his death, did not move on to the other side. According to Capone, Clark stayed with him.

Apparently, Clark made it his duty to carry out revenge even after his death. Some speculate that the ghost Capone saw was merely a result of insanity stemming from congenital syphilis, which Capone had since birth.

However, Capone's chauffeur Sylvester Barton allegedly saw the ghost on at least one occasion. Whatever the source was, a legitimate ghost, insane visions, or crippling guilt of his deeds, this is something that Capone suffered with until the time of his death.

Capone eventually was sent to prison on charges of income

tax evasion. While in prison, guards would constantly hear Capone's cries and pleads for the ghost to go away.

Of the major players in the event, only one person's life came to an unnatural end. McGurn was killed exactly three years later. Police found him with a Valentine's Day card stuffed in his mouth.

It appears Capone himself has his host of haunts. He was first seen at South Michigan Avenue roaming the fifth floor of the Lexington Hotel where he had his headquarters. That building was demolished, but his ghost apparently moved on to a boat named *The Duchess III*, which Capone used to own.

Despite the fact that the city wants to forget about this part of its past, perhaps a sign or historical marker stating the significance of the site of the St. Valentine's Day Massacre could allow the tormented souls there to rest. For years, the only acknowledgement of the past was a single brick to the left of the lot bearing graffiti: the word "SAINT." As of 2008, however, even that was removed and the park is completely fenced off from curiosity-seekers.

Life After Capone

When Capone was finally nabbed for the anticlimactic crime of income tax evasion, his successor was Frank "The Enforcer" Nitti. Nitti's reign as head of the strongest mob in Chicago lasted eleven years before coming to an end, along with his life, in 1943.

The world of organized crime is one with rules, regulations, respect, and putting your neck on the line. Vouching for someone or helping someone into that way of life can often make you responsible for their actions.

Nitti introduced Willie Bioff to the Chicago mob some years prior. Bioff collected cash from several Mafia-run unions within the film industry. He and Nitti hatched a new plan that would land a two-million-dollar take. About a million dollars into the operation, journalist Westbrook Pegler blew the whistle. To plea bargain a deal for himself, Bioff turned government witness.

Nitti feared his own imprisonment, but the information was out there and his days of freedom were numbered.

The morning of March 19, 1943, Nitti awoke by a phone call from his lawyer, A. Bradley Eden, who told him that he and six of his underbosses had been indicted on mail fraud charges. Nitti instructed his wife to go to church and pray. Somewhat puzzled by her husband's undetailed instructions, she obeyed.

With his wife gone, Nitti started hitting the bottle. After a countless number of drinks, he put on a hat and coat, grabbed his revolver, and left his Riverside home for the last time.

The next time he was seen was several hours later by three men riding in a caboose. The train they were working on was backing through the crossing at Cermak Road. Since there were no automatic gates at that intersection, men had to get off the train to flag traffic to a halt before the train could continue. With their train safely passing through the intersection, the train workers noticed a man stumbling along the tracks about one hundred yards ahead of them.

Before he was in harms' way, he stepped off to the left of the tracks. William F. Seebaur, the train's conductor, tried to get a feel for what state the man was in.

"Hey there," he shouted.

Nitti responded by raising his gun and firing a shot. Two of the men in the caboose ducked, thinking that they were the targets, but Seebaur corrected them. "He's shooting himself!"

The thoroughly drunken Nitti had fired a shot through his hat at no danger to himself. He was more careful and deadly with his second shot. He placed the gun under his right jaw and pulled the trigger. The bullet exited through the top of his skull, taking part of his scalp with it, and knocked off his hat. He fell onto his back, his head propped up by a chain link fence in a slouched over sitting position. Nitti was not yet dead.

Switchman E. H. Moran pulled the emergency brakes and

stopped the train. The three men rushed from the caboose in hopes of preventing a fatal shot. Moran and Seebaur started to slowly approach Nitti from the side while another man placed himself directly in front of Nitti but with the train between them.

The two men to Nitti's left considered rushing the fallen gangster to steal his gun. At the same time the men were understandably apprehensive about getting shot in the process.

Nitti looked up at the men, placed his gun to the side of his head, and escaped jail. One of the train workers called the police while the other two stood guard at Nitti's body.

Though most people in Chicago wouldn't recognize Nitti alive or dead, the Chicago police did immediately. Ironically, rather than move Nitti's body in an ambulance, he was placed in the trunk of a police car.

In addition, the warrant for his arrest was issued and sent from New York just minutes after Nitti died. It was returned with "Deceased" written on it.

Nitti became the first known Chicago gangster to beat a wrap via suicide. His six underbosses were all convicted and served ten years in jail. Willie Bioff served a reduced sentence and a previous sentence for assault that corrupt lawmen previously "forgot" to enforce. He became Phoenix resident

William Nelson. On November 4, 1955, the Mafia got their man as he was killed in a car bombing.

Nitti's afterlife has not been a peaceful one. He has been seen numerous times pacing along the tracks at the exact location of his demise. Like Frank Giff of the Ole St. Andrew's Inn and possibly Sharon who is associated with the Country House Restaurant, Nitti died while drunk. Nitti's blood-alcohol content was an amazing .25. More than three times today's legal limit.

Nitti's final moments played out on the train tracks just east and across Cermak Road from Woodlawn Cemetery. Ironically, the tracks are between a Toys "R" Us toy store and the North Riverside Mall.

What exactly Frank Nitti is still doing on Earth is unknown, probably even to him. Perhaps it's a residual haunting, or maybe Nitti is still struggling to grasp the gravity of the situation. His suicide may have brought him freedom from jail, but it left an eternity of second thoughts.

Your One-Stop Shopping for All Things Mafia

Rob and Susette Degen invested in an older, run-down building on that famously haunted stretch of Archer Avenue that used to be a biker bar. The dream was to turn it into a popular neighborhood pizzeria. Thus, Cavallone's West was born. It didn't take them long to realize that they got a lot more than just a building with their purchase.

The exact age of this building isn't exactly known, but a photograph was found in the basement showing the bar full of canal workers. This shows that the bar was in operation during the 1910s or 1920s (when the canal was being built).

Not only was the building haunted when the Degens purchased it, it was also lost in time. The top floor, in particular, hadn't been touched in over seventy years. By all accounts, the last people to use these rooms were men and women under the employ of the Capone gang.

Though there was a great chance for a lot of the local history to be lost with the location becoming a biker bar, it appears the bar owner only used the main floor, somehow never feeling the need to explore the second floor or the basement. The owner missed a lot.

The immediate appearance is the first clue that this wasn't intended to be your typical establishment.

All of the windows are over eight feet off the ground, intentionally over head-level, and are opaque. The reason for their frosted appearance was to prevent spying from the FBI and rival gang members while the reason for the height was to prevent drive-by shootings.

The layout of the dining area also looks strange. Instead of simply being a large square, there is a small offshoot that holds another table with four chairs. Overlooking the table is a larger-than-life portrait of a woman.

This area once had a fourth wall, creating an office. Though Capone himself didn't oversee the day-to-day operation of this business, this is the room he used when he was in town. The table and chairs are the same ones that Capone used, and the portrait is that of Capone's aunt.

The final anomalies apparent are two holes that have been filled in with putty, slightly smaller in diameter than a dime, that are in the door to the women's bathroom. According to stories passed down, a man was trying to make his get-away through this room and out the window. The gunman was in the hall when he blindly fired two shots through the door. One bullet struck the fleeing man in the neck, killing him.

Before the room was a bathroom, it was a closet with a secret passageway into the basement. In the hall outside the bathroom is a piece of furniture one wouldn't expect to find in a speakeasy—a church pew. Capone himself purchased this item from a charity auction held at the St. James Church, which is another haunted location on Archer Avenue.

Today the bar occupies the front portion of the building while the remainder of the first floor is the dining area. Once upon a time, the bar went much farther into the dining area, which used to be a casino.

The Degen's found one artifact from its casino days in the basement. Amazing in its craftsmanship and condition, they found an antique, handmade, wooden table imported from Italy. It appears to be a normal, albeit eloquent table; however, upon closer look, there's much, much more to it. The top of the table, when removed and turned upside-down, becomes a chess table. When removed entirely, the table expands to be a complete roulette table with wheel.

The table was found without chips or other gambling paraphernalia. However, at least one picture of the table, when developed, showed it covered with gambling chips. Cavallone's ownership has since changed hands, but when the Degens owned it, waitresses frequently led tours of the main floor and basement, challenging customers to get the next strange picture of the roulette table.

It almost goes without saying that this bar served alcohol throughout prohibition. The liquor closet, close to one hundred years old, is still being used to house alcohol. Indeed, even the shelves that held Capone's booze holds today's popular brands.

Notable antiques like a German WWII helmet and a glass bottle from Chicago's World's Fair were also discovered here. They also found what all Mafia hangouts need: a hidden room.

This hidden room is accessible through an inconspicuous storage room in the back of the basement. In the rear of the storage room there is a removable panel along the ground. One has to push the panel aside and crawl through a small opening to enter the secret room, complete with a peep hole to spy on the authorities as they look through the room.

Based on the puddles of wax on the shelf, they also had a hierarchical system for the hiding. The melted wax closer to the entrance is red while the wax deeper into the room is silver. During this time period, red candles were given out to poorer families that didn't have electricity. In addition, silver candles were commonly used in expensive chandeliers. Workers at Cavallone's theorized that the higher-paying customers with the silver candles were farthest from the door and would therefore have access to the peephole and be arrested last if it ever came to that.

With illegal alcohol in the basement and illegal gambling on the main floor, the Mafia made full use of every square foot of the building by running a brothel on the top floor.

Of course, they had a system for this too. After getting their customers good and liquored up, they would send them upstairs so the girls could take whatever cash they had left on them after drinking and gambling. The girls were summoned through a system of bells that ran by strings between the first floor and every bedroom on the second floor.

The final notable aspect of this building, like any good real estate agent would tell you, is its location.

Partially concealed by the woods near the Calumet-Saganashkee Canal, the area made doing business that much easier.

Located in the basement are three underground tunnels. Based on their small size, they were likely used for transferring cargo, probably via a pulley system rather than as escape routes. These tunnels have not been explored due to fears of a possible cave-in.

One tunnel went several hundred yards underground to the canal so that bootlegged booze could be stealthily loaded to or from boats. The second tunnel connected this basement with the basement of the Willowbrook Ballroom, which is located across the street and discussed in a later chapter. Even if authorities did get a tip-off that the Willowbrook was serving booze, a stakeout wouldn't reveal any incoming shipments.

The final tunnel is a little more mysterious. This tunnel simply emerges deep within the woods behind the building. Perhaps it was just a secluded spot to receive smuggled goods, though, being so secluded, anything could happen out there without fear of a witness. Many speculate that a number of people were beaten or even had their final moments in the woods behind the building.

Erin Rae Zartman had visited Cavallone's West a few times while it was open specifically for the purpose of looking for ghosts. She has a very well-developed sixth sense. Her walk through the woods, as she put it, "was like a dam breaking." She went on to explain the feelings and emotions she felt, saying that she walked around in awe and pain for the spirits that are still out there.

She has a number of photographs that she took in the woods during that evening. A number of them show literally dozens of orbs floating around her.

Orbs are suspect as it is, because they can be caused by a number of explainable reasons. The sheer number in her photographs is also an indicator that it may have been a particularly hazy evening.

As one would assume, a building housing so much vice and violence also serves as a good setting for ghost stories. One story involves a bartender who was dating Christina, one of the upstairs call girls. When he found out Christina wasn't just "turning tricks" upstairs but was actually dating another guy, he flew into a furious rage of jealousy. First, he had the boyfriend meet him in the basement. The bartender was already downstairs waiting, staked out beneath the staircase. When the other man walked down the stairs, the bartender reached through the stairs and tripped him. Reportedly, the man fell, broke his neck, and died at the foot of the stairs.

The bartender was not done with his revenge. According to the stories, he went to the second floor and brutally killed Christina. The second floor, being totally untouched, still bears a bloodstained wall.

The bloodstains could have another story attached to them. The other tales all revolve around the death of a prostitute as punishment. The variations revolve around what her misdeed was, from skimming money and walking out on a customer to stealing alcohol.

In addition to the woods, orbs, most likely a result of dust, have been photographed throughout the building, mostly in the bar and basement.

Edward Shanahan has captured his own strange photographs including a picture he took in the bar of a picture of Al Capone. The developed picture shows a strange, dark object floating in front of the picture. This strange photograph can be seen at TheUnexplainedWorld.com.

The last curiosity is the basement. Psychics have picked up on strong energy in two different areas. In both cases, psychics claim that something is buried under the floor. In the first location, not far from the hidden room, psychics claim there is some sort of a box. The box is said to be armored and contain silver certificates. Rob Degen has explored the area, digging into the floor, but his search was fruitless. There is a spot very close to where the psychic told him to dig that sounds hollow when it is tapped. Allegedly, this area has not yet been explored.

The second place psychics told the owner to dig is in the furnace room. This room is often the area that psychics are most drawn towards. Being the furnace room, it would make sense that this is the hottest room in the building, but it is often the coldest. The box buried here is reportedly the size of a coffin, but the psychic could not identify what was inside of it. This area, more understandably, has not yet been excavated.

Is this seven-by-three-foot box containing untold millions or the corpse of a very unhappy spirit? If there is, indeed, a box buried here, the possibilities are limitless.

Unfortunately, it might be quite a while, if ever, before we find out if anything is buried beneath this building and what it is. It is also quite possible that a treasure was unearthed. Naturally, the smart thing to do as the finders would be to keep quiet to avoid all of the people that would invariably come out of the woodwork to lay claim to the bounty.

The Degans have left; Cavallone's has closed. It was followed by another pizzeria, Rico D's, that has also come and gone. Most recently, the building was called Frankie's Roadhouse, but that too came and went in the blink of an eye. As of press time, this impressive building is vacant, unsure what will come next.

Public Enemy Number One

John Dillinger broke the law many times and was directly responsible for ten deaths. He was an American hero.

Dillinger's story reads like a Hollywood screenplay (partially because that screenplay has been written many times over). Innocent but misguided young man makes a mistake but tries to do the right thing. For his efforts, he is punished harder. From then on he decides to wage his own war on the criminal justice system—a system that made him a smart, ruthless, and a successful bank robber. It created him.

Born in small-town Indiana, Dillinger was nothing more than a punk kid until he started running with Ed Singleton. In 1924, Dillinger committed his first major crime. He and Singleton tried to mug a local grocery store owner. Dillinger struck the man, Frank Morgan, with a pistol. The gun accidentally fired, but no one was shot.

The unwritten rule is that pleading guilty will result in a lesser penalty compared to being found guilty in court after pleading not guilty. Singleton pled not guilty to the crime, was found guilty, and was sentenced to two years in prison. Dillinger, on the other hand, issued a plea of guilty and was sentenced to the maximum of ten to twenty years in prison.

Singleton, who had a previous record, was released in less than two years. Dillinger, with no prior criminal record was denied parole again after his eighth year. During his time in jail, Dillinger worked in the prison shirt factory as a seamster, finishing his quota by lunch and helping other workers during the rest of the day. He was social, joining the prison baseball team. Most importantly, he made friends with experienced bank robbers. The denial of parole was difficult to Dillinger. In his mind, the prison stole his youth, his wife, who divorced him while he was serving time, and even his stepmother, who died before his release.

The rulings from the judge were looked at as unjust by all that observed it—including Frank Morgan himself. A petition in 1933 containing nearly two hundred names, including Morgan's, resulted in Dillinger's early release.

After nine years in jail, Dillinger had plenty of time to organize his revenge against the system, the same system that would take his life just eleven short months later.

The scene was the early 1930s when many Americans viewed banks as the enemy, thanks to the Great Depression. Since Dillinger targeted banks and was reported to buy lavish gifts, such as cars, for his less privileged friends, he became a modern day Robin Hood.

He wasted no time, robbing a bank in New Carlisle, Ohio two weeks after his release, making his get-away with more than $10,000. Dillinger's freedom was short-lived. He was arrested in Ohio after a one-man, four-month crime spree.

The difference in this stint behind bars was that now he had a gang of experienced bank robbers on the outside working for him. Included in his gang were Walter Dietrich, Russell Clark, "Fat Charles" Makley, Hormer Van Meter, John Hamilton, and Harry Pierpont, who had all just escaped from Indiana State Prison.

Shortly after their escape, they came to Dillinger's aid. During the jailbreak, Pierpont shot and killed Sheriff Jess Saber. The gang went on to rob numerous banks over the following months highlighted by a freak accident that resulted in the death of Officer William O'Malley and a Greencastle, Indiana robbery where the gang made off with over $75,000, which today would be valued at over $1.1 million.

Most of the gang was apprehended in Tucson and extradited back to the Midwest on murder charges. Dillinger was taken to Crown Point, Indiana for the O'Malley murder while Makley, Pierpoint, and Clark ended up in Ohio for the Saber killing. Clark spent life in prison while Pierpont was sent to the electric chair, and Makley was killed in an escape attempt.

As we've seen, fires happen in "fireproof" theaters and "unsinkable" ships sink. Crown Point Prison was called "escape-proof."

Now with his gang incarcerated, Dillinger had to get out of this bind alone. According to some, Dillinger fashioned a gun out of a bar of soap. He then colored it black with shoe polish. Finally, he found a guard he could take advantage of. To add one more insult to "the system," Dillinger made his getaway by stealing the warden's car.

By driving the car all the way to Chicago, Dillinger unknowingly, or simply not caring, had committed a federal offence, allowing the Division of Investigation (which would later become the FBI) to start their own manhunt.

J. Edgar Hoover took the constant insults and his celebrity status personally, declaring Dillinger public enemy number one. This was the first time anyone was given this distinction. Wanted posters stated that anyone able to bring Dillinger in dead or alive would be awarded $10,000.

Of the many close calls that would result in the coming months, none was greater than the shootout at Little Bohemia in Manitowish, Wisconsin.

Dillinger and his remaining gang, which now included Homer Van Meter and the blood-thirsty George "Babyface" Nelson, took up residence in this northern Wisconsin lodge. It wasn't long before the owners noticed the gun holsters that their guests were sporting. Dillinger leveled with them and explained that they would do no harm to them and they would pay what they owed at the end of their stay.

However, with the truth being out in the open, new precautions had to be made. All phone calls were monitored and one of the gang members always escorted the lodge owners into town when they had errands to run.

While this arrangement worked out fine for the gang, the lodge owners weren't pleased. One afternoon, the wife had to bring their young daughter to a birthday party. With the child in the car and one of the gangsters tailing behind her, she decided to make a risky move.

She sped up to increase his following distance. When she approached an S-curve boarded by dense forrest, she pulled into a driveway and delivered a letter to her brother. She then got back on the road before the gangster noticed.

The Chicago division of the DOI was immediately notified, and they acted quickly. Several federal agents landed at a nearby airport not far from Little Bohemia a few days later to make a sneak attack on the unsuspecting gangsters.

They had a plan but soon learned that the Dillinger crew was about to head out, so the agents had to act now. With little preparation, several DOI agents crept through the woods with loaded guns in hand.

Even if things went perfectly, they still wouldn't have caught every member of the gang. Earlier that afternoon, some of the gang went into town. While they were gone, the other cars were placed in the garage. When the gang members returned, they noticed that the other cars were missing. Fearing that a raid had already occurred, they fled the scene.

That was just the beginning of the problem for the agents. To start, the agents had trouble getting to the location. In the winter conditions, one of the agents ran his car off the road. He then had to commandeer a citizen's vehicle to make it the rest of the way.

Around three o'clock in the morning, the lodge was full of regular customers having a good time. The agents waited impatiently in the cold for some sign of action. Unfortunately for them, the first action they saw came from the two dogs that guarded the property. People inside paid no attention, ignoring the dogs.

Eventually, three men exited the lodge and got into a car. Without being prompted, the agents opened fire, striking all three men. Two of them were able to scramble back inside Little Bohemia, but the third man was killed instantly. All three men were innocent civilians.

The Dillinger gang was obviously alerted by the gunfire and was able to make an escape without losing any of their own. Not only was the DOI responsible for shooting three innocent men, but they didn't achieve any aspect of their goal.

In the process, "Baby Face" Nelson shot and killed Special Agent W. Carter Baum.

Knowing that his days may be numbered if he didn't do something drastic, Dillinger and Van Meter, who was also on Chicago's Most Wanted List, went to a plastic surgeon. Dillinger wanted minor work done to change his appearance, but the details of his eventual appearance are still controversial and debated.

Among the work involved were the removal of his facial birthmarks, changing the bridge of his nose, filling in his cleft chin, and burning off his fingerprints with acid. However, the changes almost weren't made at all.

The surgeon's assistant was supposed to give Dillinger an anaesthetic. An ether-soaked towel was placed over Dillinger's face. He promptly turned blue as his tongue blocked his airway. America's public enemy number one was dead but only for a short time. The regular surgeon quickly ran into the room, pulled Dillinger's tongue from his throat with the help of forceps, and revived him.

Around the time Dillinger decided to alter his appearance, he was staying with a girlfriend named Polly Hamilton and her roommate Anna Sage. Sage was a native of Romania who twice got in trouble with the law for running brothels in East St. Louis, Illinois and Gary, Indiana. Deportation back to her homeland appeared imminent, but now she had leverage.

Sage struck up a deal with Federal Agent Melvin Purvis. She would turn in Dillinger in exchange for becoming a US citizen. The $10,000 award was also quite appealing.

The stage was set for the final confrontation between Dillinger and Melvin Purvis' DOI agents. Hamilton, Dillinger, and Sage attended a 9:30 P.M. showing of *Manhattan Melodrama* at the Biograph Theater on Lincoln Avenue. Sage wore a brightly colored orange-red dress so that they'd be easy to spot in the crowd.

When the movie ended, Purvis blended in with the crowd. Once he found Sage in her bright dress and identified the

man she was with
as Dillinger, he lit a
cigarette. This was the
"go ahead" sign for the
armed agents across
the street. Purvis
tried to give Dillinger
a chance to turn
himself in, but instead,
Dillinger ran.

Shots rang out.
Two women were
accidentally wounded,
and Dillinger was
hit twice. He barely
made it past the
theater before he was
struck down dead. He
died just feet from a utility pole that still stands today in the
alleyway known as "Dillinger's Alley."

Crowds at the scene grasped the situation and crowded
the body of America's Robin Hood. For souvenirs they dipped
their handkerchiefs in the pool of warm blood on the ground.
As bizarre as that sounds, his body was put on display for all to
see later that night. Far from a proper wake, it was more like a
carnival sideshow.

Sage was only awarded $5,000 and was promptly deported
to Romania.

After an eleven-month crime spree, Dillinger reportedly
robbed up to twenty banks but now lay dead. Some say
otherwise.

It is possible that Hamilton, Sage, and Dillinger had a very
productive night. Since only he and his friends knew his exact
appearance, there is speculation whether or not the man killed
was Dillinger.

Once examined, the coroner found that the man killed was

shorter, heavier, and had a different eye color than Dillinger. In addition, he did not have distinguishing birthmarks on his body in the same places that Dillinger did. Also, this man suffered from a heart condition that official records state Dillinger did not have. Finally, Polly had in her possession a picture of herself with the man the FBI shot that allegedly predated Dillinger's surgery.

Perhaps Dillinger altered his looks to resemble another man who would take the fall for him. Maybe Dillinger never had plastic surgery at all and the story was just one leaked to the community by Dillinger's gang members. It does show elements of an urban legend when considering how much detail there was in the story.

If not Dillinger, then who was this man? Obviously nothing is known of him, but there are suspicions that he was a regular at one of Sage's brothels. Maybe he was abusive or didn't pay his bills. The result: Dillinger killed him using the DOI while at the same time relieving himself of the title "Public Enemy Number One."

The debate has continued with most of the inaccuracies being shrugged off as semantic arguments and a poorly written autopsy report.

Nothing has been proven conclusively, and the government has no desire to reopen the case in fear that it will simply illustrate another one of their botched procedures that would add to a long list of embarrassments including the Ruby Ridge disaster and the fire at Waco, Texas. What has come to light is that Dillinger was unarmed at the time of his death. The DOI, now FBI, would later display a pistol they claimed was on Dillinger at the time of his death. However, the gun in question wasn't manufactured until five months after the killing.

The Biograph Theater came dangerously close to demolition when it closed in 2001. The gangster-era landmark displayed old newspapers of Dillinger's death, and the seat where he saw his last movie was highlighted.

Fortunately, the building was saved when it was put on the National List of Historic Places in March of the same year. After sitting vacant for a number of years, it re-opened for stage presentations as Victory Gardens at the Biograph. The actual location was used for the recent Johnny Depp film about Dillinger's tale.

While the theater isn't haunted, the sidewalk in front of the theater and Dillinger's Alley is. The spirit of the man killed that fateful day was dormant for a long period of time, but in the 1970s people started noticing a bluish gray figure running down the sidewalk in front of the theater, stumbling, and falling in the alley next to the utility pole. At this point the figure vanishes into nothingness.

The alley is also accompanied by nonvisual phenomena. In addition to cold spots, many people feel strange and uncomfortable sensations. People are uneasy there even though they may not know the history of the alley. This is a person's psychic sixth sense picking up on something that is present in the area that the individual cannot interpret.

As is evident in that the death replays itself, this haunting is likely a residual haunting. On the other hand, the feelings in the alleyway could be stemming from an angered Dillinger who is resentful Purvis finally won the game of cat and mouse. It could also stem from uneasy feelings the witnesses had of the event, much like the theory of the *Eastland* hauntings. Finally, if it wasn't Dillinger, it may be the betrayed friend of Anna Sage who might still be unsure what happened in the last fantastic seconds of his life.

CHAPTER 11

CODE 187 - MURDER

"The I-57 Murders"

Chicago is the location of some of the most interesting and mysterious murder cases in recent history.

As was previously mentioned, the strange and unique murders and conclusion of the Peterson-Schuessler case has many wondering if Illinois politicians wanted to find the killer or just be able to brag that they did, regardless of fact. There are a host of other cases that are interesting, unexpected, sad, and unsolved.

Perhaps the saddest of these elements isn't just the intentional termination of another life but the fact that these victims are still Earth-bound. Victims of violent crimes, most of these souls still haven't been able to cross over to the other side. The reasons are unknown, but maybe they are waiting for justice to be served here on Earth before they cross over. Unfortunately, this may never happen as some of the cases are hopelessly lost to time.

John Lalime, Indian interpreter and the first white settler in what became Chicago was also the first homicide victim in Cook County. In 1812, John Kinzie, a business rival, was the killer. Kinzie left town for several days but eventually returned and was acquitted of the crime… at least for the most part. Kinzie, who took over ownership of Lalime's property, was forced to care for Lalime's remains at punishment. The body was interred in Kinzie's property. Later, the remains were placed within the Chicago Historical Society, where they are preserved today. Kinzie, the city's first murderer, is memorialized today with a street bearing his name. One would hope that things have progressed more by now.

Random Acts of Violence

Some sociologists claim that murder is simply part of nature, even human nature. Animals have killed for food and survival, to protect their possessions and territory, and in self-defense. Humans are different than animals in the sense that humans also kill for sport.

Deer hunting, fishing, and trapping are accepted throughout the world. Unfortunately, another almost expected aspect of today is the random killing of innocent people. Drive-by shootings, serial killers, shooting sprees, and terrorist acts throughout the world claim the lives of innocent people who were killed through no fault of their own.

There are times when everyone has to rely on the kindness of strangers and the inherent goodness of fellow Americans. In these situations, people are the most vulnerable.

In 1973, Dorothy Cerny and James Schmidt, a young couple, were driving on I-57 through Tinley Park when they were "accidentally" bumped by a car behind them. Both cars pulled off the road on to the shoulder near the Flossmore Road overpass.

In this time before the widespread use of cell phones, this young couple had no means of calling the police to alert them of their situation. It was now that the couple had to rely on the driver of the other car to help the situation along. Instead, he engaged in an unconscionable act most people wouldn't dare think could happen.

As the couple pleaded for their lives by informing the driver of the other car that they were due to be married in just six months, the man pulled out a 12-gauge shot gun and shot the twenty-five-year-olds in the back, killing the unarmed couple in cold blood. The two victims were total strangers; the killer couldn't possibly have any logical reason for killing them. The randomness of this evil act forced people, particularly those living in the south suburbs, to look at all strangers with an air of suspicion.

The crime was not immediately discovered, but when the bodies of the young couple were finally found, an intense investigation ensued. It resulted in the arrest of Henry Brisbon. He also confessed to a third murder committed on I-57.

Brisbon was presumptuous when he claimed that he committed the third murder. The other man he shot lived long enough to identify his assailant.

Since this occurred while the death penalty was not in effect in Illinois, Brisbon did not get the electric chair. Instead, he was sentenced to 1,000 to 3,000 years without possibility of parole at Statesville Prison.

While in prison, Brisbon slashed and stabbed fellow inmates William T. Jones and mass murder John Wayne Gacy with a knife he made. In 1978, he killed inmate Richard E. Morgan. By this time, the death penalty was in effect in Illinois, and the death penalty was given to the overtly homicidal Brisbon. However, after confirming that Illinois had wrongly sentenced thirteen men to death row since 1977, then-Governor George Ryan ordered a moratorium on executions in Illinois in 2000. Then in 2003, the sentences of all of the 167 Illinois death row inmates, including Brisbon, were commuted to life in prison.

With Brisbon finally unable to cause any more damage, Southsiders were more than ready to try to move beyond the horrible murders in their community. However, they are still reminded by a vision from the other side.

At first all was quiet in the area near the Flossmore overpass, but then drivers on I-57 at night started seeing two people at the side of the road trying to flag down cars. All the wiser since the slayings, most called the police to have them check up on the two people. When police report to the scene to help, they find no one in the area.

Motorists who still felt it was safe enough for them to help watched the couple vanish from sight when they pulled onto the shoulder.

Hopefully, this is a residual haunting due to the high levels of emotion impressed on that space. The alternative is a sad one: the souls of these two victims are still trapped here and are still looking for help just like the victims of Flight 191 who are still knocking on the doors of houses near their crash site.

The best scenario is that these visions may be merely subconscious manifestations of an overactive imagination. "Phantom Hitchhikers" are a common phenomena throughout America and the world. Motorists making long nighttime journeys are the main candidates to see these visions. Generally, men see female phantoms and women see male forms that simply aren't there when they make a conscious effort to look back at the person usually seen at the side of the road. World War II pilots flying for countless hours at night saw even stranger images: gremlin-like forms on the wings of their planes. This was famously depicted in a Twilight Zone movie.

If hallucination is the cause of these sightings, it would make sense that the witnesses were people who are aware of the murders at the site.

If, on the other hand, their souls are still trapped here, this is not an isolated case. Often the ghosts of murder victims are seen after their deaths, apparently making sure they are not forgotten. These hauntings generally remain active until justice is served as we will see next with the phantom of Bobby Franks.

Bobby Franks and Clarence Darrow

Clarence Darrow, as we've seen, had no fear of taking on un-winnable cases, especially if they were in the spotlight.

His most famous case closely parallels a Hollywood film. Alfred Hitchcock's *Rope* is considered one of his most underrated masterpieces. The "master of suspense" tells the story of two well-to-do, intelligent young men who have the world at their fingertips, but they thirst for more. The two look for a challenge and that challenge is to get away with the "perfect crime." A simple exercise in shoplifting is barely enough challenge for two men of such superior intellect, so a murder is decided upon. The film, in addition to being a wonderful example of what suspense in film can be, also raises provoking philosophical questions about whether or not some people should or shouldn't have more rights and privileges than others based on intellect.

In the film, Brandon Shaw and Phillip Morgan kill an unsuspecting acquaintance named David. Although never completely addressed, there seems to be homosexual undertones in the relationship between Brandon and Phillip. Change the setting from New York to Chicago, substitute the names Shaw and Morgan for Leopold and Loeb and the victim from David to Bobby Franks, and the film would be about one of Darrow's "trials of the century."

The phrase "trial of the century" has been linked with the OJ Simpson and Michael Jackson trials recently, but it has been used to describe many major court cases that capture public attention in the media age like the kidnapping of the Lindberg baby.

Leopold and Loeb were two men with potential in every sense of the word. Loeb's father was the vice president of Sears Roebuck, and at the time Loeb was the youngest graduate of the University of Michigan. Leopold was also from a wealthy family and, amazingly, had graduated from the University of Chicago in 1923 by the age of eighteen.

Though they came from similar backgrounds, the two had different plans. Loeb had the dream to commit a perfect crime, which included murder, while Leopold's life goals were less sinister but still unconventional for the times; he was seeking sexual gratification from another male. The two made a bizarre written and signed agreement that stated Loeb would consent to Leopold's sexual desires provided that Leopold would go along with Loeb's criminal desires.

Over the next seven years, the two started practicing by successfully getting a number of smaller crimes under their belt, including stealing a typewriter from Leopold's fraternity.

When they felt their time was ready, the two came up with a plan. A half-year in the making, they felt it was ingenious. Their next step was to find a victim. A child would be ideal because there wouldn't be much of a fight. A child who they knew would also be ideal since most children—even in the innocent 1920s—were taught to be wary of strangers. At the same time they couldn't be very well acquainted with the child or they would be easily linked with the victim. Lastly, a child from a rich family would add to the criminal aspect since then the two potential killers could demand a high ransom that his parents could easily pay. This would also further remove them from the murders since these two men would have no rational reason to risk their freedom for money since they already had so much. Bobby Franks was the "perfect answer" to maintain their "perfect crime."

Jacob Franks, a millionaire, was Bobby's father. Loeb was a distant cousin to the fourteen-year-old Bobby.

It is said that in every murder the killer makes a number of mistakes. It would only take one to link Leopold and Loeb to the crime, but they made two.

Exiting his school in May of 1924, Franks happily accepted a ride home from Leopold and Loeb. All seemed well until the car pulled over several blocks from Bobby's Hyde Park home. While still in the car, Bobby was gagged and struck four times in the head with a chisel. The cause of death was loss of blood from the bludgeoning.

However, Leopold and Loeb didn't want to leave anything to chance, so they submerged his head in a bucket of water to ensure that if he were simply unconscious, he would drown.

In order for the ransom demand to work, the Franks family had to be in the dark about the fact that Bobby was already dead. They planned to hide and dispose of the body. To prevent identification, they burned his face beyond recognition with acid in the event that the body was discovered before they wanted it to be.

After stopping for lunch, the two disposed of Bobby's body in a drainage pipe near the Pennsylvania Railroad tracks.

The two killers had finally realized their crime, but they were far from out of the woods. The next phase was to collect their ransom and actually profit monetarily from their slaying. So, that night, between congratulatory drinks and hands of cards, they called Jacob Franks to tell him to expect a letter with ransom demands regarding his son.

Something Leopold and Loeb didn't know was that

Leopold's eyeglasses had fallen off and were still with Bobby's body. Also, they didn't anticipate the police being able to easily track the ransom letter back to them by finding that it was written on a typewriter that was reported missing by Leopold's fraternity. It does make sense that Leopold, who was far less driven by the crime, was the one to make the fatal errors.

In addition, their attempt at getting their hands on Jacob Franks' money never got off the ground. By the time they finally made their phone call, Bobby's body had already been found and identified.

With Leopold and Loeb on the ropes, their influential parents brought in Clarence Darrow to take on the hopeless case. A strong opponent to the death penalty, Darrow was the Johnny Cochran of his time. The decision to hire Darrow as the defending attorney basically indicated that the defendants knew there was an uphill battle.

Leopold and Loeb both confessed to the killing, so Darrow's mission was simple: prevent his clients from being sentenced to death. This was something Darrow was previously unable to do during his first murder case.

During the trial, the two defendants were as cocky as ever, often joking and laughing in the courtroom despite the fact that their lives were at stake. This gave Darrow the open opportunity to plead insanity, thus relieving the two from any responsibility.

To play on the emotions of the jury, Darrow described, in great detail, the act of killing Leopold and Loeb to the point he actually began to cry. The two young killers saw what was going on and the gravity of the situation finally sunk in. Whether this method was shameless or sincere, it worked. On September 10, 1924, the two were sentenced life in prison plus an additional ninety-nine years to be served at Statesville Prison in Joliet, Illinois.

Bobby Franks could now rest easy at his mausoleum in Rosehill Cemetery for justice was, to some extent, served. However, it wasn't until the lives of both of the killers came to an end that Bobby could fully rest in peace. His ghost had been seen on numerous occasions around the area of his mausoleum.

Prison changed both men drastically. Loeb became far more violent and actually became a rapist in jail. He was attacked with a straight razor by James Day, who Loeb was attempting to turn into his new partner, soon dying from his wounds.

Leopold, on the other hand, petitioned several times for his parole and was finally granted one in 1958 after Carl Sandburg came to his aid. After writing a book titled *Life Plus 99 Years*, he later moved to Puerto Rico where he started a mission and helped poor people. In his life after the murder, he volunteered in studies on malaria and donated his organs after death. This may illustrate how much of a stranglehold Loeb had on him, or it may show Leopold's strain to make up for the heinous crime committed against the fourteen-year-old boy. Leopold died in 1971 of a heart attack—the same year that Bobby's ghost was last seen.

One of Chicago's Great Mysteries

Frustrated civilians and press writers alike lost faith in the Chicago Police Department when a killer was not apprehended in the Peterson-Schuessler murders. Angered, they pointed fingers with claims that similar future crimes would be invited since there were no repercussions handed down to the last murderer. The police also took the blame for their outright lack of thinking when they allowed press members to walk around the crime scene before gathering all of their evidence.

Fifteen months after the Peterson-Schuessler murders, a blink of an eye in Chicago's history, the police were again called upon to solve a disturbingly similar multiple homicide.

Avid Elvis Presley fans Barbara and Patricia Grimes went to the Brighton Theater on what coincidentally would have been the thirty-seventh birthday of Chicago's Miracle Child, Mary

Alice Quinn. What ended up taking place on this evening was something far less holy.

Love Me Tender was the film. The sisters had already seen it numerous times, which was traditional for the devoted Elvis fans; the twelve-year-old Patricia and the fifteen-year-old Barbara went to see it again.

Later that evening, when the Grimes sisters were due to return, their mother became wary of their extended absence from home. She went to the bus stop where her daughters were usually dropped off and waited. She waited while three buses passed. Finally, her fears forced her to call the police and report her daughters missing.

The search that ensued was unparalleled until just recently, during the still-ongoing search for the Bradley sisters in the summer of 2001. The commonly reported statistics show that nearly a third of a million people were questioned while two thousand were "seriously interrogated."

One of the first theories was that the two girls ran away from home with the hopes of meeting Elvis. At that time, nearly fifty young girls were found each year on their way to Graceland. Presley even made a public statement directed to the Grimes sisters. He pleaded, "If you are good Presley fans, you'll go home and ease your mother's worries."

The police investigated several leads, ending up more and more frustrated. This was their chance to redeem themselves after the previous high-profile murders, and it was slipping through their fingers. The mother of the missing girls, Loretta, wasn't safe from frustration either. In addition to not knowing where her daughters were, she was victimized by fake leads and a total of nine fraudulent ransom notes, one of which was so believable that she went to Milwaukee with a bag filled with one thousand dollars only to be let down.

The general belief is that the sisters got into someone's car who they knew in order to get out of the inclement weather conditions. What happened after that is anyone's guess.

The police thought they had their man in Max Fleig, a

seventeen-year-old neighborhood boy who the Grimes sisters may have been familiar with. Fleig maintained his innocence throughout initial questioning but cracked during polygraph lie-detector interviews that bordered on attacks. Fleig was released; the law dictated that the questioning was illegal since minors cannot be subjected to polygraph testing.

With dreams of stardom, no matter how awful, a number of men then came forward with false claims of being the kidnapper. The only thing these claims did was cruelly raise Loretta's hopes and waste precious time. In that wasted time, Patricia's thirteenth birthday came and went without the ceremonial blowing out of the candles during a carefree party.

As the city soon learned, time had already run out. On Tuesday, January 22, 1957, after a period of warmer than usual weather melted the snow, Leonard Prescott saw a strange sight on his drive home. He saw what he thought were two department store mannequins laying on the ground just off of German Church Road in south suburban Willow Springs.

Upon returning home, he told his wife what he saw. Concerned, she demanded that they go back to take a closer look. What they found were the frozen and nude bodies of Barbara and Patricia Grimes.

Apparently not learning the lessons from the Peterson-Schuessler crime scene, police, reporters, and investigators trampled the scene, potentially destroying clues in the process. As Richard Lindberg wrote in his book, *Return to the Scene of the Crime*, "The investigation was botched from the moment the first squad car pulled up."

Though the bodies were recovered, the investigation was at a standstill. Then, a Tennessee man with a first grade education and a resemblance to Elvis Presley named Bennie Bedwell went public with his confession. He claimed that he and a stranger known only as Frank met up with the girls on January seventh.

The four of them went to a number of bars and flophouses along Madison. He recalled, in detail, which taverns they were turned away from and which ones served the young girls. He claims that they went back to the Crest Hotel where he had sex with the now thirteen-year-old Patricia.

According to his initial statements, the four went for a ride on January thirteenth. They ended up at a forest preserve where he attempted to force himself upon Patricia once more. According to his story, she resisted. Bedwell struck her, and she lost consciousness. According to his story, Frank engaged in a similar scuffle with Barbara.

Now scared, the men stripped the girls of their clothes and disposed of their bodies near German Church Road by a stream appropriately nicknamed Devil's Creek. They did not know if the girls were alive or dead.

Then, the reports came back from the autopsy. The girls died on December 28. It is possible they never even made it to the movie. The autopsy revealed signs of sexual abuse though this information was withheld from the press at the time. However, there was no other sign of violence. The easily disputable cause of death was listed as shock and exposure. The girls saw or experienced something so traumatizing that neither of them could will themselves to move, allowing the cold winter air to take their young lives.

Not only did Bedwell not kill Patricia, but she was also dead over a week before he claimed he met her.

She was twelve at the time of her death, never reaching her thirteenth birthday. Bedwell later recanted, stating that he was pressured by the police to say what they wanted him to say. This is likely considering Sheriff Lohman, the individual who arrested Bedwell and the person who had the most to gain politically, was the only investigator who believed Bedwell's story. Political squabbling that besieged the Peterson-Schuessler murders had also beset the case of the Grimes sisters.

Eventually, a neighbor came forth and stated that she heard screams from the alley next to her house around midnight. She went on to say that she would have called the police, but she didn't have a phone.

To this day, around half a century later, the murder of Barbara and Patricia Grimes is still unsolved. It is one of the most mysterious cases in the annals of Chicago crime.

Perhaps because the case is still open today, people near the site where the bodies were found have heard a series of sounds. The sounds include a car drive up, stop, a car door open, the thud of an object landing in the weeds, the door close, and finally, squealing tires as the car flees the area.

This usually isn't accompanied by anything visual, but on occasion, terrified witnesses have actually seen a reenactment of the dumping of the bodies.

The traditional reading interprets this as a residual haunting. An event so emotional has burned a hole in the fabric of that space so deep that it cannot heal.

Still, there are other interpretations. Though it is rare, it is possible for thoughts to manifest themselves in certain forms. This can be illustrated by thinking of a difficult problem that you may be attempting to solve with a group of people. Suddenly, everyone in the group who is thinking hard on the topic comes to the same answer simultaneously. As previously mentioned, areas of deep grief such as crash sites, cemeteries, and funeral parlors can materialize in a number of strange events such as impressed feelings like emotions and physical feelings like the burning sensation felt at the Our Lady of the Angels Memorial. As we've also seen, a strange event called a mass hallucination occurs when someone thinks they see something and it makes their emotion run so high that others in the area are able to see the same exact image that is running through the mind of the creator of the mental image.

This is possibly what is at play on this unassuming stretch of German Church Road. The visions and sounds couldn't come from Barbara and Patricia because they were unresponsive at the time they were left near Devil's Creek. That would leave only one source—the killer.

This is admittedly speculation, but perhaps the killer was so fearful and guilty at the time that he continues to think about the event where he terminated two innocent lives. As this event haunts him, it manifests itself in a visual or auditory form.

Another theory involves justice being served in the after life. As discussed, Clarence Darrow found his own heaven around the bridge now bearing his name. Perhaps this murderer is finding hell near Devil's Creek. It's a poetic and redemptive notion that his eternal fate is to relive the most horrible thing this unnamed perpetrator has ever done, therefore filling his soul with guilt over and over again.

This can never be proven, but it's definitely the one most Chicagoans hope is true.

One thing that will be interesting to note in the future involves the visual aspect of this haunting. Hopefully, one day someone will be able to witness this spectacular vision and will have the presence of mind to look at the license plate of the phantom car. New and important evidence may come about with thanks to the spiritual world.

CHAPTER 12

CITY CEMETERIES

"Rosehill Cemetery"

Chicago is known for many, many things—including museums. Between the Field Museum of Natural History, The Museum of Science & Industry, The Shedd Aquarium, The Art Institute, Adler Planetarium, and the Chicago Historical Society, among many others, one can learn just about anything without having to be in a classroom.

Another type of museum one may not think of can be found in numerous places around the city—cemeteries.

With a walk through a few of the city's cemeteries, one can visit the graves of the greatest people in Chicago's history. The cemeteries also hold monuments honoring individual lives and the lives of those Chicagoans who gave their life in every war effort since the French-Indian War.

Visiting a city cemetery is like walking through a history book. Art and architecture students find the city's cemeteries interesting as they hold some of the most renowned cemetery art in the country.

Bus tours run throughout the city's cemeteries throughout the year to highlight the important graves and impressive monuments. Near autumn, however, additional tours travel through these same cemeteries—with a different topic. In addition to seeing the graves of Chicago's past, some have seen the spirits that those graves belong to.

Bryn Mawr's Cemeteries

The street Bryn Mawr runs east to west only interrupted for a few blocks by the large sprawling Rosehill Cemetery. West from there at the Pulaski Road intersection sits two noteworthy cemeteries.

The west side of the road holds Montrose Cemetery. Within that cemetery stands a very noteworthy monument. The Japanese Mutual Aid Society Mausoleum was established in 1937 for the purpose of interring Chicago's Japanese and Japanese-Americans. At the time of the creation of the mausoleum, this was the only cemetery in Chicago that would accept these remains.

Just within the Pulaski Road entrance and very quickly to the left is a diamond-shaped monument to the victims of the Iroquois Theater Fire. The reports are sketchy and without detail, but there seems to be paranormal activity attributed to the monument similar to the phenomena witnessed at the Our Lady of the Angels Monument at Queen of Heaven Cemetery. There is also the possibility that the hauntings at the Our

Lady of the Angels Monument are mistakenly attributed to the Iroquois Theater Fire Monument.

Bordering Montrose Cemetery to the west is the LaBaugh Woods Forest Preserve. Today, this forest preserve, though surrounded by peaceful neighborhoods, is one of the more dangerous places in Chicago after dark.

In addition to violent crimes like muggings and outright attacks that take place in the area, bodies have also been found in the woods near the North Branch of the Chicago River.

Observing the area in the daytime reveals a place that could be an ideal gang hangout, but there is actually another type of group that uses this as their "home base."

"You think of cults as mostly just groups of kids getting together and messing around," starts John Garza, a police officer who was involved with an investigation of the LaBaugh Woods Forest Preserve, "but these aren't just some kids."

The investigation showed that cult members using those woods are working professionals including doctors and lawyers. The cult is also well organized. They found lookout towers in the trees with shotgun shell casings around them. In other words, they have armed guards.

Between Montrose Cemetery and the LaBaugh Woods Forest Preserve, there are additional graves outside of the cemetery fence. This place is unofficially known as "Forgotten Montrose Cemetery."

In this area, the grounds went unattended, and weeds took over the area. It was neglected and not maintained. Today, this area overlaps the backyards of some recently built houses. The graves are no longer there, but upon a visit in the summer of 1999, on the edge of one of those backyards, I found evidence supporting the stories of the forgotten cemetery. Well outside of the cemetery fence, I found a row marker that is usually used to help organize grave sites. Through the stories and physical evidence, the forgotten cemetery will never be fully forgotten.

On the east side of Pulaski Road is Bohemian National Cemetery, so named because it was created by residents of

a Bohemian neighborhood. After the refusal by a Catholic cemetery to inter one of their residents because she died before making a final confession, this cemetery was constructed.

One of the most notable sights in the cemetery is the statue simply titled "Mother" located in front of the cemetery offices. There are several other impressive monuments including one dedicated to Chicago's casualties of the Spanish-American War and another regarding the Civil War. In addition, there is an emotionally moving memorial to Hitler's victims of World War II that contains two urns. One contains ashes from the largest Nazi death camp Auschwitz while the other contains dirt from the village of Lidice, which was annihilated in retaliation for the successful assassination of the "protector of the Nazi German Protectorate of Bohemia and Moravia." A neighborhood in Crest Hill, Illinois was also named Lidice in memorial just two days after the massacre.

One of the darker pieces of cemetery art is the statue that is commonly called "Walking Death." According to a grave digger at the cemetery, legend has it this macabre-looking figure has an actual human skull inside of its head.

Several victims of the *Eastland* Disaster are interred in this cemetery. These graves are easily found because many of them have a ship wheel or an anchor on them.

Besides the national and local historical points of interest here, there are also a few paranormal events linked to the cemetery. In addition to the iron bars that make up the Pulaski Road fence, which is one of Chicago's four "hungry fences," there is also a phantom funeral.

While Abraham Lincoln's funeral train procession is still visible across the country, including in Illinois, another celebration of one's life after death is also visible at Bohemian National Cemetery.

At the northwest corner of the cemetery near the intersection of Bryn Mawr and Pulaski Road, the end of a funeral procession from the 1920s is still visible. Seen in broad daylight, the reenactment includes a black luxury car and a group of people dressed ceremoniously in black clothing from the same era. Residual hauntings are relatively common, but a display involving a number of people and an inanimate object is quite amazing and rare.

Chicago's Phantom Flapper

Forest Park's Jewish Waldheim Cemetery has a past that is far more public than any of its administrators would like. It started in 1977 when the grave of Elizabeth Taylor's third husband, Michael Todd, was exhumed by grave robbers. They were in search of a 10-carat diamond ring that he was reported to be wearing at the time of his death. His body was taken from the ground, the casket was opened, and when the thieves found no ring, his was body thrown into the nearby weeds. It seems like the evidence from this crime would be quite obvious, but it took two full days for cemetery workers to notice that one of their graves had been badly desecrated. In the end, three men, including two who were previously connected to the mob, were incarcerated for the crime.

Another unfortunate event happened in 1986 when a four-year-old boy was crushed to death when a monument fell on him. In an amazing exhibition of mind-over-matter, the boy's father single-handedly lifted the five hundred pound piece of granite off his son.

Today, there is evidence of the tragic death in hundreds of warning stickers placed on the many off-balance gravestones. The cemetery is built along the Des Plaines River, keeping the ground moist and soft, which explains the alarmingly high number of grave stones that are leaning or have already fallen over completely.

Another peculiar sight involves gravestones and other monuments near the back of the cemetery. In one wooded area, there is simply a pile of discarded and broken stones, while in an area off to the right of that it appears gravestones have been moved to form a retaining wall.

Mary Czerwinski questioned a cemetery worker about the wall that appears to be made of monuments. The worker confirmed that the wall is made of granite, but though it looks like a stack of graves, it is merely a coincidence. The cemetery worker went on to say that the wall was constructed to stop erosion caused by the nearby river.

The cemetery was again cast in a negative light when the owner made the controversial decision to sell off part of the unused land to developers who have since constructed several small businesses.

The most famous people buried at the cemetery include film producer Michael Todd and Albert Weinshenker, who was a Saint Valentine's Day Massacre victim. He is interred at the Sons and Daughters of Jacob Gate.

As previously mentioned, phantom hitchhikers have long been a part of American folklore. Indeed, the most famous ghost story is a vanishing hitchhiker tale. It's hard to pinpoint exactly how and where an urban legend gets its start, but the phantom hitchhiker story is quite possibly linked to one of two Chicago ghosts.

While the story of "Resurrection Mary," which is discussed in the Archer Avenue chapter, is the most famous ghost in Chicago, another phantom hitchhiker at Jewish Waldheim Cemetery has a longer history of hauntings.

The commonly heard urban legend tells the story of a girl at a ballroom. She ends up dancing with a man who eventually offers her a ride home. She tells the man her address, and sometime en route to her house, she simply vanishes from the car. The man is perplexed but decides to continue to the address anyway. There, an elderly woman answers the door. Out of the corner of his eye, the man spies a picture frame containing a photograph of the girl who disappeared from his car. He asks the elderly woman about her and finds that she died several years ago on her way home from a dance at the same ballroom the man was returning from.

Much of that story is the result of impressive imagination, but the first half of that story is much more common than one would assume.

From 1933 through at least the 1970s, a woman that appeared to be a flapper from the roaring twenties danced at the Melody Mill Ballroom on Des Plaines Avenue. More than one man who became captivated by the fun-spirited brunette offered her a ride home. Invariably, she would lead the driver north and then have him pull over at Jewish Waldheim Cemetery. She would tell the man that the cemetery is her home. Then, she would get out of the car and walk around to the back of the caretaker's house where she would vanish from sight. Some have followed her to see that she doesn't enter the house, but rather, she continues to walk deeper into the cemetery where she dissolves into nothingness.

She has been seen numerous times in day and night walking along Des Plaines Road and within the cemetery. Sometimes multiple witnesses see her at a time, but she always stands out due to her vintage look.

Today, the caretaker's house is gone and the Melody Mill Ballroom has been replaced by the Forest Park Mall, but some say there is still evidence of it today. Frequently, during the late evening hours, residents of nearby houses claim to hear big band music blaring.

It remains to be seen if the sighting of the "flapper ghost" will continue. There hasn't been a sighting of the girl for at least thirty years. The spirit may simply be in a dormant stage, or since her favorite dance hall is no longer in existence, she may not have any motivation to return.

The Spirits at Roe's Hill

Rosehill Cemetery is one of Chicago's two major city cemeteries, with Graceland Cemetery being the other. These two cemeteries contain some of the first settlers of Chicago. The first ever city cemetery was along the Chicago River across from Fort Dearborn. Eventually, the city started to grow and that land became prime real estate. The bodies were then moved to Lincoln Park. Again, the city grew and the bodies were moved. This time they were split up. Some were placed in Graceland Cemetery while the remaining were placed in Rosehill Cemetery, which opened in 1859.

The site of the first city cemetery is now the Wrigley

Building, while the other is now the Chicago Historical Society. Some monuments were not moved. One is the couch mausoleum on the grounds near the historical society building. Another is David Kennison's, who was reportedly the last surviving member of the Boston Tea Party and 115 years old at the time of his death. His monument was erected by the Sons and Daughters of the American Revolution. His tall tales, which followed him to the grave, have since been proven false by the Chicago Historical Society.

Unfortunately, it appears that while other gravestones were transferred to either Graceland or Rosehill, not all of the bodies made the journey. Almost every time the ground that once made up the second city cemetery is broken, additional bones are found. This compares to New York's problems when digging subway tunnels; they frequently run across mass burial sites that date back over three hundred years.

Rosehill Cemetery, the largest of the city cemeteries at an astonishing 350 acres, is full of interesting stories including the reason behind the name.

There used to be a pub behind the cemetery in the area near the east entrance off of Ravenswood Avenue. A man named Hiram Roe owned the pub. Locals and regulars began to refer to the area as Roe's Hill. Over time the name evolved to Rosehill.

Those represented at Rosehill Cemetery include an impressive list of names. War heroes include William Stephens, recipient of the Congressional Medal of Honor for his work at Vicksburg during the Civil War, sixteen Civil War major generals, and the Porters.

Jeremiah Porter was the missionary of the American Home Missionary Society. He was also the chaplain for the United States Army for seventeen years. He was the first chaplain at Fort Dearborn, and he co-founded Beloit College in Wisconsin. His wife, Eliza, was the first school teacher in Chicago, but she will forever be remembered for serving at Vicksburg and on other Civil War battlefields. Ulysses S.

Grant went so far as to say they couldn't have won without her and the few other females who were there.

A number of political figures were placed here including fourteen Chicago mayors, Illinois Governor Richard B. Ogilvie, Charles Gates Dawes, who served with Calvin Coolidge as the thirteenth Vice-President of the United States, and Evanston's successful prohibitionist Frances Willard.

The amount of important businessmen buried or interred here is even more impressive. This list includes Albert E. Goodrich, steamships; Charles Gunther, Cracker Jacks; James Scott Kemper, Kemper Insurance; Oscar Mayer, Oscar Mayer Weiners; Julius Rosenwald, helped found the Museum of Science and Industry; Morris B. Sachs, Sachs 5th Avenue; Ignaz Schwinn, Schwinn Bicycles; Robert S. Scott, Carson, Pirie, Scott & Company; P. A. Starck, pianos; Henry Haven Windsor, *Popular Mechanics Magazine*; and many others.

The massive communal mausoleum, which was the first in the world, contains the remains of three more important Chicagoans. This building serves as the final resting place for John G. Shedd, who the Shedd Aquarium is named after, and bitter business rivals Aaron Montgomery Ward and Richard Warren Sears. It is said that Sears feared an afterlife of nothingness. It appears even before death that he was planning to have an active afterlife, as his mausoleum room is the only one in the building with a door leading outside.

The business battle between Sears and Ward lasted until their deaths, which were only a year apart. Since death, Sears has been seen walking the halls of the mausoleum between his family's room and Ward's. Many believe that Sears is looking to continue debating business with his longtime antagonist.

Across from the Willard grave is the mausoleum constructed for real estate investor Charles Hopkins. It is said that on the anniversary of his death the sounds of rattling chains accompany a deep groan that seems to come from the miniature chapel.

Without question, the most popular haunting at the cemetery revolves around one of the most impressive monuments. At the young age of twenty, Frances Pearce tragically passed away soon after childbirth. Her husband's sorrows only grew as their newborn child died four short months later of the same disease that struck down her mother, tuberculosis.

The widower and grieving father, Horatio Stone, chose to immortalize the two people who he was going to spend the rest of his life caring and providing for with a monument. The monument is a strikingly detailed and beautiful life-size statue of Frances lying with her infant daughter, also named Frances, at her side.

The statue, created by prolific artist Chauncey Bradley Ives, who also created sculptures of politicians of the Revolutionary and Civil Wars, was eventually protected against the elements by a glass case. Its effectiveness is obvious as the names on the outside are almost completely worn away, but the protected statue is still as breathtaking as the day it was finished.

It is said that on the anniversary of their deaths, visitors are able to visit the grave and actually speak with the departed

in question. Some believe that twice a year the two innocent souls are permitted to return and meet new people, something they were deprived of due to their lives being cut so short.

In addition, it is said that the glass case fills with a haze as if someone was inside of it, breathing. While this may be a paranormal event that happens on occasion, it is important to note that the glass is not airtight, and similar fogs are present on humid days.

As first reported in Ursula Bielski's *More Chicago Haunts*, there are a slew of lesser-known active spirits within Rosehill's walls. A phantom grave digger is still on the clock as he is seen with gardening tool in hand near May Chapel. There is also a Chicago version of "Romeo & Juliet," evident in the suicide pact of two young lovers buried at Rosehill. These two are seen between the Smith Column in Section 11 and the memorial bench.

Another love-driven suicide took the life of Elizabeth Archer, who decided to end it all when her boyfriend died in a tragic accident. A monument bearing their last names immortalizes both of the fallen lovers. This is where Elizabeth is occasionally seen during November sunsets.

Mary Shedden's gold-colored grave stone has sometimes left more than one witness wondering if they really just saw her face (sometimes just a skull) staring back at them. One of the most remarkable tales goes all the way back to ancient Egypt.

Darius Miller was one of the lucky few who was involved in one of the most famous adventures of all time: the expedition to King Tut's tomb. Those who know their history remember that the lucky few who found the tomb and treasures left for the boy king will also remember that they became very unlucky very quickly. Every member of the "successful" expedition died within a year. Cause of death: The Curse of the Pharaohs.

In actuality, only six people present for the 1922 discovery of the tomb died within twelve years of the expedition. Contrary to proclamations to the contrary, Miller died in 1914 of appendicitis, a full eight years before the king's sarcophagus

was discovered. This Field Museum curator undoubtedly made excursions to Egypt, but he was not part of the much fabled discovery party of Tut's tomb.

Archeology and Egyptian studies were obviously the passion for this railroad president, as his tomb is a miniature replica of the Egyptian temple of Anubis. A strangely predictable ghost light is said to appear at this location on a regular basis. During early morning hours on the first of every May, a blue light emerges from this replica temple.

Strangely enough, this isn't the only time supernatural Egyptian powers have been witnessed in Chicago. There are reports of screaming mummies by security staff at the Field Museum of Natural History, and a reproduction of the pyramid Giza in north suburban Wadsworth has quite a number of unexplainable phenomena attributed to it.

While Rosehill seems to be full of actual ghosts, not residual hauntings, the haunts at Graceland Cemetery seem to come out of Greek Mythology.

Chicago's Other Prestigious Cemetery

Just southwest of Rosehill Cemetery is Graceland Cemetery. It is one of the few places within the City of Chicago that can make a person forget completely that they are in a major metropolis. Lake Willomere in the northern portion of the cemetery is the focal point as several large, beautiful, and impressive grave sites surround it.

Among those buried around the lake are piano & organ manufacturer William Kimball, famed architect Louis Sullivan, and Potter Palmer, who was the primary developer of State Street.

Also buried in this area is William Goodman. He named the Goodman Theater after his son, a playwright named Kenneth, who died of influenza while stationed at the Great Lakes Naval Training Station. Howard Van Doren Shaw designed the mausoleum and the Goodman Theater, and he is also buried at Graceland.

Merchant Marshall Fields, meat packing magnate Philip Armour, and creator of the Tribune Company Joseph Medill are also buried nearby. Medill was the prominent and controversial politician who took over as mayor of Chicago immediately after the Great Chicago Fire. Upon his death, ownership of the Tribune Company went to his heirs, the Pattersons and the McCormicks.

The small island in the lake is the family burial location for Daniel Hudson Burnham's family. Burnham is largely responsible for how some of the city streets are laid out today, most notably Wacker Drive.

An abbreviated list of others buried at this cemetery include William A. Hulbert, who founded baseball's National League, John Kinzie, and Allan Pinkerton who was the first private detective. A number of employees of Pinkerton's Private Eyes are also buried nearby.

Inventor of the Pullman Railroad Sleeping Car, George Pullman is buried in a coffin covered with tarpaper and asphalt, sunk in a concrete block, covered with railroad ties, and then covered with even more concrete. These extra precautions to seal his body were made in fear of angry railroad workers who might be seeking some sort of revenge, a final payback from the Pullman strike.

Charles H. Wacker, for whom Wacker Drive is named, is buried here as well as Cyrus McCormick, who invented a harvesting machine that nearly every farmer in the country ended up using. He is buried here with several relatives including Edith Rockefeller-McCormick, who was John D. Rockefeller's daughter.

Not far from "Burnham's Island" is the mysterious half-underground crypt of Ludwig Wolfe. It is said that Wolfe was a claustrophobic man who probably also feared being buried alive. In addition to a staircase leading from his tomb up to ground level, it also has a ventilation system.

Just as Bachelor's Grove Cemetery has phantom graveyard dogs, according to legend, black-haired, green-eyed hounds guard the Wolfe mausoleum.

Equally mysterious is the imposing statue near the front of the cemetery called "Eternal Silence." This marks the grave of Dexter Graves. Laredo Taft, who also created the "Crusader," which marks the gravesite of Victor Lawson, owner of the Chicago Daily News, sculpted this massive statue of Death. It is said that a photograph cannot be taken of this monument; of course, this led to it being one of the most photographed pieces of cemetery art in Chicago.

Equipment malfunctions of every kind including camera equipment and cell phones are commonplace at haunted locations. It appears this is not currently happening at this site. Perhaps around the time it was first erected there were camera malfunctions in this area for some reason. The phenomena could have been attached to the Graves grave or another nearby resting place. There is a chance that whatever spirit or energy surrounds it is dormant now but will return in the future. So, take pictures while you can!

Another legend is attached to this dark monument. It is said that if a visitor were to stand before Death, clear one's mind, and gaze into the eyes of the statue, the visitor will catch a glimpse of their own demise. Though many feel it is a far-fetched tale, most play it safe and don't try to prove it wrong.

A more traditional ghost story comes from a part of the cemetery near the Clark Street wall. Here, one can usually find a monument dedicated to young Inez Clark. Note the qualifier "usually" that was used in the last sentence.

Inez died early on in her childhood years. Left unattended while walking about one afternoon, she was struck and instantly killed by a stray bolt of lightning. Tragedy for her family, she was dead at the age of six.

In order to memorialize and immortalize their fallen, loved child, her parents commissioned a monument. It's a life-sized carved likeness of Inez sitting on a bench and holding a parasol.

Over the years, a strange occurrence started happening: the statue would go missing only to turn up later in the same spot. Vandals and practical jokers were the first suspects for this mystery as pranks like this by disrespectful hoodlums are all too common in places of burial.

To stop this event from happening further, the cemetery constructed a glass case around the statue as protection from both the weather and vandals.

The funny thing is, the statue still went missing. The site of the monument would be found with the glass case still intact and undamaged but also empty. Now this was a mystery indeed.

Over time, one factor seemed to be common that linked each and every time the statue went missing: there was a lightning storm in progress.

An interesting coincidence without question, but with nothing guaranteed there was still little to go on until there was finally a witness. A member of the grounds crew, while making his rounds, watched a pale white girl in the same dress as the one depicted in the Inez Clark monument walking across the cemetery grounds, parasol in hand.

Killed by a lightning bolt in 1880, little Inez is still seeking shelter from the dangerous Chicago sky.

CHAPTER 13

LIFE IN JUSTICE

"Resurrection Mary"

Considered the focal point when discussing Chicago's history of paranormal events, Archer Avenue runs through Justice, Illinois with the Cal-Sag Canal to its west and a slew of cemeteries to its east.

The sheer number of haunts along this stretch of roadway is one reason for its reputation, but the intensity of most of these hauntings is the real reason this area will always be the number one draw for ghost researchers and curious parties alike for many years to come.

Simply being on this road for the first time after learning about its legendary and world famous lore is enough to bring excitement. At the same time, eyes are opened wide because it seems that nowhere is safe on this road or in the businesses and homes around it. Indeed, there isn't a square mile in this area that hasn't seen some sort of documented paranormal activity over the years. In addition, the fact that Devil's Creek, where the bodies of Barbara and Patricia Grimes were found, is nearby still resonates in the back of everyone's mind who knows about the tragic, unsolved murders.

After hearing the lore and reading up on the stories for years, a trip to Archer Avenue is like stepping onto the set of a horror film. These "film sets" include multiple cemeteries, bars, a lake, a dance hall, a church, the road itself, and a specific intersection nearby. As already seen in the Mafia chapter, there was also the brothel/speakeasy/casino across from the Willowbrook Ballroom on this same stretch of road. The number of phenomena far outnumbers the number of haunted locations.

In the following pages, you will read about the possible source to one of America's most well known urban legends. Some of the first reports of hauntings in Chicago go back to the 1830s and happened here.

Here is the only tour of Archer Avenue and the surrounding area where you won't be at high risk of meeting the paranormal face-to-face.

A Musical Mausoleum

From Archer Avenue, the 1909-established Fairmont Cemetery does not look particularly large or unique other than an impressive stone clock tower at the top of the hill. It is very pristine looking. The hill begins its large ascent immediately from Archer Avenue. The absence of fences or walls makes the cemetery appear very open and inviting.

Reaching the top of the hill, the view is quite different. The cemetery, which once looked rather small, now appears to continue infinitely to the east, which isn't visible from the road.

The cemetery's past isn't as pristine as its landscaping. One body was disposed of here very unceremoniously. In February of 1981, the body of a nineteen-year-old girl was discovered here. A jealous lover killed her.

There were at least two restless spirits here. Only one has been identified and may now be dormant. The identified spirit was found at the White Mausoleum. One of the few large monuments that occupied the hillside of the cemetery, this mausoleum was located across from the clock tower along the ridge of the hill. Mr. White was one of the first mayors of Willow Springs. The ghost of this man was seen at least once. The only documented sighting happened sometime around 1960.

What happened much more frequently at this site is an audio phenomenon. The sound is of very old music. Some link the music style to music heard during colonial times. This music seemingly emanates from within the mausoleum without any possible cause. It has been observed during all times of day, but mostly near dusk. Reasons for this are still unknown, but it is possibly music that the late mayor once enjoyed. Some reports also state that the sounds of chains rattling follow the phantom music.

Around 2003, the mausoleum sustained fire damage from vandals. Soon thereafter, it was removed completely. Time will tell if music or other phenomena will continue at the site. As of the publication of this book, no new sightings have been reported.

The other spirit seems to have either found peace or is also in a dormant stage. In the past, it was common for people driving along Archer Avenue to see a large yellow ghost light near Archer Avenue, still on cemetery land. Witnesses claim that it was about the size of a basketball and disappeared when it was approached.

This light hasn't been seen for a number of years now, but there's no telling when, or if, it will start materializing again.

One Member of the Fire Department Still on Duty

Continuing southwest from Fairmont Cemetery, there is an intersection with 95th Street that runs to the east. Traveling along 95th Street there are miles of forest preserve land before coming to Kean Avenue.

It is at this intersection where a number of animal apparitions have been sighted. If one were traveling west on 95th Street, one would have to climb a hill that peaks at the intersection of 95th and Kean. A few yards before the top of the hill there is a forest preserve horse trail crossing. Today, there are street lights, warning signs, and a lower speed limit, but before these were in place, accidents between drivers and horses were sadly frequent due to the fact the driver of the car couldn't see the horses until after they reached the top of the hill. Often it was too late.

According to reports, some of the riders of the horses involved in accidents were killed while the horses suffered major injuries and were later destroyed.

This lesser-explored area is far overshadowed by the haunts on Archer Avenue but not to those who have had the surreal experience of almost driving into a procession of horses, some with riders, crossing the street, only to have them disappear before their eyes.

Since the increased safety precautions, accidents have all but stopped, but even so, there is still someone watching over the dangerous intersection. This could-be-hero is Felix, a dog from a nearby fire department who is buried on the northwest corner of the intersection on the forest preserve land under a grave bearing his name and picture. In addition to the phantom horses, this long deceased dog is seen patrolling the area, possibly working to keep horses and their riders from harm's way.

Another unexplained phenomenon revolves around one of the warning signs that indicates that drivers are approaching a horse crossing. This sign is on the north side of 95th Street on heavily wooded forest preserve land. Though city employees have to trim overgrowth that obstructs other street signs, they never have to bother with this sign. For the purpose of keeping this important sign in plain sight for everyone, the branches and leaves are removed by unseen hands. On close observation, it is evident that cutting tools were not used to make a clean cut, but the branches were torn off instead.

The branches in question are not close to the ground. The only way someone could reach them is if they were on a ladder or otherwise elevated. The romantic notion here is that a phantom horse is eating away at the overgrowth or a horse rider who died here is still their on horse, making sure that additional names aren't added to that intersection's casualty list.

A Very Public Ghost Light

Driving back to the west along 95th Street, one will find the largest lake in Pulaski Woods, Maple Lake. It sits just off to the left side of the road.

It is at this lake where a ghost light has been seen with surprising regularity. It is mostly reported as being red in color, but this is not always the case.

"There was something glowing and moving in and out," remembered Pete Crapia of his own encounter with the ghost light. "It was mostly white with a hint of yellow. It illuminated the lake."

There have been investigations into the source of the light, but no conclusions were made other than that there were no natural explanations for it. A number guesses relating to the supernatural are proposed, but nothing is proven.

The popular legend behind the story claims that a person was decapitated in a freak boating accident and is still looking for their head in the lake. The light that is seen comes from a red lantern that the headless person is holding while searching the lake. Overlooking the fact that it would be quite hard for someone to find anything without the use of their head and the uselessness of a light for someone with no vision, this is the legend that sticks to the location.

Though a body was found in Maple Lake in 1991, the ghost light had been seen there for a number of years prior. Other theories link the ghost light to victims of machinery accidents in the 1930s, targets of Mafia hits, and the deaths of workers on the nearby Cal-Sag Canal. Others link the peculiar light to Native Americans that lived in the hills that line the lake.

These are all possibilities. Deaths were actually very common in major construction efforts like that of the nearby Cal-Sag Canal and the Sanitary and Ship Canal before strict safety regulations were put into place. The construction of the Illinois and Michigan Canal is another story full of accidental deaths, murders, and even executions on the spot.

According to Chicago-area history professor John Laudermilk, the opening of the Illinois and Michigan Canal around 1820 was supposed to be "the thing that would make Chicago hit the big time." That wasn't the case because the canal opened during the same year that the first railroad came to Chicago, thereby shifting Chicago's main method of transporting goods.

Laudermilk goes on to explain that while everyone wants to think that people came to America from all over the world and magically got along right away, it just didn't happen like that. Long hours of strenuous digging combined with working alongside different ethnicities often lead to fights. These fights occasionally ended up in death. Crew managers would then take it upon themselves to bring justice to the killer instantly by impromptu hangings. Conservative estimations of killings and executions during the construction of the Illinois and Michigan Canal place the number in the dozens.

Reportedly, one of the best locations to view the ghost light is down a small and dark side street called Wolf Road. A number of scenic points where parking is permitted to enjoy the view dot the side of the road. The light is mostly seen near sunset and throughout the night.

The "Monk's Castle"

Getting back on Archer Avenue and going south into the little township of Lemont, just barely in Du Page County, a small but impressive church and graveyard can easily be missed by passing motorists if they don't look out for the "Historical Marker Ahead" sign.

The atmosphere seems like the setting for a fairy tale. The church stoically sits atop a gravestone-laden hill. The rolling hills on either side are where ghost lights have been seen floating among the gravestones that dot the hill.

Only about four miles in a straight line from Devil's Creek is St. James Cemetery and Church at Sag Bridge (sometimes referred to as St. James of the Sag). This is older than any cemetery in Cook County, hidden away in the midst of the Palos-Sag Valley Forest Preserve. It is actually at this site where the earliest reports of hauntings along Archer Avenue, and possibly among the first in the Chicago area, took place.

The very first reports started in the late 1830s to the early 1840s. The ghosts appeared to be phantom monks along the Cal-Sag Canal. Soon they were seen wandering along the St. James Cemetery hillside as Gregorian chanting floated through the air. These hauntings are continuing over one and a half centuries later. One of the more recent and widely talked about events occurred when police officers chased these monks through the cemetery after dark, thinking that they

were vandals. The phantom monks proved the police wrong by vanishing. The police later noted that they thought it was strange that these suspected vandals seemed to glide up the hill while the officers had a difficult time tripping over gravestones during the pursuit.

One of the earliest published newspaper accounts dates back to the late 1890s when two musicians were spending the evening in a gathering room that once stood down the hill from the church after a long day of performing. One of the musicians was awakened by the unmistakable sound of galloping horses. When the man went to the window to investigate, all he found was that the sound was intensifying, but no source for the sound could be found. After the sound died out, the musician who heard the sounds retreated to tell his partner what happened. As he was doing this, the sound started up again. This time, both musicians went to the window and found a woman standing outside the cemetery gates. Before they could speak out to her, she walked up to and through the fence surrounding the cemetery. Again, the sound of the horses faded away. For the third time, the sounds restarted. This time a horse-drawn carriage appeared. There was no driver visible.

The horses were white in color, and reportedly, a bright light emitted from their foreheads. The driverless carriage approached the woman, who floated towards the road, sinking into the ground as the carriage passed.

The spectral show they were witnessing was not yet over. The sound of the running horses filled the air a fourth time as the woman reappeared in the road along the cemetery. This time when the horse-drawn carriage arrived, the woman called out to it before sinking into the ground once more.

Many point to an event that happened sometime before 1890 when two people were going to run off together from the church. As the man appeared with a carriage to meet the woman, the horses bolted and crushed the girl to death by tipping over the coach. The man was also killed in the freak accident.

The site has tremendous historical value as far as paranormal activity is concerned. Visiting with a digital camera can be difficult because there are literally hundreds of beautiful pictures one can find at the location. Since little has changed here in the past hundred years, it is easy to envision the entire phantom carriage event while standing on the exact location of the strange occurrence.

As darkness begins to fall, nerves find themselves on edge. The parking lot is well lit which can be a distraction since reflections off gravestones can fool people into momentarily thinking they saw a ghost light.

Archer Avenue will always be thought of as the home of Chicago's most famous ghost, Resurrection Mary, but there is one unexplainable sight that is far more harrowing and intimidating.

The tale of the vanishing woman and the driverless carriage appears to have been a one-time haunting, but a similar apparition has been seen through the area starting from St. James of the Sag Cemetery.

This apparition is not of a driverless horse-drawn carriage but a driverless horse-drawn hearse. This bizarre sight is accompanied by sounds including the heavy breathing of the horses and the pounding of the ground beneath their feet. This hearse has been seen in Lemont, Justice, Downers Grove Township, and Hickory Hills, Illinois. Innumerable petrified witnesses have seen this over the years, and the most unfortunate have found themselves so close to the phenomena that they are able to look into the large windows that are on either side of this black oak hearse. What they see is the dismaying sight of a child's coffin. The coffin is said to emit a bright light.

Though the hearse begins at St. James of the Sag Cemetery, it visits three others including Resurrection Cemetery.

A Tough Pill for Skeptics to Swallow

While nonbelievers can scoff at eyewitness accounts of the paranormal, chalking it up to overactive imaginations and hallucination, physical evidence left from one of Chicago's most celebrated paranormal events isn't as easy to dismiss.

The most well known, but not necessarily the most haunted, cemetery is Resurrection Cemetery located north of Fairmont Cemetery on Archer Avenue.

It is at this cemetery where the body of Mary Bregovy is buried. It is believed that she awakens time and again from that grave to make her famous appearances.

Mary Bregovy was a dance enthusiast in life. She would frequently go to the Oh Henry Ballroom in the 1930s to dance into the early hours of the following day. On one of those nights, March 10, 1934, she left the ballroom with a group of friends to return to her home. She never made it. The car she was a passenger in struck an El train support beam on Wacker Drive.

After her funeral, she was laid to rest in section MM of Resurrection Cemetery.

Not long after her interment, a grounds keeper on duty after dark watched the ghost of a young blonde woman wearing white walk through the cemetery. The grounds keeper quickly identified this phantom as being the ghost of Bregovy. One problem though, Bregovy was a brunette not a blonde.

The die was cast, however, and the name "Resurrection Mary" stuck. Unfortunately, this also led to many researchers only investigating leads with the first name Mary.

That previously mentioned piece of evidence is Resurrection Cemetery's damaged front gate. In the 1970s, a taxi driver was passing the cemetery when he noticed a woman standing within the cemetery gates after sundown. Thinking that someone was accidentally locked inside after closing, the cab driver continued to the police to inform them of the woman inside the cemetery. When the police arrived, there was no woman, but the bars were pried apart and there were hand imprints sunken into the metal.

Quickly, curiosity-seekers gathered to view the bars. Cemetery administrators removed the bars to get them fixed and prevent further investigation by paranormal sleuths. After the bars were straightened, they were reattached to the cemetery's front gate. Strangely, when it was repainted, the white paint wouldn't take to the bars that were damaged by Resurrection Mary. The cemetery then painted the gate green, but it was still obviously darker where her hands had been. No one could explain why. In 2003, the front gate was repainted gold. Finally, they were able to make the bars one uniform color. However, the bars in question are still identifiable since there are imperfections in them and welding marks are still evident from where they were removed.

Like the staff of Dominican University, Resurrection Cemetery's administration has their own benign answer to the strange mystery. The explanation from the cemetery states that a truck accidentally backed into the gate. That could explain the bending of the bars, but there is no reason given for why paint didn't stick to them or how a truck striking the bars caused what appeared to be the impression of hand prints in the iron.

Asking the staff won't get you any further as there is also a gag order placed on staff of the cemetery regarding ghosts, Resurrection Mary, and even Mary Bregovy, whose gravestone has been removed to discourage curiosity-seekers.

Ever since the sightings began in the 1930s, everyone has known her as Mary Bregovy, but that is highly doubted by those who have taken the time to take a closer look. In addition to the descriptions not matching, Bregovy died in a car accident while in a car. Regarding the phantom in question, most signs point to this woman dying after being struck by a car.

As we will discuss in the following pages, a ghost also attributed to Resurrection Mary appears in the street, reenacting being struck by a car over and over again in the vein of a residual haunting.

There is also the very distinct possibility that there is more than one ghost haunting the cemetery, the road, and a number of area dance halls.

The menacing front gate of Resurrection Cemetery still stands for people to place their hands on the same bars where a ghost reportedly placed her hands and pried them apart with superhuman strength. It's an interesting feeling knowing that you are standing where the infamous Resurrection Mary stood and touching the bars she did.

Within the cemetery and to the left of the gate is a road that leads to the communal mausoleum. This mausoleum is also the site of paranormal events. The lights turn on and off of their own volition, and music emanates from the large building. Searches for faulty wiring or other culprits resulted in the finding that there is no electrical or other feasible explanation for why the lights turn on and off. The music that is heard is likely the same music that plays throughout the building on speakers, further linking this to being an electrical malfunction of indeterminate origin.

Where the Dead Still Dance

In addition to the random encounters along the roadside and within the cemetery, Resurrection Mary has also had several more intimate encounters with living persons. The first person to meet Mary after her death was Jerry Palus when he spent an enchanting evening dancing with her at the Liberty Grove Dance Hall in 1936, which has since been destroyed. After spending much of the night dancing, Jerry and his younger brother Chester offered to give the girl a ride home. The girl directed the Palus brothers past the main Archer Avenue entrance to Resurrection Cemetery, and then had them pull over. The strangely quiet woman now explained that she had to leave, but where she went, they could not follow. At this, the young woman left the car and walked towards the front gate of the cemetery, which she walked to, then through, before disappearing completely. It was at this point Jerry realized the woman had felt cold to the touch during their dance together.

As time went on, these stories continued with little variation. A man would spend an evening dancing with a quiet girl. At the end of the night he would offer her a ride home, and she would comply. While riding, she would give vague directions but always led the driver to pass the front gates of Resurrection Cemetery. Once in front of the gates, she would either vanish or ask the driver to pull over. She would exit the car, walk towards the front gates, and vanish into the darkness after walking through them.

The Liberty Grove Hall and Ballroom was the location where Jerry met the famous phantom, but her legend was earned a little farther south on Archer Avenue at the Oh Henry Ballroom, which has since been renamed the Willowbrook Ballroom.

The Willowbrook is mostly used for themed dance sessions, lessons, and special events. It is easily identifiable by the large vintage pink neon Willowbrook sign. Generally, curiosity seekers are turned away, though they have warmed to organized tours of late.

During my first visit to the ballroom in the summer of 1999, it was closed. Since we couldn't explore Mary's preferred dance floor, we did the next best thing. After looking around the front entrance, we walked along the front of the building to look into the three large picture windows with help of an infrared camera. As I was looking into the third window, I saw a figure standing in the room. I didn't jump, but my heart did stop for a moment until I realized that there were mirrors lining the far side of the ballroom. I turned with some embarrassment to tell my two friends, Jeff Lord and Jason Jacobs, of my near heart attack. Mid-way through my story, I was interrupted by two knocks on the large picture window that was just two feet away from me. As this happened, I jumped to the side, dropping all of the notes I was holding and nearly dropping the camera as well.

I can honestly say that I can't explain what happened without bringing up the fact that this dance hall is reportedly haunted. If I was concentrating really hard and hoping to hear something, it would make sense that my mind would let me think I did. However, the noise actually interrupted me telling the story. Also, there are no blinds, plants, or other objects close enough to make contact with the inside of the window. On the outside, I was the only person standing near the window and was actually looking at the only two other people present when the sound happened. There was no evidence that the sound was caused by Resurrection Mary, whoever she is, but I can say someone from the other side very well could have made contact with us that night.

This is actually a good example about the state of mind one should have in order to experience a paranormal event. Initially, my defenses were up since I was in the paranormal epicenter of Chicago, snooping around a notoriously haunted and vacant dance hall after dark. However, once I had the small scare and relief, I dropped my defenses. Almost immediately, I was joined by another spirit.

Mary's Other Hot Spot

Not too far north on Archer Avenue and much closer to the front gates of Resurrection Cemetery is Chet's Melody Lounge. When Resurrection Mary is in the mood for dancing and the Willowbrook is closed, she takes refuge here. The restaurant and bar welcomes curiosity-seekers who come in to sit at the table Resurrection Mary sat at, which is directly in front of the bar near the door. They can also purchase a Resurrection Mary T-shirt or pop a quarter into the jukebox to hear *The Ballad of Resurrection Mary*, an ode to the famous phantom penned by a local. To further emphasize the paranormal, the staff occasionally leaves a drink at the end of the bar as an open invitation to any ghosts that may be passing by. The drink is, of course, a Bloody Mary.

This small and unassuming pub is overflowing with character. From the cast of willing storytellers on each side of the bar to the decorative signs indicating the bathrooms, the experience is a pure delight. Within minutes of breaching the subject of ghosts, people up and down the bar exchange stories of the supernatural; many of them are first-hand accounts.

On one occasion, Mary Czerwinski was visiting Chet's when she observed a woman leaving the women's bathroom. This woman appeared pale white and shaking as if she was in shock. When prompted by Mary, the woman was unable to answer her questions. Mary immediately thought the woman may have had a terrifying encounter with the paranormal, though there was no known history of hauntings associated with the bathroom and the woman wasn't willing to talk.

This encounter could have been dismissed as simply an over-served customer coming out of the bathroom and nothing more. However, on Halloween of 2000, I visited this site with psychic Denise Guzzardo and a small group of people, and some new information came to light.

Music was loud and the bar was packed with people celebrating the holiday, but the second Denise walked through the door she was drawn instantly to the women's bathroom.

After entering it, she quickly learned that the spirit of a male with an Irish last name was still residing at Chet's. This man met a quick and untimely death. He did not commit suicide, and he did not die within the building. He was simply a regular who decided to continue patronizing this establishment.

Knowledgeable about the history of the site and a bartender for the past two years, at the time, Steve was able to deduce that there may be other reasons for the women's bathroom to be actively haunted. All he could say was, "I know that something has happened back there [in the bathroom], but as an employee, I'm not allowed to talk about it."

We were invited to view the basement where, according to Steve and other employees, most of the supernatural activity takes place. The basement is strictly off limits to the public and is rarely, if ever, photographed.

Steve talked about strange feelings and the typical stories of "things that go bump in the night." Denise picked up two areas of high energy. One was beneath the staircase, and the other was near the back of the basement where she accurately guessed that they have experienced mechanical malfunctions.

As we were wrapping things up, one person in our group asked, "Why does it smell like vinegar all of a sudden? Did I miss something?"

Everyone looked at him, puzzled. He then instructed another member of the group to lean into his airspace to smell what he called a "super strong" smell of vinegar.

Standing right next to him had no effect, but leaning into what seemed to be an invisible column of vinegar-scented air resulted in picking up the scent that was so potent it was nauseating.

One by one we all took turns standing on that location to smell the overpowering and pungent smell of vinegar. Somehow, the area of the odor was well defined. There wasn't a vinegar spill or even unopened cases of vinegar in the basement. Even if there was, the smell would spread throughout the room, unlike how this scent was completely concentrated in a definite area, much like a cold spot.

Now in the car and about to leave, we were stopped by a woman who came knocking on our window. She told us that as we pulled into the parking lot, her young daughter took a picture of the car with a Polaroid camera. The instantly developed picture showed the car veiled by bright pink and orange colors.

We decided to get out of the car and take a group picture on the spot with the Polaroid camera. When this picture was developed, there were five green orbs of varying sizes apparent. Was it simply a malfunctioning camera? It seems possible, though the orbs were completely different and in different places in the frame. Denise tends to think the camera was picking up on different energy present.

Chet's Melody Lounge is most commonly associated with Resurrection Mary, but it appears there is a small cast of spirits around this establishment with a dark past.

A Charged Road

Starting in the mid 1930s, drivers along Archer Avenue began filing police reports claiming that there was a young woman running along the street attempting to jump onto the running boards of their car. From the 1930s to the present day, this figure has been seen walking or dancing along the stretch of grass between Archer Avenue and the cemetery fence. Other unsuspecting drivers would have their cars completely invaded. With the car still in motion, the phantom woman opens the door, enters the car, and starts giving directions.

The most horrifying of Resurrection Mary's exploits includes darting out into traffic and being struck by the unsuspecting motorist. The desperate drivers often find themselves at Chet's Melody Lounge calling the police. This happens day and night and is witnessed by multiple people at the same time, including drivers not involved with the apparent accident.

Sometimes the ghost disappears on impact, but other times the struck pedestrian remains on the ground until she is approached. On one occasion, this suicidal hitchhiker was struck and witnessed by multiple people including a police officer who immediately called for an ambulance. The woman, wearing a white dress, lay motionless in the middle of Archer Avenue surrounded by a growing puddle of her own blood for long minutes before the ambulance finally arrived. It took the paramedics approaching her to finally make her vanish from sight, leaving nothing behind but an astounded and confused crowd.

It does not take any great thought to realize that Archer Avenue is abnormally active when it comes to paranormal happenings. The reason for this may very well be the same reason Milwaukee Avenue in Libertyville boasts a number of haunted locations. Archer Avenue was most likely a ley line used by Native Americans, so it may be considered sacred ground.

While this may explain why Archer Avenue is particularly active, it may also explain why a number of other locations throughout Chicago are haunted. If it is the ground itself that is considered sacred, then the ground may keep these characteristics no matter where they are. An example of moved sacred ground can be found on the Hawaiian Islands where tourists attempting to take lava rocks home as souvenirs have been followed by horrendous misfortune attributed to Pele, the God of Fire.

With these stories in mind, it is very noteworthy that this sacred ground was broken and the limestone that was mined from it was used to build the nearby St. James Church, the Chicago Water Tower, and the Beverly Unitarian Church. It just so happens that they are all considered among the most notoriously haunted buildings in the Chicago area.

A Cemetery with an Aura

Many believe that the driverless hearse that is seen at St. James of the Sag Cemetery is destined for the troublesome Archer Woods Cemetery. This cemetery is located on Kean Avenue, just blocks east of Archer Avenue.

Archer Woods Cemetery also contains a spirit known as the "Sobbing Woman." She apparently walks along the wooded areas around Archer Woods Cemetery wearing white and crying uncontrollably. Unfortunately, not much effort has yet been made to find the story behind the sobbing woman and why she appears to be doomed to great sadness for the rest of her existence.

Far more harrowing than the story of the sobbing woman is the story of the driverless hearse. Despite the oft-grotesque details regarding Resurrection Mary flinging herself in front of moving vehicles, an encounter with the driverless hearse is just as uninvited.

The thumping sound of the horses' hooves upon the ground, the mad panting of the determined, deceased animals, and the rickety sound of the hearse jolting from the uneven ground apparently ends at this unusual cemetery. However, it is often seen in the woods between Kean Avenue and Archer Avenue as well as running along Archer Avenue's shoulder between Resurrection Cemetery and the St. James Church and Cemetery at Sag Bridge. The phantom hearse is also seen along the Cal-Sag Bridge, which is just barely to the southwest of St. James in Downers Grove Township.

Upon entering the front gate, one becomes immediately cautious of the rough grounds and deteriorating roads. Many of the trees are dead, and mud covers most of the two roads that traverse the cemetery. To further heighten the uneasy feeling, a family of black cats guards the front office. There is a basic feeling that all is not right here. After getting out of the car and walking around, it is apparent that these suspicions are unfortunately correct.

After visiting the cemetery in 2008, it was apparent that improvements have been made, but this was the first positive sign in the nearly ten years of frequenting the location.

Much of the area is overgrown, and a broken-down red truck sat near the entrance, rusting away for many years. The feeling of uneasiness only grows after noticing the lack of security. Although the cemetery may be considered "closed" at dusk, the front gates remain open throughout the night.

The more one looks around, the worse things look. During a visit in 1999, we found masses of headstones that appeared as though they had been tossed aside. They weren't new headstones that simply hadn't yet been placed. Most of them were dated between the 1940s and 1980s. Some were even older. For some reason, these people weren't being treated well after death, which makes it easy to understand why this is a haunted site.

The typical story of a spirit making his or her presence known is often because they aren't being respected or properly remembered after death. Such is the case at Bachelor's Grove Cemetery, and some believe Death's Alley will lose its haunted reputation if a historical marker is ever placed at the location.

During our first visit to Archer Woods Cemetery, Jason, Jeff, and I walked around noticing the large number of trees that were dead although there was no drought that year. Then, something truly bizarre caught our gaze. It was a child's stuffed animal hanging from a tree limb by a noose. Upon further inspection of the same tree, we found a Mrs. Buttersworth syrup bottle, also being hanged, and a stuffed bear nailed to the tree. The really curious thing was how high everything was placed. This was a very large tree, and the first limb was easily over fifteen feet off the ground. The place where the bear was nailed to the tree had to have been twenty or more feet from the ground. How someone could get up there was beyond us.

Obviously, we were far from relaxed. As far as we were concerned, this was evidence of cultists practicing their craft or at the very least some people with bad intentions who visit the cemetery.

Not far from that site, we came across over a dozen empty cement vaults that were lined up against a fence. It was apparent that nothing was sensitive enough to be kept behind the scenes in this cemetery. Names of people who would be placed in the vaults were written with black magic marker on the front, facing a road for all to see.

We continued our walk to the area of the back woods. This was the area we hoped to bump into the sobbing woman. After walking a distance, we stopped to listen to a noise. After wondering if it was the sound of a whining cry, we decided that it was most likely the sound of children playing in the distance. Distant noises and lights, when in the heat of the moment and especially at night, can make it easy to jump to a false conclusion.

A walk though this unlit and nearly abandoned cemetery around midnight is a far more harrowing experience. Tall weeds poking in front of a flashlight cast a long shadow that, at first, appears to be any number of things. Then, the overgrown brush has a tendency to move before sets of hoofed feet galloping across the ground. Fortunately for us, these were not horse hooves but deer. The normally mundane sight of a deer becomes nearly traumatizing when on the lookout for a team of phantom horses.

Speaking with two Hickory Hills police officers, we were informed about their own stories around Archer Woods Cemetery. According to them, they knew an officer who was called out to Archer Woods Cemetery after dark to investigate a disturbance call that was phoned in by a resident living near the cemetery. As the officer was looking around the cemetery grounds, a semi-transparent woman dressed in white ran past him screaming. As the story goes, that officer then retired or transferred.

It seems as though the sobbing woman does more than just cry. The intense screaming of the woman was blood chilling enough to compel this law enforcement officer to leave and never come back.

Upon questioning the police of the credibility of the cemetery itself, one of the men said that he had seen bodies exposed, coming from the ground. At one time he also entered the gaudy green garage only to find about twenty bodies in coffins that hadn't yet been placed.

The police also confessed that it was very common to do a routine check of the cemetery to find people wearing black and engaging in cult activities.

Since it is well known that cults and cultists frequent this location, it seems that security of the bodies should be of high priority. Noting that at Bachelor's Grove Cemetery people have gone through the extreme measures of digging up the earth, moving the cement vault lid, and then opening up the coffin to get to the body, it seems unreal that human remains would ever be left unguarded while at a cemetery. As Mary Czerwinski and I unfortunately found out, this is just not the case.

In the summer of 2000 near the back of the cemetery, we found an area that appeared to be under renovation. There were a number of pieces of plywood scattered around the grounds. We were more than a little upset to find that these pieces of plywood were covering holes in the ground where uncovered vaults lie. There were some vaults placed in the six-foot deep holes that didn't even have the plywood hiding it. If a cultist or some other undesirables wanted to get to these bodies, they had easy access.

Understandably, it is in this area where strange and uncomfortable feelings are felt. Whether it is a psychic impression or simply the actual emotion felt by being in such a dismaying place remains to be seen. Either case can be made with relative ease.

The cast of the *Pete McMurray Show* and psychic Denise Guzzardo also visited this location on Halloween of 2000. Denise picked up a number of active spirits in the area, but surprisingly, she claims that there weren't any negative or upset spirits present. However, she did not visit the farthest back part of the cemetery where the most recent expressions of disrespect were apparent.

Two people in the group that night saw a man peeking around a mausoleum as if he were spying on us. Unfortunately, the man left before Denise was able to make any type of contact with him.

Later, an intensely bright white ghost light appeared directly in front of us just a few feet away. Denise saw the light directly, and I saw the light reflect off a grave stone right next to it.

Archer Woods Cemetery is not an abandoned cemetery like Bachelor's Grove is, but in other senses they are all too similar.

Despite the detestable nature of Archer Woods Cemetery, which, again, has improved but is far from ideal, the area of Summit, Justice, and Lemont, Illinois along Archer Avenue is a wonderful place filled with the fascinating tales of the people who lived there.

CHAPTER 14

THE NORTH SIDE
AND BEYOND

"The Sunnybrook Asylum"

SLIMPICTURES.COM/CHAPTER14.HTM

In the land north of the city, there is less traffic and the streetlights are fewer, but the history is just as rich and impressive. The mysterious past of Lake and McHenry Counties is often steeped with shocking, sad, and horrendous events.

This is already the area that claims to hold the remains of America's most legendary witch, Mary Worth. Only a street corner separates the fantastical story of "The Gate" and the startlingly real occurrences at St. Sava's Serbian Monastery. Legitimately haunted houses dot the landscape of these two extreme north Illinois counties.

This area also claims the most haunted area north of Justice, Cuba Road. Lake County's Northshore held two very haunted colleges in Lake Forest, while just south of there, a famous and exclusive haunted cemetery as well as the arguably most haunted military installation in America hold a number of stories. Both of these locations are covered here along with another tale of Egyptian spirits staking their claim in Illinois.

Also, read about the house with the longest and strongest tradition of regular hauntings and quite possibly the most psychically active and haunted commercial building in America: a long-vacant asylum.

A Critic Even After Death

Traveling north along Northwest Highway before crossing South Street in Woodstock, a sign comes into view on the right hand side of the road. After following the sign and the series of arrows thereafter through a number of slow and small streets, one eventually finds the heart of the small town. Finding a place to park on the cobblestone street, one is transported to a different place and time: Punxsutawney, Pennsylvania on Ground Hog's Day. It is in this area where Bill Murray relived the day in the Harold Ramis movie of the same name.

Chester Gould, a local and the creator of the *Dick Tracy* comic strip, is celebrated with a museum on one side while a beautiful park and gazebo comprise the focal point of this town square. On another side stands a beautiful and large building complete with a bell tower reaching into the sky. This is the Woodstock Opera House.

Opened as a theater in 1890, the Woodstock Opera House offers seasons of regular plays and musicals as well as special shows such as festivals of music and dance as well as Christmas-oriented shows in December.

Before the opera house took on its current form, it was a multi-purpose building. Among the functions it served was as a fire station. This is still apparent by the garage doors in the back of the building, which is the area where sets are now constructed. In addition to a fire department, the building also contained a library and the city hall. Even at the time of its construction, the second floor contained an auditorium for performances.

Today, the opera house is solely a theater. The venue underwent a large-scale renovation, finally being completed in 1999. When the building reopened in 1997, it did so with the new title of the Woodstock Opera House Community Center to thank those in the community who donated the half-million dollars used to renovate the building.

At first, the auditorium was used by traveling shows, but eventually shows were put on by the local Todd School for Boys. Most critics point to *Citizen Kane* as the greatest film ever made, but it may have never come to life without the Woodstock Opera House. Orson Welles, the writer, director, and star of the film got his early acting start on the stage of the Woodstock Opera House. A number of other actors appeared here after graduating from the Goodman School. Included are Geraldine Page who appeared in several films and television series including *Your Show of Shows*, *Night Gallery*, and *Kojack* as well as Betsey Palmer who appeared in the *Friday the 13th* series and Rod Serling's *Studio One*. In addition, Lois Nettleton of *Best Little Whorehouse in Texas*, Tom Bosley who was Harold on *Happy Days*, and even Paul Newman of *Coolhand Luke* and *Butch Cassidy and the Sundance Kid* worked their way up the ranks through the Woodstock Opera House.

Shelley Berman, a mainstay in television appearing in everything from *The Twilight Zone* and *The Mary Tyler Moore Show* to *Friends* and *Entourage,* witnessed a strange event in the theater while rehearsing. As he was

finishing, an entire row of seats in the balcony went up, one at a time, as if people were getting up and leaving.

This event was attributed to the theater ghost of Elvira, who is reportedly a former actress at the theater who jumped from the bell tower to her death, much like Bill Murray's character did in *Groundhog Day.* Other stories claim that she hanged herself from the belfry as a result of a personally difficult life coupled with bad reviews.

While "Elvira," as she has been nicknamed by theater staff, was the victim of poor reviews, she is just as critical when watching other performances. From one particular seat, sighs and groans of approval or disapproval are heard. The seat where these sounds seem to originate, DD113 in the balcony, has an honorary plaque bearing the name Elvira on it.

On at least one occasion, a visual apparition was evident. A black outline of a human form sent a stagehand running when it was seen coming down a spiral staircase.

According to Steve Leech, who has worked backstage at the Woodstock Opera House, just before every performance something breaks. It is always attributed to Elvira.

The theater staff that we spoke with were entirely knowledgeable about Elvira but were nonbelievers. This is strongly a "see-it-to-believe-it" case since the events are usually minor and there is no hard evidence to support or deny that a suicide took place at the opera house.

Paranormal Investigator Patricia DiPrima has concluded that the story is one made up for entertainment value by Shelley Berman that has taken on a life of its own. Dobie Maxwell, a stand-up comic and host of *The Mothership Connection*, a radio show on the paranormal, knowing Berman, sees it as a very real possibility.

The Story of the Aviator

Calvary Cemetery is located in southern Evanston on Sheridan Road. The front gates overlook Lake Michigan, though they are typically closed near sunset. It is at this location where one of the few ghost stories with a happy ending takes place.

In addition to the haunting, the cemetery is arguably the most beautiful in the region. The cemetery is the final resting place for such famous names as Edward Hines of Hines Lumber; John M. Smith of John M. Smith Homemaker; and Charles Comiskey, the first owner of the Chicago White Sox and the creator of baseball's American League. In addition, a player in baseball's inaugural season, Jimmy Hallinan, "Lords of the Levee" aldermen Michael Kenna, and "Bath House John" Coughlin are all buried here. Such high-class names as Chicago Mayors Edward J. Kelly, Carter Harison, William Dever, and Edward Dunne as well as the aristocratic Cuneo family inhabit the cemetery.

Cemetery visitors have a lot to enjoy at the site as the dual grave of Artie and Willie, Josie Lyon, and the angel-flanked family plot of the Lynch family are all museum-worthy pieces of art.

During the time of the Second World War, ships in Lake Michigan were transformed to aircraft carriers. On these transformed ships, pilots practiced landings and takeoffs to simulate landings at sea. Being training exercises, there was a rate of failure. From time to time, a plane would fall victim to a water landing. Even more rarely, the plane would sink to the bottom of the lake with the pilot trapped inside. The bodies of these unfortunate pilots who drowned to death while strapped into their cockpits were sometimes never found.

Between the 1940s and the 1960s, a man was often seen struggling in the choppy waters of Chicago's grand lake. After loosing his battle in the cold water, the man would sink only to reappear near the shoreline. He would then make his way out of the water, revealing his pilot's uniform and still-packed parachute draped with seaweed. He would negotiate his way up the piles of jagged white boulders along the east side of Sheridan Road. After scaling the boulders, he would stumble across Sheridan's four lanes while frantic drivers swerved out of the way the entire time. Upon crossing the road, he would find himself at the closed entrance to Calvary Cemetery. There, he would pace back and forth as crowds of onlookers observed.

For those who follow ghost stories, this is not the most unheard of story. Frequently, spirits make themselves known after death because they desire a respectable grave site. If this unknown pilot, nicknamed "The Aviator" and more colorfully as "Seaweed Charlie," was one of the few people who weren't recovered from crash wreckage, he obviously didn't get the burial he hoped for.

The visual occurrence of him drowning, reemerging, and walking to the cemetery gate happened for a little over twenty years, starting at the time of his death.

According to local lore, the haunting stopped one night when the grounds keeper for Calvary Cemetery accidentally left the front gates open. Popular belief states that "The Aviator" approached this cemetery and walked through the now open gates to find his own resting-place. This military person hasn't been seen since. Amazingly, he was able to find his own peace, without the help of living people.

Today, one can still walk the path "The Aviator" did. Standing at Sheridan Road, opposite the cemetery gates, one can look down at the water where he was viewed drowning on countless days, including the day he first drowned. The waves are usually calm, splashing water upon the rocks. This is the same water that filled the unknown man's lungs and stole the life from his body.

Despite the beauty of the cemetery and the reality that hauntings are no longer attributed to the site, it is still possible to leave the site at an accelerated pace at night.

This was the first location we covered for the video documentary *Voices from the Grave*. Jason Jacobs, Jeff Lord, and I found ourselves here after dark wanting to get back to the car faster than we had left it. We walked along the east gate pausing only to look at eerily sad statues of children looking out at us from behind the cemetery gate and spiders profiled in the moonlight. We also had our first false alarm when Jason thought he saw a ghost light. Upon further inspection it was simply a headlight reflecting off of a head stone.

Sheridan's Military Fort / Luxury Housing Complex

Fort Sheridan was one of the first major military bases in the United States. The cemetery on the property holds the bodies of three soldiers who rode with General Custer at the Battle of the Little Bighorn in 1876 while the fort itself trained soldiers for fighting in the Spanish-American War, World War I, and World War II.

The fort, established in 1872 on 729 acres of land, is named after the great Lieutenant-General Philip Sheridan, who captured the Shenandoah Valley for the Union during the Civil War. Sheridan was also the man put in charge of securing the "Burnt District" after the Great Chicago Fire. Sheridan led his men from the fort to the city. The path he took was later turned into Sheridan Road. It has since been expanded northward.

Unfortunately, government cutbacks forced the closing of the fort in the early 1990s. It stayed mostly vacant for several years, primarily being used to store equipment. Today, the vast majority of the land has been converted to an upscale community. Empty lots on what used to be training and exercise grounds now sell for $300,000 per one-third acre while one can purchase officer's quarters for over one million dollars.

Fort Sheridan is located between Lake Forest and Evanston in the small town of Highwood, which was once in the *Guinness Book of World Records* for having the most bars per square mile.

Sadly, most of the area that was once a mighty military base is now a community of mass-produced homes and condos. Despite ninety-four of the buildings gaining landmark status and the area being named a National Historic District, many of the buildings have still been removed, and the remaining buildings have been compromised by unnatural surroundings. The iconic clock tower still stands, but the building itself has been turned into a number of condos.

With so many active spirits, only a location with such a rich historical significance can overcome this much of a haunted reputation.

Building one was the fort's hospital. It is said that at this location a custodian is still on duty. The sound of him banging on the furnace pipes is still heard. A short and stocky man has been seen walking into the cellar there. From the basement, we venture to the top floor where the image of a nurse is often seen in an upper window.

Probably the most haunted building is building number thirty-one. This building served as the clubhouse, mess hall, and El Morocco Lounge. It is here that the most famous phantom of the fort is seen. She is known as the "Woman in Orange."

She appears in a vibrant orange dress and bears a striking resemblance to Mamie Eisenhower. In addition to appearing as a full form in front of people, swirling orange mists appear in the places where the woman is most often seen.

Psychics who have visited the clubhouse claim that the woman in orange was the wife of a senior military official who used to enjoy spending a lot of time in the building. In reality, there was a woman who fits the description and is buried at the cemetery, which is at the northernmost part of the property.

In addition to the woman in orange, footsteps are commonly heard walking across the main floor. The sound of objects being thrown around are heard in the basement, but when investigated, nothing is out of place.

An interesting vision is seen on an amazingly regular basis. At six o'clock in the morning, a cook reports to work and is seen walking up the back staircase to the clubhouse kitchen.

The cast of characters continues to grow throughout the area. On the east side is where a number of houses are. There, a man appearing to be a blacksmith occasionally wanders into a house. In one of the previous barracks buildings, a drill sergeant from the 1800s still barks out orders to surprised and startled witnesses. Reports have not yet surfaced regarding whether the barracks building, now altered, is still the home base for the drill sergeant.

Phantom accordion music originates from the site of a former German POW camp while a muffled German conversation is often overheard from the barracks.

It isn't entirely known how many of these hauntings were reported when the location was still a military base, but it is known that men who were living there decades ago first reported this phantom conversation.

Patton Road runs the length of the property parallel with Sheridan Road. It is here that the shadowy outline of a running horse has been seen. It is also here that an army photographer was taking pictures for a calendar and had the image of a man appear when the photograph was developed.

A 1974 government short on the effects of gamma rays on Marigolds was filmed in an auditorium on the grounds. The director, Frank Conway, claimed that there was a poltergeist that would hide props and cause havoc. The lighting director agreed, citing that lights would burn out almost as soon as they were replaced.

In addition, a soldier in Civil War garb is seen near some basement steps, while a maintenance man is seen in several buildings. This man was apparently shot and killed at the fort on accident during World War II.

A couple of paranormal events happened in the late 1990s and was first reported in 2003 on SlimPictures.com by a patrolman for the fort:

> There is a story of police officers seeing a woman wearing a white dress sitting on a gravestone. When the officers approached, she ran from them, exiting through the entrance of the cemetery, vanishing into the nearby woods next to the golf course. This has happened twice now and, believe me, it is still talked about by officers. The first incident happened around Thanksgiving of 1996, and the second was around Christmas of 1997.

Almost as expected, there is a story of a woman in white reported at this site. Though one worker at the fort isn't sure whether or not it is a ghost that has been seen at the cemetery. The worker went on to say, "She [visits the cemetery] everyday in the same dress. She is an elderly woman… no one knows if she passed or not."

With over a dozen ghosts and poltergeists accounted for, there are those who claim that countless others aren't seen or heard but are constantly felt.

Renovation and construction usually does one of two things. It either causes psychic activity to stop altogether or flare up intensely. So far, the lack of new stories leads one to believe that activity has quieted down since the transformation. However, one can only imagine what this already creepy place would be like if things got even more intense.

A House with a History as Eerie as its Appearance

Of all the counties throughout the Chicago area, McHenry County is the most overlooked. It is this county, however, that is blessed, or cursed, with possibly the most haunted house in the state.

The town of Bull Valley, Illinois is a small, quiet, and conservative town. This was even more evident in December of 1835 when George and Sylvia Stickney settled there.

George and Sylvia, his bride-to-be, fully embraced the spiritualist movement which, in one sense, served as the most popular form of entertainment for that era. The Stickneys started in a small cabin, but with thoughts of a family on their minds, they decided to build a much larger brick house in 1856.

There are a couple of interesting points to note about the house. With ten rooms, it was a mansion at the time. It housed the first piano in McHenry County. It is also probably worth mentioning that it has no corners.

Even before the house was built, the Stickneys knew that they were going to use the house to hold seances, as Sylvia was considered a gifted medium. There were two spiritualist beliefs relating to why corners aren't conducive for spirits. One belief is that evil lurks in corners while the other states that spirits can accidentally get trapped in ninety-degree corners.

After moving into the house, the Stickneys' luck took a turn for the worse. Sylvia gave birth to eleven children, but seven of them died in the house during infancy. While it is true that the infant mortality rate was higher in the past than it is now, having only four out of eleven children live past infancy, or a sixty-four percent death rate, was still exceptionally high.

The second story of the house was, at first, a ballroom where the Stickneys held weekly parties. On occasion, the Stickneys housed Union soldiers who were passing through during the Civil War. With seven of their children dead, however, the top room became exclusively a séance room where the Stickneys would try to keep in touch with their passed children.

Their intentions were good, but what may have been released during these séance sessions is entirely unknown.

After many years in the house, the Stickneys moved away and died naturally, thus proving a popular urban legend about the house wrong. The legend states that the house was accidentally constructed with one ninety-degree corner, and it was in that corner where the body of George Stickney was found dead of no known causes.

The history of the house only continued to get darker. In the 1960s, J. S. Watrous purchased the house and rented it to a suspicious group. It isn't known exactly what happened within the walls of the house during this occupation, but what is known is that they painted all of the walls very dark and actually held bonfires within the house. When they moved out, drug paraphernalia and graffiti were found throughout the house.

It is unknown if the group of renters were simply hippies who liked to have a good time or if these people worshipped dark entities, which was the overall feeling the neighbors had at the time.

It could be that spirits looking over the house, possibly the deceased Stickney children, were upset with the disrespect and destruction of the house that their father built. Or perhaps, these people were Satanists who intentionally awakened and invited negative spirits to share the house. It may have even been an unskilled Sylvia Stickney who allowed something to cross over to this world while attempting to contact her fallen children. What is known is that this house is very actively haunted.

The first time hauntings at the house became public was reported in the early 1970s when Rodrick Smith moved into the house. He only lasted there until 1973. His claim was that the house was uninhabitable due to all of the paranormal activity. He stated that phantom dogs would bark throughout the night and strange sounds, including the sound of a baby crying, were almost constant.

When Smith moved out, a real estate agency came to

take pictures of the house for publication in classified ads. The most interesting photograph taken was of the front of the house. Visible in the photograph in one of the top windows is a woman wearing a dress resembling

a bridal gown. In the same photograph, in another upper window, is a man appearing to be a butler. Ornate curtains are also visible in the windows. Neither of these people, nor the curtains, were present at the time the photograph was shot.

The next owner, Lucy Cordella, moved into the house with large renovation plans, but she moved out quickly and before realizing any of her remodeling plans. She said nothing about ghosts and actually denied that they factored into her quick departure, but one still has to wonder why Cordella's attitude towards the house changed so extremely and so quickly.

For a long while after that, the house lay vacant and attracted the undesirables that known haunted locations routinely attract. Soon, the small Bull Valley police force was spending most of its time responding to calls relating to trespassers at the Stickney House.

They found a surefire way to remedy this. They turned the Stickney House into their headquarters in 1985.

The Bull Valley community is primarily elderly, wealthy, and concerned with bad press that may attract uninvited visitors to their small town. In an effort to raise additional money, the village allowed a television show called *Weird America* to film a segment on the Stickney House in exchange for cash. Unfortunately for Bull Valley, the television show was cancelled before they got any of the promised money.

The mayor at the time placed a gag order on the police officers who work there that continues today. Officially, they are not permitted to go on record with any statements relating to the paranormal activities at the house. However, anonymously, a police officer we talked to acknowledges that the second floor, which is currently only used for storage, is still haunted. From the first floor, sounds of objects being dragged across the second story are heard, and they claim that if they go upstairs and, "see something out of place, [they] know they shouldn't go up there anymore that day."

However, actions speak louder than words. The police officers that work there don't have to say that the building is haunted. It is already evident as every second story window is boarded shut so that no one can see into the most haunted room of the house.

Perhaps additional photographs were taken by the police department that yielded interesting results, and that was enough reason to prevent others from gathering their own incriminating evidence.

In addition to the sounds and other paranormal events that take place within the house, there are also shadowy forms seen walking around the yard.

Every journey to the Stickney House leaves a breath-taking and impressive feeling upon the visitor.

The most memorable trip I made to the Stickney House was on Friday the 13th in October of 2001. I was leading an impromptu tour of the northern part of the state. The Stickney House served as a suitable grand finale.

The area is eerie to begin with, but there was little else to note for a long while. After walking around and panning the grounds with an infrared video camera and seeing nothing, we decided to head back home.

I was walking about three feet behind Stacey Kawolski when we passed the side of the house, which now serves as the front of the police station, when we heard a very prominent masculine groan come from behind the door. Instantly, Stacey and I froze in our tracks and stared at the door.

At the time it was nearly two in the morning, and employees had long since vacated the building.

This was the first time I had ever heard of being able to hear an adult male voice, but not long after, I went to talk to ghost researcher Pat DiPrima about my experience. Her words were quite sobering. She said, "Just a couple of days ago I had someone sitting in the same chair you're sitting in who told me the same exact story."

Apparently, this bizarre and unique structure continues to be surrounded by active spirits who are still making their presence known in different ways.

Asylum Granted

Unfortunately, fact can come in a distant second place to drama and suspense when telling a good ghost story. Such was likely the case when the story of the "Sunnybrook Asylum" was first told to us. In reality, the location did not start out as a haunted asylum but rather as something quite the opposite.

It was one of two utopian communes in Lake County (the other was based in Zion). The Spirit Fruit Society started using this plot of land in 1903, though they were in existence since the late 1800s. Jacob Bielhart was the founder of the organization and friend of cereal company founders C. W. Post and the Kellogg brothers. In addition to inventing Corn Flakes, the Kelloggs were famous for running a similar, larger camp in Battle Creek, Michigan.

Bielhart died in 1908 and was buried on the land according to historian and grave dowser, Tom Smith. He went on to add that the grounds were used as a sanatorium of some sort in the 1920s or 1930s.

The most haunted location in Cook County is either Bachelor's Grove Cemetery or Archer Avenue while the most haunted location in McHenry County is the Stickney House. Without doubt or argument, the most haunted location in Lake County is surprisingly overlooked. This is the so-called "Sunnybrook Asylum."

The best way to describe the site and the feeling around it is by simply writing a recollection of the first trip we took to this location in 2000. It was with Jeff Lord and Jason Jacobs when we were shooting the *Voices from the Grave* video documentary.

The story we were told about the location, passed from person to person, dictated that on one hidden piece of land somewhere around Ingleside and Fox Lake was, at one time, an insane asylum. Everything apparently ran smoothly there until several decades ago when the caretakers themselves, after being around insane persons for a considerably long time, snapped.

As the legend continues, the caretakers executed every patient of the asylum in a mass burning. The land has stood vacant and scarred since then. The only variation of the story claims that instead of being an asylum it was a tuberculosis sanitarium. In the end of the alternate urban legend, it was still the caretakers who were the murderers.

For all that were involved with the project, this appeared to be the most typical of urban legends. This was only backed up by the fact that research attempts continued to lead to dead ends. No evidence has been found to support the claim of the mass burning, and it's likely none will ever be found. There is also no evidence of a massacre in Fox Lake. However, ask any resident living near the area about the land, and their claim is that the story is true.

Jamie Lemm was the person who brought this story to our attention, and we cannot thank her enough for it. Arriving at night with a video camera, she and some friends captured the sounds of screams on tape along the path toward the supposed asylum. Inside the buildings, they heard the sounds of crying emanating from the room that they were standing in.

The Sunnybrook Asylum has no equal as far as a total fear factor is concerned. Like Bachelor's Grove, one had to gain access to the location by foot down a harrowing path.

Sunnybrook Lane was a small, rarely used road that comes to a dead end. From there, a gravel road continues into the woods but not before a gate prohibits driving farther. Leaving the car and walking down the long deserted road, there are telephone poles to the left with the wires actually lying on the ground beneath them. Eventually, the gravel road makes a ninety-degree turn to the left. From now on, no one can see where you are.

About a quarter of a mile down this portion of the road, there is a single chain-linked fence between two posts. Beyond that is an open meadow where the unmanicured grass stood as tall as our chests. It is obvious that this land was left with no intention of return.

From here, about another quarter of a mile of walking is needed before the first building comes into sight.

The trail leading into the woods where the asylum stands is much more menacing than the trail into Bachelor's Grove Cemetery. Anyone who has visited Bachelor's Grove can attest to what a feat this is. This is largely due to the amount of isolation this location forces upon you compared to Bachelor's Grove.

At this point, a cornfield borders one side while a lake is on the other. There is literally no civilization or safe haven for miles. Bachelor's Grove, on the other hand, is never far removed from the busy Midlothian Turnpike.

After walking a considerable distance from the safety of a car, several single-story buildings in the distance come into view. These buildings dated back to the 1930s and were constructed when the site was a sanitarium. The first structure we came to looked, from the front, far too small to house patients. From another angle, however, one can see that it is a sizable, though narrow building.

A building-long hallway acts as the spine with very simple rooms containing only a cot on either side. After every two rooms, or cells if one were to believe it was an asylum, there is a bathroom. One side of the building mirrors the other.

Throughout the night of our first visit, we were hearing things. Thinking conservatively, most were birds or other animals while the rest came from our own minds, although there really is no way to tell for sure that we didn't hear something extra. Personally, I was aware that there was something walking behind me for a large part of the night, particularly in the meadow where I frequently heard additional footsteps fall behind me while my other two partners were in front of me.

The next building was a small house about twenty yards to the right of the "asylum" building. Allegedly, this was a caretaker's house. We walked up to a large, broken-out picture window of the home. Jeff peered in first and said all he could, "Oh my God." As he said this, more footsteps landed just behind me.

With darkness and mosquitoes in abundance, Jeff demanded I look into the window and to the left. I did this and found a message scrolled in blood-red paint reading, "You will Die Losers."

After needing a moment to catch our breaths, we walked around the corner to enter the small house. We had already been taken aback by the apparent cult activity in Archer Woods Cemetery, but nothing could prepare us for this cursed place. Before we even entered the next building, the reflected light showed that there was almost no untouched wall, floor, or ceiling space left. Graffiti in the form of threats, gang signs, and satanic symbols were everywhere.

The tile floor had a large red star drawn on it, encompassed by a circle. Walking across the room, Jason slipped on the floor. He checked his shoe and the red paint rubbed off. It was fresh.

We quickly made our way through the dilapidated house, looking in every room before moving along. We saw nothing of significance other than an old rocking chair, which must have last belonged to a small child no older than eight years of age. A rusted bicycle was also found just outside the house.

On our way to the next building, which appeared to be another house, we stumbled across a garage that we hadn't before noticed. It was more tucked back into the woods than the other buildings. The large main door was torn down, so entrance was easily gained. There was nothing particularly exceptional about this location except for a grocery store freezer in the middle of the room. With the camera ready, Jeff opened the lid exposing a chunk of raw meat, still dripping blood to a puddle on the bottom of the freezer.

In order to soothe our minds, we assumed it was animal meat of some sort, but we still didn't venture a guess as to why it was here. Our fear was that it was the remains of some sort of full-moon ritual.

Finally, we approached the last house. Needless to say, we were a little disturbed by what we saw up to that point, but we were still confident.

Simply walking up to the back door of this house was unsettling to me. Perhaps it was simple fear, but it could have also been a psychic impression, telling me something that I couldn't verbalize. Whatever it was, without question, I felt uneasy just approaching the final house.

We walked onto the porch and all was well. By the time I stepped one foot into the main part of the house, we came across another message left for us to find. It read, "If we catch you here you die."

At this point, I don't know if Jeff was accountable for his actions. Instantly, he started mapping our way back. Suddenly and without discussion, his mission was to leave the location as soon as humanly possible. He was done, and it didn't take any additional convincing for us to follow him out of the house.

We left the way we came: out the porch, through the garage, and across the meadow. In total darkness, the meadow seemed to have grown. Quickly, we found ourselves bickering over which way we should go. At the worst possible time and in the worst possible place, we were lost. At one point, when we were frantically discussing where to go, additional footsteps followed immediately behind me. Again, Jeff and Jason were in front of me. I didn't mention it to them since our panic levels were high enough as it was.

Eventually, we came across some fallen power lines that we used to guide us back to safety. Knowing where to go now, we decided to run the rest of the way back to the car. This is something I'm sure the majority of after-dark visitors do.

If the story was true, then the murderous caretakers occupied the two houses while a maintenance shed and garage stood between them.

I was not content with our abbreviated visit, so I planned another excursion to the asylum. This time, however, it was definitely going to be in daylight.

This time I brought along photographer Sara Rendall. Now knowing where to go and what to expect, we quickly found ourselves walking up towards the asylum building. It was not long before we came across a strange sight. All of the grass around the building was pushed away from it as if a bomb had gone off. It wasn't just as though the plants were growing away from the shadows because all of the plant life was pressed to the ground.

While it makes sense that frequent visitors could trample the grass, the fact that the direction was so constant was noteworthy. Amazingly, this was evident regarding each and every building there.

The next strange thing we noticed came immediately after. For whatever reason, Sara could not get her manual camera to focus on any of the bathrooms in the "asylum" building.

As was previously mentioned, camera and equipment malfunctions are common phenomena at haunted locations. In all, Sara went through two rolls of film though only three of the photographs taken by this trained and professional photographer came out.

Walking from the asylum to the first house, a loud, extended and smooth, high-pitched sound filled the air. This was no sound a bird could make. If one were to replicate it, they would need some sort of electric device, but obviously there was nothing like that around.

We walked through the first house and the garage easily and without incident, but then it was time for the final house. Again, just walking up to it, I was filled by an emotion that was impressed upon me.

Just like how visitors to Devil's Creek and the Gettysburg Battle Field can suddenly be overcome by grief, the grounds of the Sunnybrook Asylum can fill an unsuspecting person with fear.

The feeling is similar to a feeling of impending doom, as if you knew you were about to be caught doing something bad and that a punishment was threatening. It's the feeling that you are in trouble and time is running out. The harsh justice awaits.

All this I was feeling even before we reached the house, but it continued throughout. I didn't say anything to Sara to make sure I didn't put her on edge as well.

My goal was to see every room in the small house, which was actually just a replica of the first house but with carpet, so that I would never have to come back.

Several minutes into looking around the house, Sara approached me to ask, "Scott, do you get the feeling that we really just shouldn't be here right now?"

That was all I needed to hear. We began our exit immediately.

Standing in front of that second house, we made another discovery. As mentioned, all of the grass and weeds around the buildings were pushed away from them as if they were magnets of the same polarity.

In the meadow in front of this house there was a large circle that looked exactly like a crop circle. What caused it is anyone's guess, but Sara decided to step into the middle of it for a few seconds until she felt uncomfortable being there.

While making our way back through the meadow, we heard that loud tone again. Coincidentally, this time the camera was filming throughout the duration of the sound. Excited, I checked the footage as soon as I got home, but somehow that sound did not record though ambient noise and the sound of us reacting to it did.

Though we have not found any link to an asylum, older maps of the area refer to the gravel road leading to the asylum as Bellvue Road. Of course, Bellvue is a very common name throughout the United States for asylums for the insane.

What can be said for sure about the grounds commonly referred to as the Sunnybrook Asylum is that there were definitely active spirits on the land, and they aren't particularly pleased with the way things are. Between the negative emotional impressions forced on visitors there and the sounds of agony that come out in the form of phantom screams and cries, it is quite evident that this area is still holding some tortured souls. Perhaps the area even collected more negative energy inspired by the people who frequented the site for the purpose of vandalizing it. It could even be the ghost of Bielhart, who created these buildings out of passion and remains there in an unmarked grave.

In the mid 2000s all four of these notable buildings were

demolished. The expansive farm field that bordered the property on one side is now yet another of the many subdivisions of Lake County. The precise land where the buildings stood is the three-way intersection of Spruce Drive, Magnolia Lane, and Autumn Drive. The residents of the houses in the immediate area, who are most likely unaware of the haunted history of their property, just may want to keep a watchful eye to see if the hauntings continue.

BIBLIOGRAPHY

The author visited all locations covered in the book at least once, but generally three or more times between 1999 and 2008.

Anderson, Ashley. "Mundelein legends come alive at

Halloween." The Mustang Oct. 1996. Vol. 36:8.

Aguinaldo, Teresa. "Archetypes and Ideology." Women in

Literature. College of Lake County, Grayslake. 30

Sept. 1999.

"Barat College." Wikipedia, The Free Encyclopedia.

29 Aug 2008, 03:46 UTC. Summer 2008

<http://en.wikipedia.org/w/index.php?title=

Barat_College&oldid=234921620>.

Bielski, Ursula. Chicago Haunts: Ghostlore of the Windy

City. Revised ed. Holt, MI: Thunder Bay Press, 1998.

Bielski, Ursula. More Chicago Haunts : Scenes from Myth

and Memory. Holt, MI: Thunder Bay Press, 2000.

Binder, Frederick M. and David M. Remiers. The Way We

Lived Volume 1: 1492 - 1877. 4th ed. New York:

Houghton Mifflin, 2000.

Bradbury, Andrew. "Clarence Darrow: 'Attorney for the Damned' or just another Damned Attorney?" The Scopes Monkey Trial. 23 May 2008 <http://www. bradburyac.mistral.co.uk/tennes14.html>.

Chicago Park Dist., ed. "Peterson Park." Chicago Park District. 2006. 23 May 2008 <http://chicagoparkdistrict.com/ index.cfm/fuseaction/parks.detail/object_id/433b5e34-bd4e-4fe5-a74e-81dedbacc96d.cfm>.

Chitownads, ed. "Captain George Wellington Streeter." ChiTownAds.com. 8 Apr. 2008. Mustang Internet Services, Inc. 20 July 2008 <http://www.chitownads. com/k/idx/15/013/famous_chicagoans/article/ captain_george_wellington_Streeter.html>

Danielle, Dell'Olio, comp. "Timeline: John Dillinger." PBS. 2002. 31 May 2008 <http://www.pbs. org/wgbh/amex/dillinger/timeline>.

"Darius Miller Dead." New York Times 24 Aug. 1914.

DiPrima, Patricia. Personal Interview. 15 Oct. 2000.

Filas, Lee. "Fact or Fiction." Pioneer Press 5 May 2000: I39.

Gentner, Dan. "Gentner Family Tree." Rootsweb. 11 Apr. 2003. 14 July 2008 <http://homepages.rootsweb. ancestry.com/~gentner/indi/1381.html#p13815>.

Geringer, Joe. "Phantom Killer: Texarkana Moonlight

Murders." The Phantom Killer. National Crime

Library. 8 July 2001. <www.crimelibrary.com>.

Gruel, Rick. "Showmen's Rest." Showmen's League of

America. Showmen's League of America. 1 July 2008

<http://www.showmensleague.org/showmens_rest/

showmens_rest.html>.

Hillewaere, Karel. "Frank Capone." La Cosa Nostra Database.

2007. 31 May 2008 <www.lacndb.com/php/info.

php?name=frank%20capone>.

Kaczmarek, Dale. Windy City Ghosts : The Haunted History

of Chicago. Decatur, IL: Whitechapel Press, 2000.

"Last of Loeb." Time Magazine 10 Feb. 1936.

Lindberg, Richard. Return to the Scene of the Crime : A

Guide to Infamous Places in Chicago. New York:

Cumberland House, 1999.

Lord, Bernadette. Personal Interview. 15 July 1999.

Meier, James. "Haloween Haunts." The Sun 26 Oct. 2000:

LMV

Melone, Dan, and Buzz Speakman. "Robinson Woods."

Personal interview. 14 July 2008.

Mercado, Carol, and Richard T. Crowe. Chicago's Street
Guide to the Supernatural : A Guide to Haunted and
Legendary Places in and Near the Windy City. New
York: Carolando Press, Incorporated, 2000.

Mikkelson, Barbra. "Bloody Mary." Urban Legends
References Pages. San Fernando Folklore Society.
Snopes.com. 27 Apr. 2001.

Mikkelson, Barbra. "The Hook." Urban Legends References
Pages. San Fernando Folklore Society. Snopes.com. 2
Dec. 1998.

Mikkelson, Barbra. "Satan's Choice." Urban Legends
References Pages. San Fernando Folklore Society.
Snopes.com. 14 May 2000.

The Mothership Connection. Tom & Patty Smith Interview.
WLIP, Pleasant Prairie, WI. 6 June 2008.

NBC Universal, Inc., ed. "Hancock Scaffolding Investigation
Picks Up." NBC5.com. 12 Mar. 2002. 5 May 2008
<http://www.nbc5.com/news/1296726/detail.html>.

"Poltergeist curse." Wikipedia, The Free Encyclopedia. 21
Aug 2008, 20:42 UTC. Summer 2008 <http://
en.wikipedia.org/wiki/Poltergeist_curse>.

Reiff, Janice L., Durkin Keating, and James R. Grossman,

    eds. "David Kennison marker in Lincoln Park,

    1903." The Encyclopedia of Chicago. 2005. Chicago

    Historical Society & The Newberry Library. 31 May

    2008 <http://www.encyclopedia.chicagohistory.

    org/pages/11268.html>.

Richards, Tori. "Shotgun Slaying of Millionaire Couple

    Solved 15 Years Later." TruTV. 2 June 2008 <www.

    trutv.com/library/crime/notorious_murders/family/

    dd_802_rouse/11.html>.

Strong, William D. "Indians of The Chicago Region."

    Access Genealogy. 2008. 23 May 2008 <http://www.

    accessgenealogy.com/native/illinois/chicago>.

Taylor, Troy. Haunted Illinois : Ghosts and Hauntings from

    Egypt to the Windy City. Decatur, IL: Whitechapel

    Press, 1999.

Thieme, C.T. "Chicagoland Haunted Sites." Heathen's Haven.

    2008. Summer 2008 <http://www.heathens-haven.

    com/>.

INDEX

A

B

C

D

E

F

G

H

I

J

K

L

M

N

O

P

Q

R

U

V

W